THE
WORTH.
BOOK OF

THE WORTH® BOOK OF

SOFTBALL

A CELEBRATION OF AMERICA'S TRUE NATIONAL PASTIME

PAUL DICKSON

Photographs by
RUSSELL MOTT

Facts On File®

AN INFOBASE HOLDINGS COMPANY

The Worth Book of Softball

Copyright © 1994 by Paul Dickson
Photographs copyright © 1994 by Russell Mott

Facts On File, Inc.
460 Park Avenue South
New York NY 10016
USA

Library of Congress Cataloging-in-Publication Data

Dickson, Paul.
    The Worth book of softball : A celebration of America's true national pastime / Paul Dickson.
        p.   cm.
    Includes bibliographical references (p.   ) and index.
    ISBN 0-8160-2897-4 (alk. paper)
    1. Softball—United States.   2. Softball—United States—History.
I. Worth Bat Company.   II. Title.
GV863.A1D53   1994
796.357'8—dc20   93-19312

A British CIP catalogue record for this book is available from the British Library.

Facts On File books are available at special discounts when purchased in bulk quantities for businesses, associations, institutions or sales promotions. Please call our Special Sales Department in New York at 212/683-2244 or 800/322-8755.

Text and jacket design by Catherine Rincon Hyman
Composition by Facts On File, Inc.
Manufactured by R.R. Donnelley & Sons, Inc.
Printed in the United States of America

10 9 8 7 6 5 4 3 2 1

This book is printed on acid-free paper.

Books by Paul Dickson

(Underlined titles published by Facts On File)

Think Tanks

The Great American Ice Cream Book

The Future of the Workplace

The Electronic Battlefield

The Mature Person's Guide to Kites, Yo-Yos, Frisbees and Other Childlike Diversions

Out of This World

The Future File

Chow: A Cook's Tour of Military Food

The Official Rules

The Official Explanations

Toasts

Words

There Are Alligators in the Sewers & Other American Credos
(With Joseph C. Goulden)

Jokes

Names

On Our Own: A Declaration of Independence for the Self-Employed

The Library in America

Family Words

The Dickson Baseball Dictionary

The New Official Rules

What Do You Call a Person From . . . ?

Slang!

Timelines

Baseball's Greatest Quotations

Dickson's Word Treasury

Dickson's Joke Treasury

On This Spot: Pinpointing the Past in Washington, D.C.
(With Douglas E. Evelyn)

Baseball: The President's Game
(With William B. Mead)

The Congress Dictionary
(With Paul Clancy)

Official Dimensions for Softball Diamonds

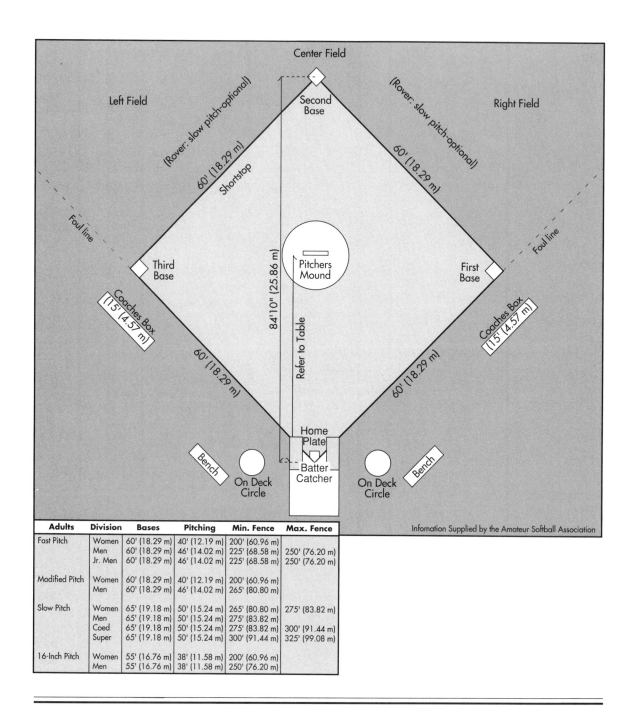

Adults	Division	Bases	Pitching	Min. Fence	Max. Fence
Fast Pitch	Women	60' (18.29 m)	40' (12.19 m)	200' (60.96 m)	
	Men	60' (18.29 m)	46' (14.02 m)	225' (68.58 m)	250' (76.20 m)
	Jr. Men	60' (18.29 m)	46' (14.02 m)	225' (68.58 m)	250' (76.20 m)
Modified Pitch	Women	60' (18.29 m)	40' (12.19 m)	200' (60.96 m)	
	Men	60' (18.29 m)	46' (14.02 m)	265' (80.80 m)	
Slow Pitch	Women	65' (19.18 m)	50' (15.24 m)	265' (80.80 m)	275' (83.82 m)
	Men	65' (19.18 m)	50' (15.24 m)	275' (83.82 m)	
	Coed	65' (19.18 m)	50' (15.24 m)	275' (83.82 m)	300' (91.44 m)
	Super	65' (19.18 m)	50' (15.24 m)	300' (91.44 m)	325' (99.08 m)
16-Inch Pitch	Women	55' (16.76 m)	38' (11.58 m)	200' (60.96 m)	
	Men	55' (16.76 m)	38' (11.58 m)	250' (76.20 m)	

Infomation Supplied by the Amateur Softball Association

Dedication

Go Timberwolves!

We were the Timber Trails Timberwolves of Sherman, Connecticut, and we were the motliest group of uncoached teenage softballers who had ever dragged themselves onto that field of overgrown crabgrass abutting Route 7.

How good were we?

Not very . . . at least not until we got a dream pitcher with a mow-'em-down windmill fast ball and a wait-until-dark change-up that took us to the top of our league for a month of unbeatability.

This book goes out to all the members of that team—my brother Peter (Pete in those days), Fitz and Tony, Jay, the Read Brothers, Dave, Steve and all the rest of us whose greatest "baseball" memories came from a 12-inch Clincher ball and a flimsy pancake glove.

Contents

Notes and Acknowledgments

It should be noted clearly that the name of *the* leading manufacturer and distributor of softballs and softball equipment appears in the title of this book. Sponsorship is nothing new to Worth because it is the nation's prime sponsor of softball teams and tournaments. In fact, as this book was being finished, Worth had just announced that it was going to sponsor its own all-star men's slow pitch team to make a serious run at top national ranking under the Worth banner.

But a book of this nature is a departure for the company. *The Worth Book of Softball* is a valentine to a game and to the softball culture, not to a specific company. Worth has supported this project and enabled the writer and photographer to travel extensively to get a beat on their subject. Other than the company's name appearing in the title, the book is totally under the editorial control of the author and his editors at Facts On File and, yes, other manufacturers' goods appear in pictures and are mentioned in the text.

Lest there be any question, the author and publisher are honored by having the Worth name on this book. There are many reasons, but one puts it all in perspective. Through the leadership of John Parish and Jess Heald, Worth has been the industry leader in softball and baseball safety and in making the game we know today.

A Note on the Photographer

Russell Mott, a very old friend of the author and a very talented photographer, took more than 10,000 photographs over a two-year period in his effort to capture the look and action of a game that helps define Americana. He was asked to shoot sports pictures that captured a phenomenon that has worked its way into every nook and cranny of the nation.

All of the photos in this book were taken by him except for the historic images. It should be noted that it was not his assignment to photograph stars and celebrities, but to get a handle on the game and bring it to life. To do this, he spent many days on the road and many days in the darkroom to achieve splendid results. From his home in New Hampshire he traveled as far afield as Quebec, California, Tennessee, Florida, Ohio, Oklahoma, New York City and Cairo, Egypt.

The toughest part of this whole process was selecting the images that work best because so many of them worked well.

Many, many people helped bring this book to fruition. The author would like to thank Orie Chandler; the one and only Herb Dudley; Les Duncan; Michael L. Harris, President/Publisher of *Softball Masters* magazine; Arnold "Red" Halpern, Idaho ASA and past President of the ASA; John Hulen of Dudley; Bobbi Kadesch; Dave Kelly of the Library of Congress; Frank La Teano; Roger May for the use of his files; Harry L. Marsh, Director of Communications and Media Relations, United States Slo-Pitch Softball Association; as always, Bill Mead; Ron Menchine for his generosity in loaning me books and images from his unparalleled collection of baseball ephemera (which harbors its share of softball goodies); Dave Metheny of the Minneapolis *Star*; Jim Mulfelder of DeBeer; Bill Plummer, III of the Amateur Softball Association; Roger May; the late Bill Newman; Hall of Famer Don Rardin; Joe Reilly; Floyd Slater, U.S.S.S.A. National Umpire-in-Chief; Bob Staples of Mainly Sports, East Wilton, Maine; Milt Stark of the International Softball Congress; and Ed Waite, General Manager Lady Blue Softball, Carrollton, Texas.

Russell Mott prepared his own thank you list, which may include a few names that are repeated. So be it; some folks deserve to be thanked twice.

"My heartfelt thanks to my wife Kate for her marvelous support and assistance, and to my parents, Mary and Hollis Chenery. And, to so many more for their kind help along the way from the beaches of southern California to the sand lots of Brunswick, Maine: Frank and Phyllis La Teano, Ray Molphy, George Vivieros, Padma Mott, Les Duncan, Mike LaJoie, Conrad 'Sully' Sullivan, Anne and George Flannery, John Holms, Jim Schwendeman (deceased 12/92), Tom Wilson, Brian Williams, and Nelson Eddy. And, Irene and Jim Lanigan, Lou Ciota, Francie Von Mertens, Emil Frankel, Paul Johnson, Chuck Cole, Skip Bradeen, Hank and Betty Sprouse, Mike DeVita, Dean McNew, Dick Handy, Maury Povich, Tricia Mendoza, Fran Pierce, Bill Langlois, Bill McCluskey, John Sousa,

John Pond, Bob Baird, Larry Mahr, Winston Lee, Bill Plummer III, Harry and Connie Marsh, Steve Freedman, Lynn Morrell, Mike Gaffney, Elizabeth Littles, Bob Barden, Wahnetah Stamper, Bob Summers, Denise Legault, Wayne Esty, Charlie Beach, Melissa Jarrell, Linette/Peter/Herb/Lisa-CSS, Mike Hipp, Buddy Mantia, Louise and Al Dichard, Sonny Anderson, Jim Desmarais, Bob Ayersman, Guy Schevenell, Miguel Ferrer, Chuck Vokul, Rick Fortenbaugh, Lorelle Bryson, Walt Sturtevant, Fred Elliott, Wayne Thomas, Doug Dicey, Richard Bourgault, Gaston Grenier, Berg Frederick, and B. J. Wixson in Escondido. And, to all the terrific folks at Worth who so generously supported this project from the outset. And, lastly, to my friends of 30 years, Paul and Nancy Dickson, for asking me to travel with them on what was a most joyous trek."

¹ Introduction:

FEATURING

A FEW VOICES

FROM THE FIELD

It is the most American of things and it is everywhere.

But you have to know where and when to look for it.

You can always see it at twilight on a summer evening driving along those lesser rural roads that seek out small population centers rather than bypass them.

It blooms in the suburbs like crabgrass and it stays downtown long after the commuters have gone home. If your windows are down you can not only see but hear it—yelling, cheering, squawking and laughter in a blend of male and female voices. You can hear dogs and babies,

What Is Softball?

too, and if the wind is blowing in the right direction you may get a whiff of something on the grill.

Softball is a firmly established bat-and-ball game that originated in the United States more than 100 years ago. It was created as a variation on baseball by a group of young men killing time waiting for a football score.

Since then it has changed in many ways and has branched out in every direction. The game has been adopted and adapted by so many people that softball today is, in fact, two major games and a number of lesser variations operating under a single name.

Underdogs *The University of Massachusetts team celebrates after beating Long Beach State—to whom they were the certain underdog—during the 1992 NCAA Championships in Oklahoma City. Left to right are: Danielle Walsh, Holly Aprile, Jen Devlin, Stacy Nichols, Kelly Daut, Tabitha Williams, Lisa Metz, Darlene Claffy and Catcher Sheri Kuchinskas. (Russell Mott)*

It has been organized into church leagues, co-ed leagues, industrial leagues, urban leagues and too many others to mention quickly. Besides the United States and Canada, it is a popular game in Japan, the Philippines, New Zealand, Australia and most of Latin America.

But there is a lot more to it. For one thing, softball is a passion and has been for a while now.

The Modified Game *Boston city championships— women's modified-pitch softball. Featured is Terri Carilli, a senior software engineer playing for a team called Silhouette. A softball vet, Carilli has been a consistent lead-off batter and has played for 20 years. (Russell Mott)*

. . . here is a sport played by the greatest number of people in the history of the world. And, if you consult any one of them, you'll find it's also the greatest game in the world.

—Lowell Thomas and Ted Shane from their 1940 classic, *Softball! So What?*

Softball is a religion (at least during the warm months) . . .

Normally, I'm dead set against tinkering with the institutions that got us where we are today, but I feel strongly that we should face the facts: The separation of church and state just isn't working anymore.

I think we should get it over with and declare amateur softball the official American religion of the 1980s.

Certainly it has the requisite characteristics: elaborate ritual, bright costumes, a sense of community among people who could otherwise be expected to ignore one another, the promise of immortality and, for the evangelists among us, a prodigious allotment of fantasy.

—Albert Oetgen, *Knight-Ridder Newspapers* columnist, June 1, 1986.

Softball is not baseball. Although it was created from baseball, it now stands on its own as a thing apart.

I like playin' softball . . . but watchin' [baseball]? I don't want to knock the national pastime, but, mister a lot of nothin' happens.

—Elvis Presley, *The World According to Elvis*, Jeff Rovin.

The core of baseball is the professional game; professional softball is, despite several ill-fated attempts to go pro, an oxymoron. Baseball is tradition and unchanging ritual, while softball is ever-changing, ever-adapting and tolerant of new ways of doing things.

Softball today is remarkable in that its identity is so diverse and that the word softball means so many things to so many different people. In the red clay of Valdosta, Georgia, softball is hulking men who hit a slow pitch homerun poke every other time at bat; but a few miles away it's a bunch

Teeing Off   Leah Brann, of the "Steelers-Phillies"
Peterborough, New Hampshire,
Midget Girls Tee Ball League.
(Russell Mott)

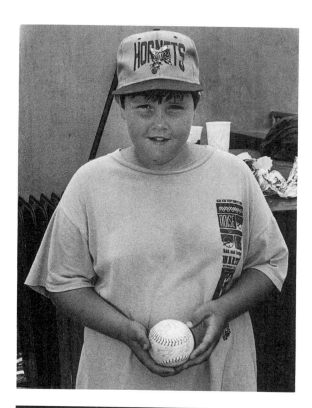

come a professional sport. Except at the highest skill levels, softball attracts few spectators save for an occasional friend or family member. People who come to watch often end up playing.

Softball is a sport for the masses.
—Tom Petroff. The first seven words in his book *Softball Hitting: Fast and Slow Pitch* (1990)

Softball is also a business fast moving into the billions:

You won't see the economic impact of softball in any econometric model. But it's already a sizable business and growing fast . . . softball uniforms [alone] are a $225 million-a-year business.
—*Forbes*, July 15, 1985

Softball is also a matter of intensely personal feeling:

Clearly, the game is about grander, more transcendent issues than exercise: identity and immortality, courage, mastery and the joy of skilled cooperation. It's about proving you don't throw like a girl even if you are one. Or proving you can still turn a double play as quick as you could in seventh grade, even though you're fat now and smoke cigarettes and are losing your hair, or that you're really mean and tough and a little crazy, even though you have a wife and 3.2 kids and a lawn to mow waiting for you at home, or that you're still a regular guy even though you spend most of your waking hours working on something so esoteric you can't even explain it to your friends, or that you can still achieve moments of amazing grace and true greatness even though you spend most of your waking hours doing things so mind-numbing you can hardly believe it.
—Patricia McLaughlin, *Indianapolis News*, Universal Press Syndicate, May 8, 1988

Autograph Hound *For young fans, one difference between softball and baseball is that in softball you can get more names on the ball. At the Salem, Virginia, September ASA Men's Fast Pitch National Championships in 1992 young Rett Smith got a ball autographed by all team members. (Russell Mott)*

of 8-year-olds having a whack at tee ball. It is Olympic-bound U.S. college women windmilling a sinker for a fast pitch shutout over the Cubans, but it is also the big spring intramural sport on those same campuses. It's a 100-year-old player featured in a television commercial for athletic shoes and a 9-year-old catcher on home plate. It's pickup play, picnics and celebrity charity events. It's a weekend respite for truckers and plumbing supply companies, network television workers and advertising executives or a tournament made up of players who are all women filmmakers. It is Jack Nicholson passing time on the set of a movie and American troops playing on the sands of the Middle East.

Softball is a game that is meant to be *played* and, despite a number of serious attempts to the contrary, it does not seem to be destined to be-

Fast Pitch Ace

In the uniform of the
Raybestos Brakettes,
Lisa Fernandez
pitches in a Stratford,
Connecticut, tournament
in the summer of 1992.
(Russell Mott)

The Pleasure Principle

Softball is also a pleasure that ranks with the other pleasures of the flesh.

Some years ago novelist Les Whitten was playing in a Washington media league and poled a ball into right-center way over the deepest fielder. Whitten arrived at home plate at the same moment as the ball, and the umpire bellowed "Safe!"

The writer lay in the dirt for a few seconds, smiled and said, "That's the second best feeling in the world."

It is also an intensely social sport. In 1989, when the city of Sacramento (with 3,708 teams) overtook Detroit (with 3,575 teams) the local softball director, Ron Radigonda, was asked why his program was growing at the rate of 20 percent per year and he replied, "People don't have a lot of time, so they want to socialize while they recreate. A game takes only an hour."

From a practical standpoint, softball requires less playing space than baseball, the pace of play is generally faster, less equipment is required and the equipment is relatively inexpensive (although serious players demand more elaborate equipment).

All one needs to get started is a bat and ball.

There was a time not long ago when softball was seen as the game for the guy in the ugly Bermudas who always took the beer can into the outfield. That guy is still out there, but his image as the soul of softball is going the way of the wooden softball bat and the mushy beaten-up ball and is being replaced by a man or woman playing a fast game in which hitting, running and defense overwhelm pitching. The guys with the big bellies are still there but some of them are pounding

Pounder *Jeff "Beaver" Norby, of the Peterborough Co-Ed "A" League softball team, The Duffy Electric Pounders, of Jaffrey, New Hampshire. The Pounders have been winners for three straight years, the amount of time they have been in the league. (Russell Mott)*

out over 100 home runs a season with a high-tech "power generator" made of aircraft aluminum. The ball that person hits will fly off that bat and has about as much in common with a ball of the past as a propeller-driven plane has to a jet.

It is important to remember that today's softball is not soft, it is heavier and larger than a baseball. The basic ball is 12 inches in circumference, but some forms of the game use balls that are up to 16 inches. The center of the ball is made of either a mixture of cork and rubber or long-fiber kapok or of a concoction of polyurethane that helps the ball fly off the bat. The polyurethane balls are becoming more and more common with each passing season, although some favor the traditional cores. Many of the folks who play 16-inch softball swear by kapok and actually like the fact that it gets mushier during the course of the game.

The center is in turn enclosed by a taut hand or machine winding of fine-quality twisted yarn, with the cover cemented to the yarn by a latex or rubber adhesive. The covers are usually genuine cowhide or a synthetic approximation of cowhide that's sewn on by hand.

The bat is round and for the most part made of aluminum; but it can be hard wood, graphite, carbon, magnesium, fiberglass or even a ceramic composite. For some time now the preferred bats at all levels of the game have been those made of high-grade aluminum. For all practical purposes, the short-lived wooden bat is no longer used by those who play seriously. The bat cannot be more than 34 inches in length nor more than 2¼ inches in diameter at its largest part. It does not exceed 38 ounces in weight.

But softball is first and foremost a game—a dynamic,

fast and enchantingly unpredictable game—with complicated rules and competing rulebooks. It is so simple and direct that its essence can be understood in a few hundred words.

The fundamentals of softball are the same as baseball. Batting (scoring runs) and fielding (getting outs) strategies are similar. There is, however, an important difference in pitching technique. The underhand pitch is a distinctive feature in softball.

There are a number of variations in the game, but the most important distinction is between the traditional game of fast pitch softball, which favors good pitching and features low scores, and slow pitch softball, which favors the batter and features scores that often seem to resemble those of football games.

The fast in fast pitch likens it to baseball. The slow in slow pitch likens it to pitching horseshoes. Heat vs. a toss.

Fast pitch softball is a defensive game because the softball pitcher has more mastery over the hitter. In major fast pitch softball competition the scores are usually low and get lower as players' skills improve. Special skills have been developed in this art and pitchers display baffling windups followed by a release of the ball that achieves a speed comparable to an overhand baseball.

In the fast pitch game bunting and base-stealing are the major factors in softball team play. The sacrifice bunt is used to advance runners from first to second and from second to third, in addition to the run-scoring squeeze play (bunting a runner home from third). Sacrifice bunting and base-stealing are closely allied, since in each there must be cooperation between base-runner and batter.

The idea in slow pitch is to get the ball into play—to make everybody a hitter and everybody a fielder. The best a pitcher can hope to do is get the batter to pop up or ground out; he or she can't even dream about strikeouts (although they do occur, albeit rarely).

Softball is traditionally played on turf with an infield area that is usually "skinned"—or cleared—of its grass. The playing field is in the shape of a baseball diamond with a home base and three bases numbered first, second and third.

Unlike other sports, there are different standards, rules and measurements for the game's many variations. These variations can be daunting and require some time with a rule book to fully

Coach on a Harley   Dale "Bo" Guyer, coach, sponsor and part-time player for the Guyer and Son Roofing softball team in the Keene, New Hampshire, Greater Softball Association, makes out his lineup card. (Russell Mott)

comprehend. The distances marked off differ depending on the level of play. Softball diamonds come in two basic sizes: a 55-foot or a 65-foot diamond as measured from home plate to second base, depending on the dominant form of play.

Power Cut The "Crusher" of Ritch's/Superior of Windsor Locks, Connecticut, Rick Scherr, now retired from the highest level of men's slow pitch. This photo was taken in Sherbrooke, Quebec, Canada during the summer of 1991. (Russell Mott)

The home base is at least 46 feet from the pitching point for men and 40 feet for women. Homebase and bases one, two and three are, usually, 60 feet apart (in slow pitch the distance is 50 feet). In men's major slow pitch play, the bases are 65 feet apart, but only 55 feet apart in the version of slow pitch played with a 16-inch ball.

The object of the game is to score runs. This is done when the batter attempts to hit the ball into fair territory and, after doing so, circles the three bases to return to the home base. In order to score the run the batter-runner cannot be tagged with the ball while rounding the bases.

The playing area of the diamond extends from the home base down two foul lines for approxi-mately 200 to 275 feet (depending on the age group and the type of ball used), which is usually marked in-bounds by a line or fence. The outfield area extends from the bases, which are stationed in the infield area to the distance marker that indicates in-bounds and out-of-bounds.

The players in the field consist of a catcher, who squats behind home plate, and a pitcher, stationed on the pitching rubber. Each of the three bases is covered by an assigned fielder plus one additional player, the shortstop, who remains within the infield area between second and third. Players in the field are permitted to use gloves except in Chicago. There they play their own game called "16 inch" and the use of a protective piece of leather is disdained. The same bravado holds for an odd softball offshoot called Over the Line where gloveless fielders dive in the sand to make spectacular catches.

The outfield area has three players in fast pitch and four players in slow pitch. The extra player is traditionally called the rover or shortfielder and plays in the shallow outfield or in left center.

Each team is allowed three outs while taking its turn at bat. When three outs have been recorded the two opposing teams change sides. The length of the game is recorded in innings; one inning consists of each team having a turn at bat. Seven innings constitutes a complete game. The team with the most runs at the end of the seven innings of play is declared the winner.

The ability to skillfully play softball is, as the coaches say, primarily governed by innate factors. Nevertheless, the techniques can be learned or improved by practice and by using sound fundamental skills.

The basic skills in softball are pitching, catching, throwing, batting and base-running. But it is also a game that requires—for most of us—a sense of humor and humility. Anyone can muff a routine fly ball, a peculiar bounce can turn a routine ground ball into a double and a team can have a good time even when on the short end of a rout.

Softball is, after all, a game. It is played for fun and it is there for just about everyone. As a sports book, *The Worth Book of Softball* is intended as a valentine to a sport that almost as many women as men enjoy and hopefully will appeal to people of both sexes and all from ages five to 105. It dwells on the history of the game because so little has been written on its history.

Finally, it is hoped that you the readers see yourselves in this book because it was written for and about you the players.

MVP Terry Shea of Club 110 in a New Bedford, Massachusetts, co-ed team tournament. She was the most valuable player on the women's side.
(Russell Mott)

² The State of

42 MILLION AMERICANS CAN'T BE WRONG

The Game for Everyone

The 1992 season was long over and, as it has done every year since 1934, the last Sunday *New York Times* sports section of the year carried a summary of the winning teams that would go into the record book. Quoting directly from the *Times* of December 27, 1992:

the Game

U.S. men's fast pitch: National Health Care Discount, Sioux City, Iowa.

U.S. women's fast pitch: Raybestos Brakettes, Stratford, Conn.

U.S. men's super-slow pitch: Ritch's/Superior, Windsor Locks, Conn.

U.S. men's major-slow pitch: Vernon's, Jacksonville, Fla.

U.S. women's major-slow pitch: Universal Plastics Inc., Cookeville, Tenn.

U.S. college women: U.C.L.A.

Tagging One *Chris Sircar tags one for Sam's Sports Bar of Springfield, Massachusetts, at the co-ed tournament in New Bedford, Massachusetts, at Ben Rose Field in the summer of 1992. (Russell Mott)*

Simple end-of-the-year listings like this are among the few times that softball gets in the sports pages. The fact is, there's hardly much room for softball, because the off-field antics and media

coverage of Major League Baseball and its many owners, agents, free agents and lawyers need space to tell their sides of the story.

Baseball has become a grand opera, with personalities and issues so strong that they sometimes seem more important than the game itself. An event as non-athletic as baseball's winter meetings in December now overshadows coverage of football and basketball.

For years baseball has been dubbed the National Pastime, America's National Game. It has held this position in American culture since the years just following the Civil War and survived—some would say thrived—during two World Wars, the Depression, the Cold War, several major scandals and some of the prickliest owner and player egotists ever to walk on North American soil.

But playing softball—actually making contact with the ball, actually taking a header trying to get hold of a sinking line drive, actually coming home from a long day at work to get the grass stains out of your uniform—makes it, as the folks at the Amateur Softball Association have termed it since the 1930s, the "Game for Everyone."

It would seem as if everyone in contact with the game comes up with the same secret and the same conclusion. The secret is that you can be a poor player and still enjoy the game. The conclusion, which follows, is that it *is* a game for everyone regardless of gender, age and athletic ability.

Family Man Second baseman Ernie Montgomery of the Steele's /Sunbelt Hitmen and his 18-month-old daughter Megan at the Worth Conway Twitty Classic in Hendersonville, Tennessee, in the spring of 1992. The tournament is named in honor of the country music star . (Russell Mott)

Dugout Scene Excitement at the Falmouth, Maine, girls' District 6 Little League Fast-Pitch Championship in July, 1992. They would win it all and graciously pose for the next picture. (Russell Mott)

If the motto uttered constantly by those atop softball organizations seems self-serving, it is because it also happens to be true. The men and women who bring us all the coverage of baseball play softball, as do many of the front office staffs of Major League Baseball. Facts On File, the publishing house that is bringing you this book, has a softball team that has been a powerhouse in the New Publishers Softball League. Teams in this league play in Central Park along with teams from the Broadway Show League and with those bearing the names and colors of funeral homes, auto body shops and taverns.

Someone once said that softball knows no gender—that it is a game that looks beyond the sex of its players. Nonsense! If anything, softball *celebrates* gender: femaleness, maleness and—for lack of a better term—co-edness all have a niche.

There is one particular game played by women under 30. It is their version of baseball and it is played with passion. It is a tough, fast game of bang-bang plays and nerve-wracking pitching duels. Ever wonder why the women at Berkeley, Vassar or the University of Oklahoma are not running around demanding a baseball league of their own?

The answer is that they already have one and it is called fast pitch softball; it is crisp and will make fans lightheaded just to see it. The best place to see it now is probably at the National Collegiate Athletic Association Women's College World Series in May. There won't be a lot of homeruns, but it is a delight for those who like spectacular pitching and tight defense.

An interesting phenomenon occurs when sports writers attend a game for the first time and then go home and write an article to let their readers know that it is a stunningly athletic form

Pennant Winners   Left to right, the Windham All-Stars: Amanda Fish, Cecilia Baston, Katie Bernier, Allison Brooks, Chrissy Birt, Kelli Works, Laurie Witham, Rebecca Brasier, Kati Morrell, Shalyn Graves, Katie Crisaffi, Amanda Bowdon, Tracy Toner, Jill Eastman and Lynn Morrell.

(Russell Mott)

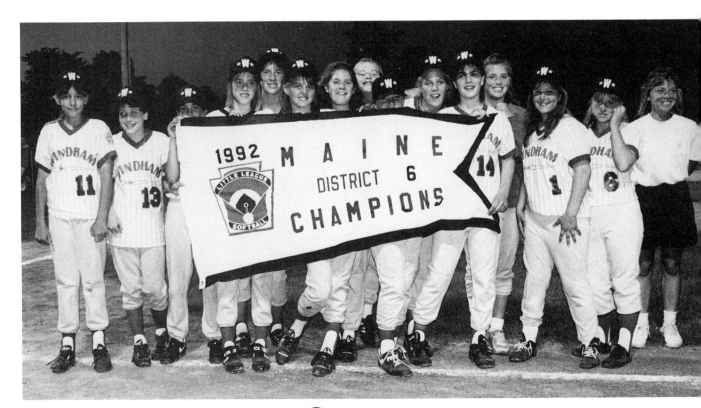

of the sport. One writer recently repeated the litany:

> The pitchers *do* throw hard.
>
> The fielders *do* know where to play and where to throw.
>
> The batters *do* know where to run.
>
> The players *do* know how to handle the various situations.
>
> The base coaches *do* know why they are out there.

The homeruns that do come are spectacular. In extra innings of the opener of the 1992 Women's College World Series in Oklahoma City, Kansas pitcher Stephani Williams served up a rising fast ball to Fresno State's Michelle Bento, who belted it over the left field fence for a game-winning three-run homer. What one should know

is that Williams had not allowed a homerun all
season (over 254¼ innings) and only one other in
her career (over 454 innings).

Another extreme is the game played by the
monster male who would rather park a hunk of
leather-covered plastic over a distant fence—in the
315–325-foot range—than almost anything else

in the world. One fact cuts through it all. As the United States Slo-Pitch Softball Association got ready for its 1991 World Series, in which the top 16 male slow pitch teams in the world would compete, it prepared a fact sheet with one item that overwhelmed all the others. Based on earlier World Series, it noted:

Teams average 50 runs combined and 22 home runs per game.

Those associated with the organized game are totally aware that softball has long been the game of choice for homosexuals and lesbians. A *Boston Phoenix* cover story on lesbian softball in July, 1992, termed it "the lesbian national sport" and talked about what teams from Boston's Alternative League would head to the Gay World Series in Los Angeles. Before this, a book from the softball shelf, Yvonne Zipter's *Diamonds Are a Dyke's Best Friend* (Firebrand Books, 1988), billed itself a report on "the lesbian national pastime."

This is not to say that everybody in the game is altogether comfortable with this publicity; but lesbian and gay people are accepted and the players are quietly acknowledged as another interest group. The attitude seems to be one of "We don't care who you are. Shut up, observe the rules and play ball."

Diversity Celebrated

Softball celebrates diversity in other ways and did so long before it was in fashion. Black teams played white teams in national competition a decade before baseball was integrated in the late 1940s.

It is played by folks in wheelchairs who have their own tournaments. Deaf kids play the game, and there is an offshoot of softball for the blind called "beep ball" in which the batter "sees" the ball by hearing it beep on its approach to the plate. New Amateur Softball Association rules that took effect in 1993 go a long way toward accommodating the physically challenged athlete. For instance, as a result of one of the new rules for slow pitch softball a player can—as a result of his or her disability—play *only* offense or *only* defense.

Softball has become an increasingly important part of the Special Olympics, which did not traditionally offer team sports to its athletes. Frank Kolarek, a former minor leaguer in Major League baseball's Oakland A's organization, had been working with the Special Olympics since he was a player in the 1980s. He now heads the softball program of Special Olympics International, which involves 30,000 Special Olympians, including a number who play on Unified teams that combine individuals from the Special Olympics with those from the larger community. A number of states now have tournaments, and Kolarek predicts significant growth in the next few years.

Softball seems to be played by every group imaginable . . . and under every circumstance. For more than 20 years the town of Priest Lake, Idaho, has sponsored a winter tournament in which the players use a bright pink ball and wear snowshoes.

In Boston a team of police plays a team of priests to raise money for charity. In 1992 Cardinal Bernard Law led his Law Men in a contest

Blue *Jean-Paul Pepin, chief umpire from the Sherbrooke, Quebec, tournament in 1991 when he was 60. At any major tournament the chief umpire is the final arbiter. (Russell Mott)*

against the Real Law Men police team. That city can also boast of the Boston Softball Sober League in which players represent groups such as STEP, a North End center for recovering drug and alcohol addicts.

The Little People of America—an organization of midgets and dwarfs—play softball at their annual conventions and at various locations around the nation. There is also a two-team circuit in Florida in which all of the players are more than 75 years of age.

Murfreesboro, Tennessee *The Riverdale High School Warriors, in a game against Manchester at their home field in the state regionals. The Warriors won this game and later went on to the state quarter finals in Chattanooga, losing in the top 16 bracket AAA girls' fast pitch. Left to right are a sliding Michelle Duncan of Manchester, umpire Ken Chapman and Riverdale catcher Suzanne Gibson. (Russell Mott)*

The scoreboard reads:

BROADWAY SHOW LEAGUE
1992 CHAMPIONSHIP GAME

TEAM	1	2	3	4	5	6	7	8	9
Garrison	0	0	0	3	1	1	0	0	
Hals	0	0	0	0	0	0	3	0	0

Central Park, N.Y.C. *Bruce Grossman, second baseman of the Garrison Protection Security team, which won the Broadway Show League title that afternoon in 1992.* (Russell Mott)

There are Hispanic, black and Indian invitationals. The 1992 All-Indian tournament in Oklahoma City's Wheeler Park drew 78 teams from all over the U.S. and Canada. It has been held every summer since 1952 and long ago took on the title of "the world's largest Indian sports event."

Some of these culturally and socially diverse games take on their own special importance. Advertising guru Jerry Della Femina has been quoted to the effect that winning the Advertising Softball World Series (drawing teams from 17 cities) is "the equivalent of getting a $10 million account."

Families also play the game. Not long ago *Balls and Strikes*, the magazine of the Amateur Softball Association, told of the Godards of Saginaw, Michigan, and a team that features members of the family ranging in age from Joe Godard, 64, the pitcher, to Mike Godard, 16, who plays the outfield.

Given this diversity, there are more than a few leagues and tournaments that are not necessarily watched for the quality of play, but rather, for who is playing. The most glamorous of these:

The Summer Matinee The Broadway Show League marks its 40th season in 1994. Its games are on Thursday afternoons when the theaters are dark and the games fill three diamonds in Central Park. Each year as many as 21 Broadway and Off-Broadway Teams struggle for the championship along with teams from the press, two theatrical unions and other affiliated groups. Team names have reflected the hottest plays of the time dating back to *Hair*, *Hello Dolly*, *The Great White Hope* and *My Fair Lady*. It has a star-studded history, having involved such diverse celebrities as Sammy Davis, Jr., Merv Griffin, Robert Klein, Woody Allen, Joe Namath, Meatloaf, Robert Redford and Phil Silvers. Over the years passersby and a small gaggle of fans have been privy to such sights as George C. Scott pitching to former Giants slugger Monte Irvin; Scott admitted in a 1971 issue of *Balls and Strikes* that Irvin was "still a pretty good hitter."

Each team is allowed five outsiders, but these can be show business people as well. Just after shooting *Ironweed* a few years ago actress Margaret Whitton, a ringer brought in for Barbara Cook's *Cook in Concert*, stopped a bad hop with her face and sported a very traditional black eye for much of the rest of the softball season.

Opening day first pitches are reserved for the likes of Lauren Bacall and Alan Alda.

Also in New York, personalities such as David Letterman and Maury Povich have regular teams. If one was to pick up one of the tabloids in early June of 1992 it would have been possible to see Marla Maples and Donald Trump in their pinstripes playing in a charity softball game at Yankee Stadium.

The Real Washington Senators

One little-heralded crisis in official Washington is the shortage of softball fields. Often men with law degrees and dressed in suits are ordered out into the June sun to hold onto a field for the boss. Softball has become the game of national politics involving everyone from powerful Senators to White House clerks. There is a Congressional League with more than 160 teams, a Congressional tournament, media teams and much play behind the White House on the plot of park land known as the Ellipse. This whole business has a long set of traditions of its own, including grudge matches, which have presumably replaced dueling. Controversial Interior Secretary James Watt once fielded a team—named "Watt's Right!"—that he would unleash on teams bearing the name of his most vocal foes in Congress.

One still talks about a battle that took place in 1983, when two Congressional offices—those

Show Biz Buddy Mantia holding up the winner's trophy from the Show Business League Championships in Central Park in the summer of 1992. (Russell Mott)

The State of the Game

of Robert Kasten (R.-Wis.) and Robert Dole (R.-Kans.)—got into a mock-grudge softball game over divergent positions each took on an important provision of the tax bill. The bases were made from letters from constituents on the provision in question, proving, if nothing else, that they do things differently inside the Beltway.

The Bat Is Mightier

Long Island softball is a long and established Hamptons' tradition featuring a writers vs. artists matchup that, according to local lore, was started by artists Willem de Kooning and Franz Kline. Over the years, it has involved the likes of George Plimpton, Willie Morris, Peter Maas and Carl Bernstein. It is also very informal with many scattered pickup games; this casualness is typified by the announcer who some years ago stood up and said, "Welcome to either the 21st or 25th annual Artist-Writers Softball Game."

Hollywood Ball

Softball—along with Frisbee—also seems to be the game of choice when movies are being made. There was a rather fascinating photo in *Newsweek* a few years ago of Jack Nicholson pitching to Cher while filming *The Witches of Eastwick*. Over the years the softball magazines have carried photos from the sets of films as diverse as *Parenthood* and *Dances with Wolves*.

Sliding Home
A play at the plate at the U.S.S.S.A. Black National Invitational Tournament in Cleveland, 1992. (Russell Mott)

Local Motion   *Local 265, women's slow pitch team at the Black National Invitational Tournament, Cleveland, Ohio, in the summer of 1992. This is the "post-winning dance" they have done regularly for several years after each victory. Local 265 out of Cincinnati won the tournament.*

(Russell Mott)

The Leisure of the Theoried Class

In June in Washington there is a benefit Think Tank Softball Tournament in which the Centers, Institutes and outfits with names such as the Alliance to Save Energy and the U.S. Public Interest Research Group vie for "thinkie"—a trophy replica of Rodin's *The Thinker*. A few years ago major news coverage was accorded to a matchup between the Heritage Foundation and the Institute for Policy Studies, which are about as far apart as any two groups ranging from political right to left. In 1992 no less than 24 teams took part and two teams— the Urban Institute and the Logistics Management Institute—posted their first tournament victories.

The Corporate Game

A 1988 *Washington Post* round-up piece on the game told of an athletic local high school girl who at first was turned down trying out for the school team. Late in the season, she asked the coach if she could try out. He said yes, but asked why she changed her mind. She replied, "Because softball is the executive sport,

and if I ever work for IBM or a company like that, I'll need to know how to play."

It seems that there is a move afoot that is taking the game even deeper into the corporate realm. The new Pepsi corporate headquarters softball diamond boasts an electronic scoreboard and the same Jersey dirt that fills the basepaths at Yankee Stadium. Companies such as Hertz and Coca-Cola sponsor major tournaments, while others recruit players for high-visibility teams.

Softball is the most popular team sport in modern history because almost everyone fits into a uniform. It is a pole apart from baseball, which has granted glory to a limited number of youthful almost universally male athletes. Softball shares

Team Facts *(Below) The feared team in the New Publishers Softball League is fielded by Facts On File, Inc., publisher of this book. Here it poses in Central Park, New York City, in 1992. Left to right in the top row: Michael Goldman, Jill Friedman, Ken Park, Ron Monteleone, Jackie Massa, Marney Fuller, Dave Storck, Bill Bissett, Jeff Golick and Coach Oliver Trager. Bottom, left to right: Matt Heimer, Ken Rosenberg, Chris Larson, Chris ("Chief") Walklet and Ivan Moses. Members of Team Facts missing from the photo: Lori "Line Drive" Klein, Liz "the Preacher" Prager and Melissa "100%" Cotton.*

(Russell Mott)

its glory with almost anyone willing to work hard and find the right level of play.

Consider hypothetical twins born this year. One is a boy and one is a girl. Between them they could play organized softball beginning with tee ball, a simple form of the game in which the ball is driven from a large tee. This simple no pitch game will be played for a few years until they are older and relegated to the senior divisions. If the boy is good enough he may leave the game for baseball, and if she is good enough she can play highly competitive fast pitch softball. Given exceptional talents she might even have an opportunity to play softball in the Olympics. On June 13, 1991, the International Olympic Committee (IOC) approved women's fast pitch softball as a medal sport beginning with the 1996 Olympic Games in Atlanta.

Someday, the two will lose that edge and they will want to play on a team . . . have a few laughs . . . put the ball into play a half dozen times on a weeknight . . . and top it off with a nice fielding play. They will have come back to the game—the slow pitch division. Maybe they will play in the same co-ed league.

And just maybe—if they stay in shape and keep active—there will come a day when both of them will be old. Old softball players.

This book about softball is intended to be a celebration and appreciation of an American phenomenon replete with good yarns, strong personalities and dazzling feats. Babe Ruth and Kirby Puckett are mentioned here but in a new context, and there is a softballer's view of two U.S. presidents, Franklin D. Roosevelt and Jimmy Carter, who led their own teams.

This is not mere trivia. F.D.R. not only managed a team, but he helped create a mania for the game during the New Deal by letting his social engineers go forth and create softball diamonds.

And those games between Carter's people and the media were no mere "photo ops" but real people playing a real game for keeps. These games were famous, observed one writer ". . . not only because the President himself was a participant, but because the games were hard-fought, give-no-quarter affairs where two proud adversaries in the nation's business were not about to concede anything on the playing field. . . ."

Kids and Kubs   (Opposite) Undergoing a ceremonial beard shaving at the end of another successful season: 1961–1962. These gents love publicity stunts like this one. On the ground is Walter D. Lebengood, 82, of Orwigsburg, Pennsylvania, about to lose his whiskers grown for the season. (Amateur Softball Association)

Laughter   (Below) Keene, New Hampshire, Mohican Senior League, slow pitch activist Dick Sault enjoying the summer of 1992. (Russell Mott)

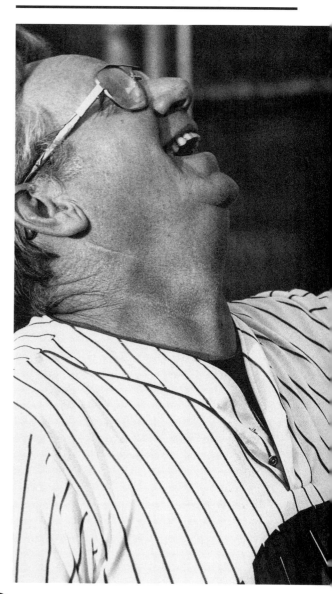

The State of the Game

George Bush is a softballer. In fact, the Bush family ties to the game can be considered a birthright. George Bush's mother hit a softball homerun in Kennebunkport the day she gave birth to his older brother, Prescott Bush. After circling the bases, the late Mrs. Bush let it be known that it was time to go to the hospital.

To the Numbers

"Softball is an American icon. It's baseball before money brought it down," says John Parish, Chief Executive Officer of Worth, Inc., the Tullahoma, Tennessee, company that manufactures and sells more softball equipment than any other. It manufactures baseball equipment as well, but Parish and his family have long been identified as leaders in the softball field. With the recent addition of John Parish's three sons to the company, a fourth generation of the founding Lannom family is in place.

Parish sees softball as an entity that was born of baseball, but that now stands independent outside the game that sired it. "I'm still wrestling with that question," continues Parish, "but I have concluded that softball is truly the national pastime. Americans may watch baseball but they play softball. More than 42 million men, women and children play the game of softball. With apologies to Ernie Harwell, softball—and not baseball—is the game for all America. It is as individual as the regional accents, architecture, cultures and culinary arts of the different places that make up America." He adds: "Its individuality and variety symbolize America's diversity while its essential uniformity—a bat and ball game—is an embodiment of democracy. There's a reason why the great image makers—the beer companies, cola ad men and presidential spin doctors—have all employed softball as an action visual and a photo op."

The numbers speak for themselves:

- It is the nation's *number one team participation sport* according to those who oversee the game, who also claim it has "the most consistent and sustained growth" of any team sport in America. Based on Commerce Department numbers and Gallup polls, some 39.8 million, or 16 percent, of all men, women and children in America play the game on a sustained basis. (By contrast, volleyball is played by 37.3 million, basketball by 32.3 million, baseball by 24.9 million and soccer by 9.9 million.) That number of 39.8 million, which was based on 1986 numbers, has, based on the same sources, been re-estimated to have grown to over 42 million in 1991.

- There are over four million "die-hards," softballese for those men and women who play in six or more competitive softball tournaments a year.

- The largest sanctioning body, the Amateur Softball Association, has 259,139 teams registered in the U.S. with 60,000 umpires. These Amateur Softball Association (ASA) teams will play more than five million games this year. This is only a small part of the team count, since there are an additional 11,000 high school teams, more than 56,000 Junior Olympic teams, the 85,000 teams of the United States Slo-Pitch Softball Association and the thousands of unregistered and unsanctioned teams.

- One series, the Budweiser National Triple Crown Softball Series, runs from March through July and in 1992 involved more than five million men and women slow pitch enthusiasts in 25 states.

- The game is increasingly co-ed and co-equal. At the organized level the game is now approaching sexual parity; 45% of those playing in the 18–34 age group are female and of the 17.7 million players who are on ASA–sanctioned teams 9.7 million are male and 8 million are female. After track and basketball, it is now the third most popular women's collegiate sport.

- At last count, there were more than 25 regular softball publications, ranging from a tabloid newspaper devoted exclusively to Chicago-style 16-ounce gloveless softball to a slick four-color magazine, *Softball Masters*, which is a national news and features magazine "for all softball players." There are many local softball periodicals that maintain exhaustively detailed statistics and standings in their areas. To name some of them gives one an idea of the breadth and depth of this world: *The Sandbagger* (covering slow pitch softball for the Greater Southwestern Division); *Cincinnati Softball News*; *Lone Star Softball*; *Softball West* (which publishes features with titles such as "Heavenly Diamonds" on church teams); *Sierra Softball* (which proclaims itself "The West's Leading Softball Publication"); *Minnesota Amateur Sports Review* (which, despite the name, has had issues focusing 90 percent on softball); *Slo-Pitch News* (out of Seattle); *The Softball News of the Diamond State* ("Delaware's award-winning softball newspaper"); *Chicago Metro Softball*; *Softball News* (covering Missouri, Illinois, Nebraska, Kansas, Wisconsin and Colorado); *Southern California Softball Magazine*; *Southwest Softball* (a slick magazine from Buna, Texas); *Let's Play Softball* (out of Bloomington, Minnesota); *Nebraska Softball News*; and *Georgia Softball*. One monthly, the Amateur Softball Association's *Balls and Strikes*, has 300,000 subscribers (who pay through membership fees) and is in the midst of a drive that its editor claims will get them to 450,000 by year's end. At least 50 newspapers have writers with a regular softball beat or column (to name a few, the *St. Petersburg Times*, the *Richmond News-Leader* and the *Kansas City Star*).

- There are many more numbers, ranging from the statistic that 4.7% of those in organized softball are over 45 years of age to the fact that the game is now being played in 70 countries.

These numbers look even more impressive when reduced to the local level, suggesting that one of the real problems facing the game is that there are not enough places to play it. Looking at the greater Washington, D.C. area, for instance, one finds information like this: Between 1983 and 1988, the number of organized adult softball teams in Fairfax County, Virginia, leapt from 640 to 2,200; there are now 2,000 adult teams in Richmond, Virginia, and more than 10,000 teams in the Washington, D.C. area.

There is also the case of Las Vegas, which has been accused of being softball crazed; in recent years it has been host to more than 100 softball tournaments and features the nation's only regular softball radio show. Those tournaments, by the way, are attractions that cities and towns bid and beg for in order to raise funds and increase tourism. In 1991 the Amateur Softball Association held 57 national tournaments, which alone had an economic impact on their sites totaling $19,173,182.

Organizer *Sonny Anderson, a.k.a. Mr. Black Softball. He directs many tournaments in the Cleveland, Ohio area. (Russell Mott)*

The State of the Game

But are there any problems here?

There are two.

The first is that the violence that has infected society has had an effect on the game. Some of the worst has been addressed at umpires. Underscoring this point is the following paragraph from an article in the August 2, 1991, *USA Today* on violence against officials.

Connecting *Steve Kirby of the California Gold 16 Inch Softball Team gets hold of a mush ball during a U.S.S.S.A. tournament in Sturdevant, Wisconsin, in September, 1992.* (Russell Mott)

In Seattle, where a softball umpire was chased in his car by three players and kicked until he bled, there are reports of officials carrying Mace. The Associated Press reported one keeps a gun in his car and another works under a false name and backs his car into the parking space so he can make a fast getaway.

To curb violence in this particular case, the Seattle arm of the U.S. Slo-Pitch Softball Association created a safety committee that has acted to suspend some players.

From 1983 to 1989, the number of registered umpires in the Amateur Softball Association of America fell from 62,000 to 56,500. The total has started to go up again—59,668 in 1992—but Merle Butler, the ASA's national director of umpires is on record with his concerns: "Basketball has the technical foul and football the penalty, but umpires have nothing to combat the abuse," says Butler. "With the economy down, more and more leagues can't afford two umpires. How is one umpire going to handle a confrontation with a 6-foot-7 player?"

Some have said that a portion of this violence was inevitable as the game grew, but the fact remains that the problem has to be dealt with.

Big Guy *Clyde Guy at the Smoky in Maryville, Tennessee, in 1992. At the major slow pitch level he is one of the dominant players.*
(Russell Mott)

Limits to Growth

The growth of the game has and will present some problems that are quite real. Those who look at the game for trends find that there are limitations to its expansion because, as the number of players continues to rise, so do the number of teams demanding a place to play. Or, as a 1988 *Washington Post* headline on softball in the area put it, "DIAMONDS FAST BECOMING SCARCE."

The number of ASA–registered teams increased ninefold between 1963 and 1980, and

Dust Up   (Above) Dust, sand and assorted debris kicked up in a Cambridge, Massachusetts, municipal fast-pitch league. Despite what slow-pitch aficionados say, the fast-pitch game is still played with passion by both men and women. (Russell Mott)

Angel at Bat   (Opposite) Cleveland, Tennessee, Angel player Mrs. Vetta Ware at the Black National Invitational Tournament, Cleveland, Ohio, in 1992. (Russell Mott)

during that period municipalities kept pace with the demand. Federal and state funds helped increase the overall acreage, and more and more amenities such as concession stands and bleachers were added to the mix. To ease the weekend demand, old and new diamonds were equipped with lights.

Then, all of a sudden, in the late 1970s things changed. Recreation departments throughout the country suffered cutbacks or remained stable in the face of double-digit inflation. Measures created in a "taxpayer's revolt," led by

Proposition 13 in California, eased the tax burden for homeowners but caused budgeting setbacks. At the beginning of the 1981 season, *Balls and Strikes* lamented, "More than one perfectly good softball field has been abandoned by cities with over-stretched budgets because there is no money to maintain it and no money to staff it." It was also pointed out that "horror stories" were emerging of players spending entire winter nights waiting in line at the Recreation Department, waiting and hoping to be among the lucky ones able to sign up for a league during the upcoming season.

All of these problems required further study, and in early 1992 the Forbes Consulting Group delivered its preliminary report on the "softball marketplace" for the Sporting Goods Manufacturers Association of the U.S. After addressing the appeal and growth of the game—something that boiled down to the six words: easy, exciting, healthy, sociable, nostalgic, affordable—and determining that it appealed to a very broad spectrum of people, the report got into the challenges or limitations facing the game.

Softball has gradually evolved away from the highly skilled and competitive fast-pitch game of the '50s and '60s to a much more broad-based and recreational game. In the words of the study, the "skill threshold had been lowered" and the officials in charge encouraged more people to get into the game. For instance, the Amateur Softball Association's "re-entry rule" encouraged coaches to replace first-string players with second stringers during a game, since the rule permits a player to re-enter the game if his or her skill is later needed. More and more softball associations have also changed the format of their tournaments to render them more participative: "Champion/consolation" tournaments allow pairs of losing teams to play additional, consolation games.

The report even looked at the sociology of the game and concluded that from a social scientist's point of view, the ever-growing appeal of softball may in part be a reflection of two sociological trends in the United States today: "neo-traditionalism," and "cocooning."

Neo-traditionalism   For many softball players and officials, softball seems to embody certain traditional American values that have recently regained importance in American society: Softball is described as "good, clean fun," an American pastime suitable for the whole family or for members of one's church. Many parents see softball as having a positive influence on their children's character development. As spectators or players of the sport, children, it is felt, can learn critical "life lessons" about the value of discipline, teamwork, respect for authority and how to win or lose gracefully.

Cocooning   Softball also mirrors the greater importance that the "baby boom" generation now places on family and home and on social activities that are close to home ("cocooning"):

- Softball can involve all family members in either the role of player or spectator. Post-game social events can be geared to families, e.g., family picnics or barbecues
- Reflecting the desire to stay close to home, players with families now prefer local tournaments rather than regional or national ones that require weekend travel. Recognizing this limitation on tournament participation, some softball organizations now tailor regional/national tourneys to families, offering family-oriented accommodations and activities.

The most important findings of the report were disturbing:

1. *Current playing space cannot accommodate more players.* A stunning conclusion. A considerable number of officials reported that they did not need to promote softball since their fields were totally booked each season; these administrators typically turned teams away.

    Some have suggested better scheduling of teams as a partial remedy but as expansion of

---

Media Bash   (Opposite) Mary Carillo, sportscaster for CBS and a member of the CBS softball team, playing versus the WFAN team at the Volvo tennis tournament in New Haven, for the Special Olympics. It rained throughout the games. WFAN, a New York City all-sports radio station, won. (Russell Mott)

Big Men *Mascot for the 1991 U.S.S.S.A. Sherbrooke Tournament at Desranleau Field greeting Dennis Graser, the first baseman of the Ritch's/Superior team of Windsor Locks, Connecticut.* (Russell Mott)

the game outstrips these measures for better usage of current playing space, private funds may be needed to help finance the building of new facilities.

2. *Funds are short for new program development.* Some park and recreational officials cited lack of funds as a reason for little or no additional development of softball programs. Program sponsorship by the private sector would clearly be helpful to their developmental efforts.

3. *Funds are lacking for direct maintenance of fields.* The report indicated that players became "spoiled" from the high-level maintenance of playing fields in the '80s when municipal budgets were much more generous. Some park and recreation administrators reported a loss of players to private sports complexes, as players sought the field conditions and amenities they grew accustomed to in the past decade.

It went on to suggest: "Involving the local community in field maintenance and improvement (in the spirit of a traditional barn raising) would be one approach to keeping up these playing spaces."

4. *The weak economy has put a financial squeeze on local business sponsorship of teams/tournaments.* Some administrators reported that in recent years teams had dropped out of leagues and tournaments had been discontinued because local businesses were no longer able to subsidize them.

There is relief for some of these problems in the continuing emergence of privately owned softball complexes. These new multifield softball complexes come replete with lighted diamonds, restaurants, video playback systems, playrooms for the kids and more. The new Twin Creeks Sports Complex in the heart of Silicon Valley, California, and the Cocoa Expo Softball Complex, on Florida's East Coast with seven fields, are prominent "state-of-the-art" examples. The Twin Creek facility is home to 650–700 teams in a season and boasts a disco, while the Florida location features a lit 5,000-seat stadium. However, two of the largest softball centers are in Kansas— Miller's Woods in Overland and Fun Valley in Hutchinson.

Dream Teamer
Chris McKuhan, a
player for the
softball team of WFAN, a
New York City sports
station. She is playing in
a celebrity softball game at
the Volvo United States
Tennis Association
Tournament. The game was
played in the rain at Yale
Baseball Stadium before
3,000 fans for the benefit
of the Special Olympics.
(Russell Mott)

Where Is the Money Going?

Who are these people that can't seem to get enough of the game? Data generated by the Sporting Goods Manufacturers' Association tells us that even when kids are thrown into the equation, 64.1 percent of those who play the game regularly make over $25,000 per year; 48.7 percent make more than $35,000; and 26.2 percent make over $50,000 a year.

Even more to the point, there is lots of money being spent on this hobby/sport; according to the ASA, the annual expenditure for new equipment is more than $500 million and growing. Some years ago it eclipsed the amount of money spent on baseball equipment. By the end of 1992, 12 million softballs had been bought and the number was projected to keep growing. As companies such as Rawlings, Dudley, Louisville Slugger, Wilson, Spalding and Worth have discovered, softball is soon to be a billion-dollar-a-year business. There are a number of top-of-the-line items out there. Worth's RD2-ll softball glove retails for $129.00 and there are a number of aluminum or graphite softball bats that cost close to $100.

As a matter of fact, there are those in the business who claim that the ASA's $500 million for new equipment is on the low side because many of the gloves sold with large webbed areas are counted in the sporting goods industry as baseball sales, but are actually being bought for softball use, especially those purchased by women and men over 30.

There is a sensual quality built into the equipment that is a distant cry from the klutzy, company-picnic equipment of a generation back.

Sleek, high-tech aircraft aluminum and ceramic bats are a blend of gleam, color and bold graphics; shoes are designed with the same eye on

---

Bats   Two bats at rest in the "B" Slo-Pitch Tourney, Agawam, Massachusetts, in the summer of 1992. High-quality aluminum bats have completely overtaken wooden bats for the simple reason that they are long-lived. If these had been wood they would probably have been retired a long time ago. (Russell Mott)

style as those used in basketball; and the balls have been re-engineered for their audio qualities. Aerospace engineer and chairman of Worth, Inc. Jess Heald, inventor of the Worth Blue Dot ball, was quoted in an interview in the ASA's monthly tabloid *Balls and Strikes*: "In testing we discovered there was a prescribed sound that translates in the player's mind as the sound of power or a solid hit. We actually tuned the ball to enhance its performance with a more powerful sound."

The fielders' gloves are works of art sculpted of leather and the uniforms are handsome, snug and colorful. There are also customized bat equipment bags and beautifully designed batting gloves made of "English tanned Cabretta leather." The video camera and cassette have become vehicles for showing it all off—including the pop of the ball. Lest there be any question, video recording has become an important element in the game for those who take softball seriously, from batting analysis to season highlight tapes, even if a team is sponsored by an out-of-the-way tavern. And that tavern is likely to use the tapes of Saturday's games to stimulate business on Sunday when it replays the game. (Incidentally, the emerging protocol of the game seems closer to rugby than traditional softball—players drink after the game with the team, not on the field during the game.)

Where is all of this going? If there is a direction in all of this it is toward increased performance and safety. Injuries are still a factor in the game, despite continuing attempts to make the game safer. For instance, the ASA rule changes for 1993 included new requirements for the catchers in youth divisions to wear throat protectors, helmets with ear flaps and shin guards that protect the knee caps. "Safer balls, bigger diamonds, helmets for runners, breakaway bases are all things being instituted without changing the character of the game," says Jess Heald, who is responsible for a number of key product innovations in baseball and softball including RIF (Reduced Injury Factor) balls for baseball and softball.

There are a number of reasons cited for the growth of the game but most of these—the baby boom, the rise of the suburbs—are the same factors that fueled other pastimes. One unique factor is the rise of the slow pitch version of softball. Fast pitch was the dominant form of the game 25 years ago, but slow pitch is now the game of 90 percent of the adult players in the country.

Kicking Up Dust *A play at home at the Sherbrooke Tournament in Canada in June, 1991.* (Russell Mott)

Heroes and Television

In spite of all of its growing popularity, the game of softball gets precious little attention from the media. The problem the people involved in the sport have grappled with since the late 1940s is that television has turned a cold shoulder on softball. Games have been televised from time to time by the networks (although this hasn't occurred in many years) and a few tournaments have shown up on cable television; but the small screen has never been a factor, despite the chorus of those who have pushed to have broadcast coverage.

A few have come to see, however, that it is not likely to become a television sport even in an era when it seems like every imaginable sport is getting television and cable time. Worth's John Parish, who advertises softball equipment on television, has given this matter some thought:

Softball is about participating and not spectating. And yet it's more than that. Softball replaces television. In baseball, television allows us to watch a sport we dreamed of playing as a child. Television is a vicarious means to play in the big leagues or return to our childhood heroes. But while television is a passive means to live our big league dreams, softball is an active means. It is the home run trot, beating out an infield single, turning or breaking up a double play, high fives and wearing a uniform—all the motions and emotions of baseball. Lived. So softball is an active replacement for television's passive big league dreams. In fact, most softball players don't watch baseball because they're playing softball.

I think the character of softball would change if it were televised. The game would be altered for the spectator's pleasure rather than the player's, for the network's benefit rather than the game's. And with television would come more and more money, and we've seen what money has done to baseball. Money changes everything. Gone would be much of the color, spontaneity, character and fun of the game.

Some think that the biggest tragedy of televising softball might be that it would lure participants into the easy chair of spectating. Senior softball players might retire early in the televised glare of younger players.

But the real heroes and heroines of softball are not movie or television stars but folks who earn wages or salaries or live on pensions, and in some cases play the game when logic dictates otherwise. There are softball teams that literally defy the imagination. Consider a game played in 1991 in Washington, D.C., between the Heart Throbs and the New Pumps. The teams were dominated by 13 men who had *undergone heart transplants.*

Then there was the case of Susan Craig of San Diego who in 1976 was famous for her statement to the Associated Press that she hoped to have her second child after the next game her team would play, so that she would be ready for the game after that. As for the first child, she said, "I played the day before I delivered and was playing again two days after she was born." And what about her condition? "It's not hard to get down

Celebrity Swing Connie Chung of CBS swinging a Worth bat at the Landon School class of '57 reunion in June 1992. Her husband, television personality Maury Povich, was in the class of 1957. (Russell Mott)

for the ground balls but it is sort of hard to get back up."

There are, in fact, vast numbers of older people playing the game and some who are truly old. The hero of the old players is George Bakewell who turned 100 on April 27, 1992, and claims the title of the oldest active softball player in the world, a title he still held in 1993.

At the time of his birthday, there was a lot of hoopla about Bakewell—Nike featured him in a television commercial—but what seemed to get lost in it all was that this man had been playing for the Kids & Kubs softball club since he began as a batboy in 1967 at 75, the *minimum* age for playing with this team. Slowed by a prostate operation, he was not playing full games at the time of his centennial, but vowed to the *Tampa Tribune* that he would stage a full comeback at age 101. According to the president of the club, he was not too pleased when the team cut him back from a full game to four innings.

Bob Chick of the *Tribune* described Bakewell as catcher a few years earlier: "In his mid-90s, when he caught every day and squatted behind the plate, his rear a dozen inches off the ground, he merely flicked his wrist, returned the ball to the pitcher and never left the crouch position."

One story written by DeNeen L. Brown in the *Washington Post* in the spring of 1991 may be as heroic as a softball story can get. To quote the first few paragraphs of the article, which was reproduced in a number of softball publications:

It's the top of the seventh and the batter cracks a pop fly over the first baseman. Harry McCary takes off from his position at second, his 77-year-old legs moving him left to the foul line, his 77-year-old arm stretched above his head, determined not to miss the softball arcing toward him.

He makes a running catch, and the crowd explodes. He throws to the pitcher, and smiling

from ear to ear, walks back toward second. Then Harry McCary's heart gave out.

"He died doing the things that he wanted to do. He was not ready for the rocking chair or T.V. He wanted to go on the ballfield. He couldn't ask for anything better than that," said Raymond J. Kaminski, manager of the 70 Plus Virginia Cardinals, who played in a tournament Saturday afternoon in Fairfax.

"You should have seen him after he made that catch. He walked back to his position with a very content and happy look on his face as though to say, 'Gee, I knew I could do it. Did you see that catch? I know I can play ball at 77.' When he got back to his position, he seemed to wilt."

Before the game, McCary had demanded more playing time.

Octogenarian *Maynard Van Horn, 80, gets hold of one in this picture of a Kids and Kubs game from 1973.*
(Martin Luther King Library, Washington Star Collection)

Flexibility Counts

What the game possesses and what gives it health is that it is adaptable.

Searching for a league for folks over 65 only? Competing groups such as the Amateur Softball Association and the United States Slo-Pitch Softball Association will knock each other over trying to give a newcomer a hand. And what about a game that is played in the sand and seems to borrow some of its spirit from volleyball? It exists and it is called Over the Line softball. Suppose a group of folks wanted to hang onto the game the way it was played in the 1930s? That is precisely what they do in Chicago with a melon of a 16-inch ball. Maybe there should be a version for the little ones? These games would include tee ball and bonk ball—simple skill games that teach youngsters the rudiments of batting and fielding.

Then let us suppose that there were some people who wanted a game that was not quite as fast as fast pitch, eliminating the demon

The Worth Book of Softball

pitches of the fast game—the windmill and the sling-shot—but not quite as slow as slow pitch. It exists and is called modified and the Amateur Softball Association alone signed up 8,370 modified teams in 1992.

Co-ed softball provides a similar case in point. Large numbers of people wanted to play on teams with male and female members and the game embraced the idea. The growth in co-ed teams has been nothing short of phenomenal.

The game thus engrained is hard to remove. Folks in softball love to talk about die-hard softball places, such as Hendersonville, Tennessee, where two of the greatest slow pitch tournaments are held; or Maryville—in that same state—where they hold the Smoky; or York, Pennsylvania, which lost its minor league baseball team a few years back and filled the old ballpark with softball games. In 1991, when York was offered a new minor league baseball team, the town decided to take a rain check and stick with softball.

Heresy? You bet, but many softballers think all of the *Field of Dreams*-y "baseball as metaphor" stuff has gotten a bit too overblown and precious.

But it should be pointed out that the game played by Kevin Costner, the star of that film, is softball. In fact, he was the cover boy for May–June 1990 *Softball Masters* magazine.

People who play the game tend to be amused but not awed by the fact that Costner, Cher, Alan Alda, President Clinton and others play the game, but the stars tend to simply be seen as other players and not much more than that.

What is important to softball is the season itself—the months in which the game is played. For most people, the softball season is brief and sweet, beginning to roll in May and mostly wrapped up by Labor Day weekend, a very important time for tournaments. There is also a longer season. It begins with the high school and college women's first scrimmages in the early spring and extends to the last invitational, which is likely to be played after Halloween. In 1992 the last ASA slow pitch tournament was the Firefighter's Invitational, which was played until November 12th. That tournament in Las Vegas ended the game's 105th season, which was a far cry from its first in Chicago.

Barnstormer *The eternally fast Eddie Feigner showing his form. Feigner has been on the road since 1946 with his four-man team, The King and His Court, which takes on all comers.*

(Amateur Softball Association)

3 The

BEFORE SOFTBALL COULD BECOME SOFTBALL IT HAD TO MOVE OUTSIDE

Hancock's Game

Unlike baseball, whose origins have long been a matter of debate, there is no disputing the exact moment at which the game of softball was invented. It was late on the cold afternoon of Thanksgiving Day, 1887, in the gymnasium of the high-Gothic Farragut Boat Club at the edge of Lake Michigan in Chicago in the 3000 block of Lake Park Avenue.

A group of 20 or so young men had gathered there for the reading of a series of telegrams that would reveal the progress and final score of the Harvard–Yale football game. Small wagers were made between telegrams.

Primitive Game

These were single young men with simple honest jobs. Among others assembled there were: a cashier, Frank Staples; a bookkeeper, Carl Bryant; a salesman, Ogden Downs; and a watchman, Edward Palmer.

When the final score was announced—Yale, 17; Harvard, 8—bets were paid off and, as one historian of the moment put it, "Animal spirits came to the fore. Horseplay was rampant."

At one moment during all of this, one of the Yale boosters picked up a stray boxing glove and lobbed it across the gym at one of the Harvard fans. The target saw the glove coming, grabbed a pole and whacked it back across the room over the pitcher's head. The batsman howled with glee.

Indoor Team   *Image of the men who played the early game. Rediscovered recently, it is one of a very few photographs of the early game that has survived.*

(Library of Congress, Prints and Photographs Division)

Seeing this, a young reporter for the Chicago Board of Trade named George Hancock said, "I've got it. Let's play ball." Hancock shaped and bound the glove in its own laces so that it resembled a ball and then chalked out a crude diamond on the gym floor. The dimensions were much smaller than those for regulation baseball so the game would fit the confines of an indoor gym. A broom handle was broken off to form a bat.

Teams were chosen and play began. It was a frolic and the sport was played "without rule or wisdom." Time has obscured the winner of that first game—each team scored more than 40 runs—and no record remains of how the teams were divided, although it has always been assumed that players were separated between followers of the Harvard Crimson and Yale Blue. This odd game of "scrub" baseball lasted for more than an hour.

It might have ended then and there at the Farragut Boat Club if George Hancock—who had been thinking about this game since they had started to play—hadn't gathered the lads around him and made a little speech. "I believe this affair can be worked into a regular game of baseball which can be played indoors," he said, "and if you come down Saturday night I'll make up some rules and have a ball and bat which will suit the purpose of the sport and do no damage to the surroundings."

True to his word, he created an oversized ball and an undersized rubber-tipped bat, wrote a set of rules and went back to the boat club to paint permanent white foul lines on the gym floor. He named his game indoor baseball and it was different from baseball in a number of specific ways right down to its specially crafted bat and ball.

The Saturday game was played with the odd new ball and the small rubber-tipped bat. As recalled in a later *Indoor Baseball Guide*: "The contest was one of the funniest performances ever witnessed and members and visitors went away loud in their praises of 'Indoor Base Ball' as the new sport was christened."

By mid-winter the game had caught on all over Chicago and was being played in gymnasiums and lodge halls around the city. Hancock ruled that almost any inside space 40 by 60 feet or larger was acceptable, including "the waxed floor of a dancing hall."

By the end of the winter there were regularly scheduled games at the boat club against other newly formed teams.

Then as now, Chicago made the claim that a new game had been created there. Unlike baseball, whose creation story involving Abner Doubleday has been proven to be mythological, the story of softball and the Farragut Boat Club has never been debunked or challenged. Organized softball celebrated its 100th Anniversary in Chicago throughout 1987 without a single claim to the contrary. One reason for this unanimity may have been that Hancock in his various rule books and articles was extremely specific as to other people involved in the development of the new game. To cite one example, Hancock even recorded the name of the man, Augustus J. White, who created the first ball "which could be seen at night and fill all the requirements of the game."

Nor has Hancock's role ever been disputed. He was "Mr. Indoor Ball" for years to come and wrote about the growth of the game in official guides that were published well into the 20th century.

Indoor baseball filled several needs. For one, it bridged the gap between the football and baseball seasons. It was also something other than calisthenics and straightforward exercise that could be staged inside a gymnasium.

At the time the game was created, gymnasiums existed for the serious activities of physical education. It was a place for Indian club drills, rope climbing and gymnastics, including work on the parallel bars and suspended rings. The business of physical education was an intensely serious one and the nation's school systems seemed to be divided into two camps—those using the German system of gymnastics (featuring repetitive/Indian club drills) and the Swedish system (which stressed the idea of "medical" gymnastics through a prescribed series of exercises).

Games, on the other hand, were played outside, without adult supervision and depended on the simplest (and cheapest) of playthings: jacks, jump ropes, marbles and dice.

It is of more than passing interest to know that basketball was invented in Springfield, Massachusetts, four years later to fill these same needs. A young Canadian instructor at the Y.M.C.A. Training School by the name of James Naismith was given a problem to solve. The school was having disciplinary problems with some of its young men who seemed to be having a particularly hard time facing a long, cold and sportless New England winter. There was a bleak icy gap between the end of the football season and the first day of baseball practice, which made the lads restless.

After experimenting with indoor variations on outdoor games (football, soccer and lacrosse), it became apparent to Naismith that he wanted a new game—one that used a ball and had a goal. He came up with the notion of wooden boxes into which players could toss a soccer ball. The day the idea was tested there were no boxes to be found and he had settle for a pair of peach baskets, which he had nailed to the underside of the gym balcony ten feet off the floor.

Suddenly, the winter sports schedule started to fill up. With the advent of the steel ice skate in about 1885, organized hockey was poised to take off. In 1893 the first U.S. college team was organized on the Yale campus in New Haven, Connecticut. Meanwhile, indoor baseball was on the move.

Out of the Boathouse

In the spring of 1888, the game of indoor baseball moved outdoors, where it was played on a small diamond and started to be called indoor-outdoor.

Hancock could see that he had created something important and published his first set of indoor-outdoor rules in 1889. A few excerpts from that first set of published rules:

It can be played in any hall or room of dimensions which will permit of a proper distance for bases and fielding, the composition of the floor being immaterial, as the rubber-soled shoes required to be worn are equally suitable for a smooth surface or carpet.

The game is played like ordinary baseball with special rules and regulations to equalize the difference in size of grounds and surroundings.

The ball is of large size, made of a yielding substance, especially for this purpose. The bat is 2¾ feet long and 1¼ inches in diameter at the large end. The four bases are each 1½ feet square, half filled with sand.

The catcher should always play up close to the bat as foul tips are frequent, and the composition of the ball will not allow a serious injury if a player should be struck in the face with it.

Masks and gloves are not essential, but it is a good idea for players to have their suits padded all around the knees, as the frequent slidings and bumping on the hard floor would otherwise be hurtful.

In addition, there were 19 special rules that were needed to fully refit baseball to the indoors. As adopted by the Mid-Winter Indoor Baseball League of Chicago on October 24, 1889, these special rules called for: a smaller diamond (27 feet between the bases—unless the hall was too narrow; then the distance between first and third base could be reduced); rubber-soled shoes; straight-armed underhanded pitching with no curving; teams of eight or nine to a side; two umpires; and no leaving a base until the ball has reached or passed the catcher. As if to prove that the inside ball was soft, the rules said: "A pitched ball striking the batter is a dead ball, but does not entitle him to a base."

Players eagerly learned the sport and the 80-plus runs scored in the first game were due to the fact that this was new and everybody lacked experience. But as the introduction to the 1890 *Rules for Indoor Baseball* pointed out, "As the play of the athletes improved the result was much smaller figures and more on the professional basis of baseball . . . the game has reached a scientific standpoint hitherto unsuspected of fulfillment."

The Windy City embraced the game with a real zest. It was, as guidebook writer George E. Moran put it in his 1892 *Dictionary of Chicago and Its Vicinity*, "An amusement which is purely Chicagoan, invented by a Chicagoan, and little known outside the city limits. . . ." Moran said that there were more than 100 organized clubs in Chicago, adding that "their games attract thousands of spectators of the best classes."

Indoor baseball was very much a game for the social and athletic clubs of the area, as evidenced by the names of the leading teams: the LaSalles, the Kenwoods, the Harvards, the Lincoln Cycling Club, the Idlewilds of Evanston, the Carletons, the Marquettes, the Chicago Cycling Club and the Oaks of Austin. It was billed as "a great game . . . played by good fellows."

Indoor play was a novel feature until just after the turn of the century. In 1899 the National

Indoor Baseball Association reported leagues in 16 states from Maine to Oregon. C.G. Sinsasbaugh of the *Chicago Daily News* wrote of the game ". . . it has grown out of its swaddling cloths, until now it is the recognized winter sport of those base ball enthusiasts who are not content to remain passive during the winter months. The game has always been popular, and at the start of the 1899–1900 sèason prospects are that it will be played in cities in the United States where three years ago the game was practically unknown."

Organized indoor baseball became international with the formation of a league in Toronto in 1897. This was the same year that the earliest *Indoor Baseball Guide* was published by the American Sports Publishing Company in New York. Publication would continue for a decade. The previous rule books had been published in Chicago, and this was the first nationally distributed publication on the new game.

It was a major diversion in the Canal Zone, was embraced by the firemen of Colorado Springs and attracted leagues in such far-flung locales as Savannah, Georgia; Concord, New Hampshire; and Brooklyn, New York. Others came to the indoor game fairly late in its development. In the fall of 1909, for instance, the St. Louis Railroad Indoor League was founded.

Pitching was key. That first season played by the St. Louis Railroad Indoor League, for instance, was won by the Rock Island Railroad team. Bart Holland pitched all 14 of the team's games, losing only one. In the process he pitched two no-hit games, threw 247 strikeouts and allowed only 14 hits.

As it moved west into California, Hancock adjusted a few of his rules for the outdoors, such as extending the base lines to 45 feet. In California the game was played indoors and outdoors; but the indoor game was primarily reserved for evening games played in armories and gymnasiums.

In Chicago, however, the game became so popular that a problem arose: the best players wanted to be paid. Leagues that had been playing every night during the winter were collapsing. Journalist C. G. Sinsasbaugh, writing in the *Daily News*, attributed this to "rowdyism and the 'grafters'"—men who put a price on their talent, causing every decent team in the Windy City to balance a payroll. Managers bid for players and

there was a lot of team jumping. Even by charging admissions, few teams could support its players and one by one the leagues died out to be replaced by "guerrilla teams" finding competition where they could.

New starts were made, but problems of professionalism kept cropping up. The beginning of the 1910 season, for example, was a mess because of wrangling between promoters, amateurs and teams entirely composed of professionals. An amateur association was formed that year under the control of the Amateur Athletic Federation, and that association saved the game temporarily.

Early in the 20th century interest in indoor baseball began to die out—or, as one critic later said, "Folks stayed away from it in large numbers"—despite several organized attempts to give the game some new life. In February, 1914, *Sporting Goods Dealer* magazine suggested that dealers go out and help start new indoor leagues. The magazine suggested that a good place to begin these leagues was where basketball was being played.

It was too late.

Quite simply, the indoor game was being bounced out of the gymnasium by basketball. Basketball had become such a consumer of gym time—and so rough and tumble—that in 1896 the YMCA was forced to temporarily ban it from its floors. By 1920 it had become the winter game for all of North America south of Toronto.

One of the few places that indoor seemed to be winning out over basketball as a gym sport was among Americans working in the Panama Canal Zone, where it was simply too hot to play basketball.

A Bat of Her Own

For most of the 19th century in America it was not considered proper for women to play team sports. Croquet, lawn tennis, archery, ice skating and gymnastics were considered properly feminine. Physical contact was out.

Basketball changed things. Beginning with Smith College in 1893, basketball was eagerly adopted by many of the same female physical education leaders who had shunned baseball as "unladylike."

Baseball had a rotten reputation at the end of the 19th century and players were regarded as carousing crude men admired for their ability to curse, drink and gamble.

Some of the Eastern women's schools tried to play baseball. Vassar had a baseball club as early as 1866 that operated for a number of years. Students at Smith College formed a club in 1879, but it was forced to disband before the season was over when the school said the game was too violent and that it would cause windows to be broken. (To be fair, Smith College had a long baseball history, including an annual Field Day game between students and faculty. This game was converted to softball in about 1940.)

Indoor baseball, on the other hand, was initially little more than a pale imitation of baseball, lacking even the hint of violence—or at least that was the common perception.

The early balls tended to be dumpling-soft spheres 15 to 17 inches in circumference, to be hit with a shorter and smaller bat. The rules were seemingly set to protect people and property rather than provide action. The ball tended to be hit on the bounce and players weren't allowed to bunt. It was a pleasant alternative to calisthenics and Swedish-drill periods, and no one got in trouble for breaking windows.

More than one observer noted that indoor was not taken seriously by many of the men and boys who played outdoor sports and who were unaware of the rough and tumble reality of Chicago-style form of the game. Regulation baseball was king and the male gym rats were not satisfied with an indoor game that attracted nicknames such as "sissy ball" and "dainty drawers." The names also alluded to the fact that by taking baseball indoors it had ceased to be an all-male domain.

Indoor baseball—and its followers, kitten ball and playground ball—gave American women a turn at bat. Once allowed to participate, women would be a key element of the sport at every juncture.

In 1895, eight years after Hancock first invented the game, the first women's team was organized at Chicago's West Division High School, signifying the beginnings of the woman's game. It was a slow and lackluster start, but still a genuine beginning. That Chicago team did not get a coach for competitive play until 1899, and later on players and coaches had a hard time creating interest among fans. The 1904 *Spalding Indoor Baseball Guide* said that the first few years were discouraging because of the "lack of natural ball playing ability of the girl," a point that would be disproved in the 20th century after the women's game had gained strong footing. But that same *Guide* devoted a large section to discussing and reporting on the women's game. It was argued that 90 percent of the schoolgirls exposed to the game played it with enthusiasm. (The remaining 10 percent were women who were not interested in competitive athletics—about the same percent found in the male population.)

Hancock himself was enthusiastic and deeply pleased with the degree to which the game had become a women's game. He wrote about its development and noted just after the turn of the century: "It is surprising to note the expertness with which girls can play the game after short practice."

Basketball broke the ice for women's team sports, indoor baseball was right behind it and by about 1900 field hockey came along. Volleyball and soccer would follow later. But it was indoor baseball that put the bat in a woman's hand and let her hit the ball and run the bases. Many years later Joel Zoss and John Bowman, the authors of *Diamonds in the Rough: The Untold History of Baseball*, wrote, "What finally seems to have done in baseball as an acceptable sport for young ladies, though, was its own offspring—softball."

But basketball was attracting more women than indoor baseball, and by 1908 the *Spalding's Official Indoor Base Ball Guide* was focusing on the reason why. The *Guide* cited several factors, including the specious argument that basketball was more understandable to American spectators than baseball.

But then women began to play indoor baseball outdoors. From early on it was seen as the vehicle by which women could play a game that had, for all intents and purposes, excluded them: baseball. There would be a moment in 1933 when softball would become a nation wide phenomenon through a national tournament. At that moment, women's softball would reach full status, as the male and female champions were crowned with full equality.

The Primitive Game

Kittens and Rats

While Chicago is where the game was born, softball experienced an important part of its infancy in Minneapolis. In 1895 indoor was reinvented for the outdoors by a fire department officer named Lewis Rober, Sr. who needed a game to keep his men in shape and occupied during their idle time. The problems of inactivity and boredom were genuine. Rober's men lived in the Fire Company Number Eleven building and served as a single platoon, meaning that they were on duty 24 hours a day. He had tried to interest the platoon in boxing but that had limitations as a routine daily activity. His use of heavy medicine balls, tossed for conditioning exercises, may have added to rather than alleviated the boredom in the fire house.

It is still not clear whether Rober knew of the Chicago game, but there is really no reason to think that he did. Indoor-outdoor was still largely confined to the greater Chicago area, and the sports pages were hardly interested in this compressed version of baseball. What appears to be true is that Rober was creating his own game for confined outside spaces such as the vacant lot attached to his firehouse.

Rober created a diamond half the size of a baseball diamond, set the pitcher's distance at 35 feet and had a woodworker turn out a pile of bats two inches in diameter.

The game was immediately popular among the city's firefighters. The next year Rober was given a new unit, Fire Company Number Nineteen, on the campus of the University of Minnesota, and a new team to manage. This group called itself the Kittens.

The name Kitten League Ball was given to the game in the summer of 1900 by Captain George Kehoe of Truck Company Number One in honor of Lieutenant Rober's original team. The League was formalized for the Kittens, Rats, Whales and others who by this time could routinely draw crowds of 3,000 a game.

To be sure, the game was played with intensity and feeling. "Sometimes two brothers would belong to different teams," reported the *Minneapolis Tribune*, "[The] spirit would be so intense that families would be divided on the merits of the two teams, and some members of a family would go a whole season without speaking to one another."

The name Kitten League Ball was later shortened to the sport kitten ball, which came under the Park Board program in 1913, when leagues were formed among the boys of city playgrounds. The limited time, space and equipment the game required soon led to its adoption by commercial firms and athletic associations throughout the city. Because a game could be played in an hour or less, it was deemed to be particularly well suited to the working person who could enjoy a game after a day's labor.

The year 1915 saw the new game taken up actively in Minneapolis's twin city, St. Paul. The *St. Paul Pioneer Press* of August 15, 1915, wrote:

Kitten Ball has at last come into its own in St. Paul. The popular game—a first cousin to the great American sport and half-brother to the indoor baseball game—has secured a foothold in this city. It has been played here for the past two or three years, but not until the Park Board officially recognized it at the start of the present season did it really display a healthy growth.

Kitten Ball is faster than baseball. Games of nine innings duration have been frequently played in 45 minutes. It is an ideal after-dinner sport which may be indulged in by any person, man or woman, without danger of injury or lameness.

This season has found many well-organized leagues in St. Paul. Whenever there is a playground or a plot of ground large enough to lay out a diamond, there the Kitten game will be found. Nine leagues are now finishing their schedules in St. Paul.

The game was known as kitten ball until 1922 when the park authorities, feeling that the name was not appropriate, changed it to diamond ball.

Like indoor baseball and other infant forms of softball this one attracted female teams. In 1920 in Minneapolis there were 64 men's teams in 11 divisions and 25 women's teams in four divisions entered under the Park Board.

In addition, the game was long-lived and remained fairly constant well into the 1930s when it essentially merged with the national game of softball. The *Minneapolis Tribune* of May 24, 1936, compared the modern game with the original:

A comparison of the first rulebook (*Official Kitten Ball Guide*) published in 1906 with the rulebook in use today shows only minor changes: Baselines in 1905, 45 feet; in 1936, 45 feet. Pitching distance in 1906, 35 feet; in 1936, 37 feet, 8½ inches. Size of ball in 1906, 7 ounces, 13 inches in circumference; in 1936, 6 ounces, 12 inches in circumference. Size of bat in 1936, 34 inches in length, 2 inches in diameter; in 1936, 34 inches in length, 2¼ inches in diameter. Number of players in 1906, 10; in 1936, 10. Number of innings in 1906, 9; in 1936, 7.

Because it was home to the first formal leagues, Minnesota has laid claim to being the "birthplace of *organized* softball." It has also been argued that Minneapolis was where the game was created for the outdoors.

After the turn of the century, the game evolved all over the country with interesting and totally confusing variations in everything from ball size (from 10 up to 20 inches) to what the game was called. Many of the names were prissy or insulting and did nothing to help the game. It was known by such diverse titles as mush ball, melon ball and panty waist.

Headed Outdoors   *An early form of softball as it emerged from indoors to the schoolyard.* (Ron Menchine Collection)

The name softball did not come into play until 1926 when a meeting was held in Colorado to standardize that state's rules under a common name; the term softball was suggested by Walter C. Hakanson, the Y.M.C.A. director for Denver. Before this moment the term did not appear as a name for the game, but as a way of describing the ball used in playground ball. For instance, in 1918 *Playground* magazine outlined the ways in which playground baseball differed from regulation baseball, including the phrase "A big *soft* ball is used." Ironically, the term was applied to the game at a point when the ball was large and light, but not at all soft.

However, it would be years before the name was used elsewhere, and the effect of the Denver decision was to add another name to the ever-growing collection. Many held on to the name indoor baseball for several years after the game had moved outdoors.

Running Backwards?

There were many different sets of rules that came into play at this time. Perhaps the most interesting, and certainly the most popular, were those created for a game called playground ball. In 1908 the National Amateur Playground Ball Association of the United States was formed in Chicago. It immediately created a handbook for the game, which seemed more like a set of options than a list of rules.

The most bizarre option allowed the first base runner in each inning to determine which direction his team would move during that inning. In other words, the first runner could start by running to first base or to third. A legal game could be played in five, seven or nine innings depending on the agreement of the teams, and the ball could be anywhere from 14 to 16 inches in diameter. A game could be played for runs or points, with a point being awarded for each base achieved by a runner. Its oddness notwithstanding, the game was well suited to its time and was destined to grow. The following paragraph, taken from the 1909 *Official Playground Ball Hand-book*, is interesting to those who have watched the game develop and finally arrive as a major sport:

Playground Ball has more than a bright future. Its prospects really appear so good that within a few years it probably will have gained more than a marked position in the athletic world. The reason for this is it is being boomed throughout the country by men who realize its importance and are energetic in its promotion. In addition to that, Playground Ball is a sport which is better adapted for the large crowded cities, where the men and boys encounter difficulty in obtaining space sufficient to permit them to play the regular national game. This is one of the great advantages of Playground Ball and before many seasons have gone by it is asserted by the promoters its general advantages will assert themselves.

Morris A. Bealle, the sole historian of early softball, pointed out that this game with its short bases, larger ball and flexible rules was particularly adapted to playgrounds and that following 1908 ". . . the playground program of most municipalities, and many counties, grew by leaps and bounds."

Playground ball had become enough of a factor that it had officially sanctioned balls, bats and other equipment. One manufacturer insisted that the Spalding No. 1 Sheepskin Knee Protector was essential.

Because of its various options, the game took off as different games in different places. In some areas leagues simply borrowed the official rules of baseball and played with them on smaller fields. Youth groups loved it, and it was hard to find a Y.M.C.A. or a Y.W.C.A. that did not have a program. Others created their own rules, and as the game became more popular in the teens and 1920s the situation became more and more confusing.

In his 1940 book *Softball*, Arthur T. Noren described the game as it existed in the 1920s and early 1930s: "Softball was being played in every hamlet, village, town, city and state in the nation, and in many foreign countries. A dozen sizes of balls were in use, as well as many different bat-

lengths, every conceivable base-length, and a bewildering array of variations in rules."

In Detroit, an early hotbed for the game, baselines ranged from 25 feet to 75 feet depending on which part of town one was playing in.

Even with all of this variation, the game was becoming more and more popular. A number of factors came into play, including the advent of daylight saving time, which was introduced during World War I. In 1918 *Sporting Goods Dealer* magazine saw the potential and suggested that retailers sponsor "sunset" leagues to encourage men to play after work.

The war itself spread the game, as many large ball variations were played in the camps. Indoor baseball was the dominant game—but it was also played outdoors in the streets of the camps. There was no question what the game of the hour was, since it was played with the large ball, the slim indoor bat and—most important—the indoor rules.

In the 1920s playground baseball grew in various parts of the country, as increasing attention was paid to the concept of public recreation and municipal parks to support them. It was very much a part of a national playground and recre-

---

Doughboy's Game   *Early softball was so popular among American troops during the First World War that it took on the nickname of "the Army Game."* (Ron Menchine Collection)

---

ation movement. The Playground and Athletic League brought the game to Baltimore and it got its start in New Jersey in the Elizabeth playground department; it first appeared in Pennsylvania in 1928 in the children's playground program. Although there is scant record of it, a form of "court" or alley softball was reported to have come out of the alleys and streets of New York at an early date.

Youth organizations also got behind it. The game took hold in 1924 and 1926 in Missouri and Iowa respectively, both promoted by the Y.M.C.A. In New Orleans and other cities, the Jewish counterparts, the Young Men's Hebrew Associations (Y.M.H.A.), were early boosters. The first two Louisiana State Champions (1932 and 1933) were teams from the New Orleans Y.M.H.A.

Postal clerks were the first to play a new game called big ball in Louisiana in 1931, which

was still another version of the same game with a new name and slight variations in the rules.

People were discovering that hard ball had its limitations and that there was a need for a new ball game. In 1927 the first interstate association, the National Rules Committee on Playground Baseball, was founded. The Committee studied the many rules being used around the country and created a uniform set of rules in 1928, which, history would soon prove, had little impact on the game. One reason may have been that the rules they adopted were simply those of Major League Baseball with ten vague exceptions that begged not to be taken too seriously. The ball, for instance, was to be "not so hard" as a baseball. In their entirety, here are the ten rules adopted in 1928:

1. Base lines—45 feet instead of 90 feet.
2. Ball—12-inch ball instead of a 9-inch ball and not so hard.
3. Underhand pitch only allowed.
4. Bat—Smaller, both as to length and thickness.
5. Number of Players—10 instead of 9 with no restraint as to their positions in the field.
6. Length of Game—7 innings rather than 9 innings, with an official game 4 complete innings except in championship series.
7. Dead Ball—A pitched ball that hits the batter. Batter does not take his base and it is called a ball.
8. Stealing not allowed until the ball has reached or passed the plate.
9. No scoring on a passed ball.
10. Bunts may not be attempted.

The women's game got a tremendous boost from an unexpected source—something identified as women's baseball but which was actually almost identical to softball in the modern sense. In

April, 1923, a delegation approached Mrs. Herbert Hoover and obtained her help in calling a conference in Washington. It was there that the Women's Division of the National Amateur Athletic Federation was created.

Three years later, under the sponsorship of this organization, Gladys Palmer of Ohio State University came up with a special set of baseball rules for women, recognizing the fact that those of standard baseball would not be appropriate. The reasoning was that baseball would be too strenuous and dangerous for "the weaker sex."

The name baseball notwithstanding, this game was softball. In his 1956 thesis *The Evolution and History of Softball in the United States*, Irwin Kawarsky concluded "The American Physical Education Association, through its National Committee on Women's Athletics, recommended that Mrs. Palmer's rules be adopted for and used generally by women. The principal items in the Palmer Code were smaller bats, shorter bases and pitching distances, and a larger and not quite-so-hard ball. This is practically the softball structure of today."

After seeing these principles in practical application for six years, Mrs. Palmer wrote in 1929:

From the educational standpoint baseball, because of its highly organized nature, has a great deal in its favor as a game for girls and women. It teaches them what the boys have learned from time immemorial in their sandlot games—the ability to think quickly, to coordinate thought and action, to exercise good judgment, and a certain faculty in divining in advance the thoughts of others. The development in girls and women of loyalty and self-confidence, as well as a sense of responsibility and good sportsmanship, are not the least of the advantages of the game.

This women's game was sometimes known as women's baseball and at other times as diamond ball. The latter was breaking out in many places and was a fast, tough game much like the fast pitch game played by American college women today.

Diamond Ball in the Sunshine

Diamond ball became extremely popular in certain places. Probably the leading case in point was Sarasota, Florida, where a Department of Public Recreation came into being in late 1925 and by the summer of 1926 was being called one of the city's greatest assets.

David B. Wright, Sarasota's new director of recreation, immediately began looking for a game that was patterned after baseball and could be played on sand, which was a common playground surface of the time, especially in Florida. There was a baseball field in town, Payne Park, but it was often reserved for the likes of the New York Giants, who used it for spring training, and the local Florida State League team.

Wright latched onto a 14-inch indoor ball with an outside seam that was very soft and began to promote the game as outdoor-indoor ball; however, it very quickly attracted the name kitten ball and then diamond ball (described in the papers as nothing more than "indoor baseball played outdoors").

A special field was put into use and lighted for night play, and there was a large and immediate following for the game with leagues formed for men, women and children. A local sporting goods dealer found a 12-inch outseam ball that was better suited to outdoor play than the bigger ball. It had one serious drawback: it lacked durability and players were literally knocking the covers off of them. Barney Dreffus, the Southern representative for Goldsmith Brothers, a Cincinnati sporting goods manufacturer, took an interest in the new game and asked if his company could develop a new ball for the city. After experimentation with covers, contents and colors, a durable 12-inch ball with an inside seam was put in play.

Soon there were powerful leagues, as other cities in Florida adopted the Sarasota game. Tampa and St. Petersburg fielded powerful diamond ball teams for inter-city play, which attracted the attention of tourists. These teams quickly became loaded with professional baseball players, either retired or in Florida for the off-season. The ringer problem was finally settled when league officials ruled that only two professionals or former professionals could play on any one team.

The Sarasota game so influenced the development of softball that it has been argued that the city was responsible for the end of the game's long infancy. "The tourists carried the game back north," said Wright in a 1963 interview with the *Sarasota Herald Tribune*, "and in many cases got jobs in their cities for skilled players. A young man in Sarasota who was a really good player would usually get some pretty good job offers. They wanted to start company teams and they would hire them so they could teach the game up there."

Companies doted on the game for many years to come. As most games lasted less than an hour and sometimes no longer than 40 minutes, a full game could be played during lunch hour. Night workers coming out of a plant at seven or eight in the morning would play before heading home to dinner and bed. Many companies built their own fields and some installed floodlights.

Most folks played in ordinary clothes with gloves and bats they already owned, insuring that this game would require few new expenditures at a time when money was so scarce.

Lively Ball

Unintended help for Depression Era softball also came in the form of a livelier and higher quality baseball. Much has been written on the influence of the so-called lively ball in professional baseball, but little attention has been paid to the sandlot and playground versions of baseball where a cheap nickel-rock baseball—one that cost a nickel or so and acted more like a rock than a ball—was no longer acceptable. The quality of gloves, bats and the playing field were improving and players were no longer content to play with cheap dead baseballs whose only resemblance to the Major League ball was its size and shape. With this new higher quality ball there was an overnight change in many vacant lots, public parks and sandlots. These places were simply too small for a Major League–quality baseball and many baseball play-

ers converted to softball—although few if any knew it by that name.

In Minneapolis, park space was used wisely and emphasized the importance of a smaller playing area. Seven full-sized baseball diamonds in the open area known as the Parade Ground were erased and reconfigured into 24 softball diamonds.

The ball became so important sporting goods manufacturers had to work hard to come up with models tailored to the needs of amateurs. The most clever and enduring of these was the "Clincher," an invention of Frederick deBeer of Albany, New York. It was created for city play on pavement where the exposed thread of the ball was more likely to break—especially if used for a number of games. The Clincher seam was created by cutting the leather in a slightly different way so that the seams lock and the thread is protected. In fact, no thread at all is exposed.

New York City softball may not have had much of a chance without the Clincher; in that city it quickly became the only ball that made sense for the paved public school playgrounds where the game developed with its own set of rules (no sliding, no bunting and no stealing). Although in the 1990s patent protection has long expired, the deBeer 12-inch Clincher is still the most popular ball in New York City, and the 16-inch deBeer Clincher remains the most popular ball sold in Chicago where today, as in the 1930s they play with a larger ball.

What is more, softball had the flexibility to do things that organized baseball could not. Softball could be played under the lights. In 1940, when night baseball was still severely limited and experimental, Leo Fischer of the Amateur Softball Association could report: "Hundreds of softball fields from coast to coast have presented night games for years and the number is growing annually."

Invented in Chicago and developed in Minneapolis, softball had to be reintroduced twice again in Chicago. It was first invented in 1887 and history would repeat itself in 1908 with the creation of playground ball in Chicago. The final and most dramatic re-introduction would occur in 1933.

The sport was thriving and begging for a standard set of rules and organization. It seemed like anyone who wanted to could stage a tournament and crown a champion. In 1930 Minnesota organized no less than three state championships, one each at Minneapolis, Hibbing and Crookston.

The rules were a constant source of debate and discussion. For instance, there was the very important business of the distance from the pitcher's box to home plate. It ranged from 30 to 46 feet and, as Edward Claflin put it in *The Irresistible American Softball Book*, ". . . it depended on the state you were in, the size of the field, the mood of the players, and the mental aptitude of the gentlemen who marked out the field."

All of this came to a ludicrous conclusion in 1932 when a tournament was held in Milwaukee under the auspices of the National Diamond Ball Association of Minneapolis. Forty teams were invited from six states; 40 teams showed up and with them came 40 sets of rules.

But first the game needed a proper name.

Army Ball *The game they played most often during the First World War was an early form of softball. A group poses with one large ball and two small bats.*

(Ron Menchine Collection)

This point was driven home by the cover of a 1931 rule book from Spalding's Athletic Library, which looked like this:

OFFICIAL RULES OF
PLAYGROUND BASEBALL
ALSO KNOWN AS
KITTENBALL, SOFT BALL AND
TWILIGHT BALL.

What was being demonstrated—and would continue to be demonstrated—was that this game of many names would reflect changes in the nation's recreational needs. In *A History of Recreation* writer Foster Rhea Dulles eloquently summarized this ability to change:

Recreation in America may be compared to a river—its course adapting itself to the nature of the country through which it flows, the main stream continually augmented by tributaries, and the river bend itself ever growing both broader and deeper.

4 Fair

FAST FORWARDING

THROUGH THE

GREAT DEPRESSION

Only a Dime to Spend . . .

The game really began to take hold during the Depression thanks to the 1933 World's Fair, the assistance of a major newspaper chain, a rule book, a little organization and the social and economic tinkering of "that man" in the White House.

It began as simply as this: two guys with an idea.

Sportswriter Leo Fischer, of the *Chicago American*, and M.J. Pauley, a local Chicagoland sporting goods salesman, attended a game and

"COON" ROSEN

Game

saw a venue for it. It seemed like something that could be successfully promoted.

The game was already popular in the Midwest and the venue was a once-in-a-lifetime opportunity. In early 1933 these two envisioned a tournament at the Century of Progress Exposition, more popularly known as the Chicago World's Fair. A meeting was held to adopt a set of uniform rules and give the game a common name. Softball, the name which had been created by Walter Hakanson and adopted in Colorado, was formally proposed and accepted; a common set of rules were adopted; and the World's Fair organizers were approached. The game had al-

ready had its first—albeit confusing—national championships in 1932. It was assumed that the Fair directors would be willing sponsors.

But Fair officials deferred any decision and showed a real lack of enthusiasm for the idea. Fischer and M.J. Pauley pushed the idea again and

again and each time were rebuffed. In late August, however, the Fair administration said that it would put up $500 and create a playing area on the grounds for this odd game.

The two men were left with 10 days to organize their national tournament. M.J. Pauley later recounted what happened next:

This looked like a whale of a job, and would not have been successful if it had not been for the efforts of Leo Fischer. He wrote stories tirelessly, and besieged the wire services with articles, which they took only as a favor to him and not because they thought that softball deserved the time and money it required to send the stories out.

We climbed in our car, and every state that we heard of where any sort of a softball tournament was being conducted, the winning team was invited to this first national softball championship event. The meet attracted 16 teams of men and 8 in the girls' division. They came from Colorado, Louisiana, Georgia, Connecticut, Kentucky, Illinois, Indiana, and nine other states. We had a cross-section of the nation represented.

The tournament was a totally amateur affair, and teams and players were invited without the promise of transportation, room or board. Some drove, others biked and a few hitchhiked. The 20-odd teams camped out in tents near the softball diamonds and lived on a diet of bread and bologna. The $500 from the Fair had been spent on advance promotion, and there was not even enough left to buy a trophies for the winning teams.

Hall of Famer *(Opposite) The late Charles Justice on his induction to the National Softball Hall of Fame in 1974, the year he died. His softball career spanned three decades and he became a national force in the game when his team, the Pontiac Big Six, an African-American team, played in the World Tournament repeatedly, beginning in 1937. Justice played with the Harlem Globetrotters in the late 1930s. (Amateur Softball Association)*

The fact that teams showed up at all was all the more remarkable, considering that the summer of 1933 marked the economic bottom of the Great Depression. There was so little work to be had that it was later suggested that many had come to Chicago because they had nothing else to do.

Once there, and a new set of rules notwithstanding, confusion reigned. Not only did each team arrive with its own set of rules in its collective mind, but each was trying to accommodate the others. The sole team from Florida reported that it had played 10 games in 10 states under 10 sets of rules as it barnstormed its way to Chicago.

In addition, it seemed that each used different kinds of equipment. Some teams played in shorts and short-sleeved shirts, while others played in baseball longs. The variety of balls brought in could have supplied a museum, ranging from a model that was six inches in diameter to a 16-inch melon-sized ball. The tournament ball was a 14-inch model.

Despite all of this confusion, the tournament was a smashing success as was the World's Fair that surrounded it. More than 20 million people attended the grand festival, which was described as a "sleeper" that surprised both its financial backers and just about everyone else. Gaudy and upbeat, it mixed the grotesqueries of its famous midway with historical exhibits and a gleaming view of the future. Here you could see a genuine Mayan temple, an Army camp populated by 410 real soldiers or a monorail. But you could also pay two bits to see a mouse circus or, for a quarter more, the tiny "Midget Village" populated and operated by living midgets or a world-class collection of freaks.

Some years later Cabell Phillips of the *New York Times* wrote of the Fair, "By some strange alchemy of chance or psychology it seemed to offer just the kind of release that a depression-bogged society needed."

The Fair was a showcase for things such as the baseball All-Star Game, which was created here, and this new game billed as softball. Many fairgoers got an eyeful of this game, with its underwhelming and misleading name, and were surprised that it was played by women as well as men. The softball diamonds were prominently located at the base of the East Tower of the Sky Ride, which—along with the Streets of Paris and

Miss Sally Rand, the fan dancer—was among the most popular divertissements of the fair.

The tournament was helped considerably by publicity. It was backed by William Randolph Hearst and promoted heavily in his newspaper, the *Chicago American*, which was also where Fischer worked. The national softball tournament, with separate divisions for fast pitch, slow pitch and a women's league, was touted by the Hearst papers as a success even before the first ball was thrown.

On the opening day of this tournament the pro-softball *Chicago American* claimed:

It is the largest and most comprehensive tournament ever held in the sport which has swept the country like wildfire . . . Fifty title winners from Colorado to New Jersey, and from Minnesota to Florida, have sent in their entries. Admission will be free to those within the grounds of A-Century-of-Progress. The diamond is located on Northerly Island, near the east tower of the Sky Ride and bleacher space is available for thousands of spectators.

Some 70,000 spectators saw the first round of play and more than 350,000 had gone through the turnstiles before it was over three days later. There were even a few softball heroes to follow. Pitcher Harry "Coon" Rosen won eight games in three days. His local Chicago team won the World's Fair Tournament and Rosen posted a record of 108–11 for the year (while batting a very strong .368 for the season).

One of the things that the Fair proved was that softball had a "gate" and that it could attract a crowd. Again and again this point would be made as the sport mushroomed. At the end of the decade *Time* called it the "spectator sport for folks with only a dime to spend."

Fischer, in later years, declared:

We just didn't know what we had a hold of back there in 1933. We liked the game, wanted to popularize it, and keep it alive. It was in its infancy. We never thought it would grow into a tremendous giant almost overnight.

Girls had taken up play at almost the same time as did the men. And they played it well. This was so because many had participated in playground ball during earlier years on the recreation grounds.

When we sketched out the rules for the men's world series of 1933, we decided to include one for girl teams as well. We didn't think it would go very well, but we didn't want to slight the ladies. They could have their chance, if they wanted it. It developed that they wanted it, and the play for the ladies' championship of 1933 really featured our program.

Triple Threat *(Below) Three members of the Cleveland Rosenblum women's softball team. Left to right: Roma Merck, catcher; Ann Koenig, pitcher; and June Feldtz, short center.*

(Cleveland State University)

Champs *(Opposite) This team was the 1934 national champion from Kenosha, Wisconsin. Even though the rest of the world was calling the game softball by this time, the team's original caption on this photograph from the Amateur Softball Association archives was "World's Champion Kittenball Team."*

(Amateur Softball Association)

Organized Softball

The tireless Leo Fischer and M.J. Pauley, who had pulled off the World's Fair Tournament, decided that there was more missionary work to be done. They reasoned that the game would best benefit from an organization of cohesive state and metropolitan groups. They set up shop in the Morrisey Hotel in Chicago; soon they were promoting the game with a special zest. The formation was official in the fall of 1933 and it had a name, the Amateur Softball Association of America. From the start the ASA would be the prime mover in organized softball. But it was, as cofounder M.J. Pauley explained at the time, a great idea without any money to support it.

The Athletic Institute, a nonprofit organization of sporting goods manufacturers, came to the

rescue. The *Chicago American* agreed to pay the bill for the office space with lights and telephone included.

State associations were formed, state commissioners were appointed and the game of softball under the guidance of a national organization went forward with tremendous initial success.

Fischer and other Chicago sports writers gave the pioneer championship series of 1933 a good deal of post-event publicity, and much space was given to the new game later, when the Joint Rules Committee proceeded to lay down rules to govern the game throughout the nation. As a consequence, when the time neared for the 1934 World Series, every area that had a snappy team wanted it to be given a chance to play in the tournament.

Pauley later wrote about what happened next:

The 1934 national tournament was in sight, and again the "no money" sign was in our face. Again we went to Mr. Hearst, and he donated $5,000 towards the world's softball championships for 1934, and this time we could give the players at least the money for their room in the hotel, and a little entertainment while in Chicago.

The Chicago park district set up the diamonds for us at no expense to us, and we charged no spectator for seeing the second national soft-

ball tournament of the Amateur Softball Association. Thirty states were in this tournament, and we handled 1,001 players, and their managers and coaches, and played to over 200,000 people, in the three days. It was won by the Ke-Nash-A team of Wisconsin, and the girls' title again by the Hart Motor Girls of metropolitan Chicago.

With the founding of the Amateur Softball Association, the Joint Rules Committee went to work. Since women were playing the game with enthusiasm in all parts of the country, and because

Men's Champs   *Pohler's Cafe of Cincinnati was the men's World Champion team in 1938 in Chicago. The team was led by pitcher Clyde "Dizzy" Kirkendall, third from left, front row.* (Amateur Softball Association)

they had been such a factor in the World's Fair Tournament, it was decided that two world series would be set up—one for men, one for women—when the winners of the state, or regional, championships had been determined.

It was only a matter of months before the ASA's infant newspaper *Balls and Strikes* was reporting on the rapid spread of the game through its many state and local commissioners.

Typical was this item from May of 1935:

INTEREST GROWING.

Membership applications have been received from 42 teams in Atlanta, Ga., where a year ago the game of softball had never been heard of. A lighted park also is being built in the city, Commissioner Joe Stears reports.

With the standardization inspired by the 1933 Century of Progress Exposition, the game was becoming a national phenomenon rather than a local curiosity. A continuing boost came from the Hearst newspapers, which had supported softball beginning in 1933 when it backed the idea of a national association.

In 1934 William Randolph Hearst gave the Amateur Softball Association $7,000, enough to pay the hotel bills for the 1,001 team members who played in the national championship. Before its sponsorship ended in 1938, the Hearst papers had given the ASA $50,000 and as much newspaper publicity as any fledgling sport could ask for.

This point was driven home five years later when Chicago was host to the 1938 national championships. It was an event of such magnitude that the papers were calling it "Chicago's most spectacular sports event."

Softball was on the move and finding its way into parts of the country that had not been exposed to the larger ball game. In *The Evolution and History of Softball in the United States*, Irwin Kawarsky noted that it came to the District of Columbia in 1934 through the medium of the William Randolph Hearst newspapers, which backed its organization in the nation's capital. The man who organized the first softball team to play in Washington was Morris Bealle, who staged his first game with a group of students at the Catholic University, and started the first league in the Capital City Circuit. He obtained the help of the chairmen of both the Senate and House committees of the Agriculture Department. Bealle went on to write extensively on softball and become a major unpaid promoter of the game.

Three-peaters
The Zollner Pistons, the 1945 ASA World Champions. This would be the first of three ASA titles in a row.
(Amateur Softball Association)

Workers of the World Play Ball

In the experimental period during the depth of the Depression, the games were generally played in the afternoon. When industrial conditions improved and men went back to work, they did not quit playing softball. They simply changed their hours so that they could play after work, thus ushering into existence what became known as "twilight softball."

Before long, industrial leagues flourished and special rules were written for them. Typical was this rule from a group calling itself the Midwestern league formed in 1937: "Any team that rules it compulsory for any employee to play on their team shall be barred from securing a franchise in the league or be barred from securing return of entry play."

Major efforts were also made to ensure that the better players actually worked for the companies they played for.

An important—if overly tongue-in-cheek—point was made by Lowell Thomas and Ted Shane in their 1940 opus *Softball! So What?*

KARL MARX, EXTREME LEFT FIELD

Were old Karl (Whiskers) Marx alive today, we venture to guess he'd have to do something about softball. Looking around the industrial cities of this country, he'd probably be more than a little disturbed by the prospect of thousands of teams of men and women factory, office, store, ditch, and market workers, taking off valuable time from arguing about the union to devote to arguing about the dead ball with an umpire. When he learned that the wise men of Capital have sensed the value of softball as an antidote to the worker's troubles and are devoting thousands of dollars to its development, he'd fly off his clever head, probably start muttering something about softball being the opiate of the masses, throw out *Das Kapital* and start writing *Das Softball* instead. Unless of course he got sucked into the game himself. That would cook him completely as an economist, for the game has a deadly effect on the player. Poor Marx'd grow content and

Hot Corner Evelyn Paeth, third basewoman for the Hydrox Girls, seemed to exemplify the spirit and raw athleticism of women's softball in the 1930s and '40s.
(Amateur Softball Association)

placid playing the game himself, but would have his skill as a player to comfort him. Undoubtedly, he'd play left field, extreme left.

For, it's unquestionably true that softball is the game for the masses and is having a tremendous effect on the laboring man and woman of today. There are rumors around that Detroit, spawning bed of the hottest softballers and unionists and a swell place to start a revolution, has been pretty well tamed by softball.

Fischer and Pauley guided the game through its precarious years, and saw it mushroom from something little known to a sport of gigantic proportions. According to the ASA, it had five million or more known players by 1938 and could be indulged in by boys, young men, those of middle age and, often, the oldsters. The girls took to the sport in a remarkable way, and there were well over one million female players, who played at the game either regularly or sporadically.

In 1938, when Wilbur J. Landis succeeded Fischer as president, the latter stated: "Landis was associated with one of Detroit's large automotive companies. He had helped greatly to introduce the sport as a morale builder for industrial workers, which became a field where the sport enjoyed tremendous growth."

The world series grew considerably from the first audacious event at the 1933 World's Fair in Chicago into the war years. They were lavish extravaganzas with increasing media attention. In the 1937 tournament, 88 teams from the United States and Canada participated. This was the first series to be broadcast over a national network, with both Columbia and the National Broadcasting Company doing play-by-play broadcasts of the important games.

Meanwhile, the national ASA tournament in Chicago's Lincoln Park was beginning to draw crowds over 100,000. And, for the first time ever, the game was attracting attention in the national press. "Anybody who travels of an evening through the Middle West can testify on the subject," reported *Collier's* magazine in August 1935. The subject was this game—this "jazzed up version of baseball"—which had seemingly come out of nowhere and was being played by all sorts of ordinary Americans. "There are girls' teams, league teams, church teams and teams which have wandered out on an open lot and are endeavoring to break all the windows in the apartment house across the street," *Collier's* noted.

New Deal for the Bigger Ball

If you are a softball scoffer, try playing it.
   Then if you don't like it, try having your head examined.

—Lowell Thomas and Ted Shane,
from *Softball: So What?* 1940

Night Games

During the early years of the game, the sport was played on any available field, and there was no admission fee. The crowds filled small stands if the parks had them and then overflowed onto the playing field. The immensity of some of the crowds made it difficult for the players to perform their duties satisfactorily.

The result was a fenced-in playing field here and there, with games continuing until darkness came. Later, some of the more daring parks installed floodlights, built stands of real size and charged admission fees in order to meet the expenses. The experiment was a great success, proving that the game had enough appeal to entice folks to pay to see the players in action under the lights.

There was also a revolutionary social and political factor that came into play at exactly the moment when softball became organized. Without it, softball might have grown gradually, but it never would have exploded into a game of the masses—played by millions. In 1936, for the first time ever, the Amateur Softball Association could report that more than one million Americans were playing the game in organized leagues. Two years later more than five million played the game.

But 1936 was a key year; by then, softball's backers and boosters were claiming that the game

Enjoying Himself (Opposite) Catcher Kenny Anchbrick of Ferguson's Columbus Auditors takes a break.
(Amateur Softball Association)

Fair Game

led the national parade of sports because it was being played in every village, town and city in North America.

The revolutionary factor at work here was Franklin D. Roosevelt's New Deal and its tenet that public works should boost the standard of living. One of the ways to do so was through recreation; and the way to increase recreation was through the building of athletic facilities.

Between 1935 and 1940 the Works Progress Administration (W.P.A.) spent a billion dollars building athletic fields—3,026 of them to be exact—with a major emphasis on the dimensions of softball. Many of these were lighted and especially suited to softball and its ability to hold two or three games on the same diamond on a school night. Even before the W.P.A. got into the act there were approximately 1,000 lighted softball parks. In 1935, it was said that with government aid, the number of lighted parks was growing "by the hour."

The W.P.A. figures only tell a small part of the story. Consider, for example, the National Youth Administration (N.Y.A.), which put youngsters to work building cooperative softball diamonds on private property with donated equipment and technical advice from the W.P.A. Churches, P.T.A.'s, Lion's Clubs and the like backed these projects

According to a 1939 report from the Youth Administration's Chicago Recreation Commission, softball fields were being constructed in and around Chicago in a labor-intensive blitz. Quoting from the report:

If a resident of Hyde Park, one of Chicago's communities, had chanced to be walking past the vacant lot on the corner of [certain] streets on a certain spring morning in 1938, he would have seen thirty young men engaged in clearing and processing the lot. They were digging up weeds, picking up stones, leveling the ground, under the general supervision of a slightly older man.

After the lot was entirely cleared, saws, hammers, lumber, nails and paint emerged from a nearby truck. Now the boys began to measure, saw, plane, and hammer. That afternoon a softball backstop and several "bleachers" were erected. These were painted a cool green. The boys then departed.

All of this was done under the aegis of District Recreation Committees uniting all sorts of local people. Who are the typical members, the report asked itself? "Anyone in the Community interested enough to want to help: The local preacher, a fireman, a few school-teachers, a haberdasher, representatives of every organization in the community which indicates interest."

Eduard C. Lindeman, W.P.A. recreation chief, advocated "democratic leisure," and softball fit the bill. To erect a softball complex was seen as an almost perfect piece of social engineering. Jobs were created to produce something that would work against ennui and the forced idleness of the time. The standard of living of Americans was enhanced by grass to play on and bleachers to watch others play on. And the work was labor-intensive; the planners wanted to put wages in people's pockets rather than put the lion's share into equipment and materials. The economics of it were stunning—a lighted park with seating for 4,000 could be erected for $3,500. Even at a dime a game, parks could pay for themselves in no time.

Moreover, the lighted parks necessary for night games were ideally suited to the Federal Rural Electrification Program whose goal was to bring electric power to all parts of the nation, no matter how rural. As the decade wore on, lighted softball fields started to spring up in farming centers across the nation.

There was something very important occurring in this softball boom of the 1930s. Jesse Steiner, a leading historian of sports, has written that ". . . leisure in such large measure and so widely distributed among all classes of people [was] a new experiment in the modern world."

Softball became a symbol of this new participatory leisure, and its powers to revive and refresh seemed to be special. In the late 1930s, for example, there were those who saw softball as a promising vehicle for criminal rehabilitation. The Illinois State Penitentiary could brag of a host of teams with names such as Knit Shop, Warden's Laundry, Stragglers and Print Shop.

None of this was lost on those running organized softball. As the W.P.A. began to run out of steam in 1940, *Balls and Strikes* magazine urged its readers to write to their congressmen to ask for an increase rather than a cut in the W.P.A. appropriation.

The record was indeed impressive. Besides the diamonds, the W.P.A. could also boast that it had created 1,883 wading pools, 103 golf courses and 3,076 tennis courts.

If the game was a break for the out-of-work American, it was a breath of relief for the employed American. Softball was seen as an answer and, if it sounds odd today, it seemed to fit with the idealism of the era. It was not merely a game. Consider a statement issued by the Intramural Sports Department of the University of Michigan during the Roosevelt years:

It is a health contributing and invigorating game; one that presents numerous educational possibilities, and one that offers untold recreational and social advantages (and) has no outstanding hazards. It is a scientific game demanding the use of mental alertness as well as physical skill; it allows individual skill and yet instills cooperation; calls for judgment and quick thinking; it develops coordination; and it permits action for all players at almost all times.

From a community standpoint the game has real merit, for in our many leagues, classified as sandlot, playground, interscholastic, industrial, church, minor and major city, players of all nationalities, of all strata of civic life, are brought together . . . the game is interesting not only to the players but also to the spectators . . . finally, softball has a real carryover value, for informal games may be organized at outings and picnics, and almost every city with a recreational program will want to include softball for adults as well as for the younger groups. It can be played successfully for a much longer period in life than can regulation baseball.

The rising recreational tide helped sporting goods manufacturers float as well. Early in the Depression, they suffered, as Neil Hamilton detailed in *Visions of Worth*, his biography of G.S. Lannom, Jr. The value of sporting goods production declined from about $58 million in 1929 to about $25 million in 1933. But a steady upturn then ensued. The figures substantiate a claim by *Business Week* magazine at the time that in the mid-1930s more people spent an increased amount of money for athletic goods. In 1939 the value of sporting goods produced in the nation reached nearly $65 million, and the number of workers employed in sporting goods factories increased from 10,793 in 1929 to 13,816 in 1939.

More people were playing baseball than ever before. In 1939 Little League baseball was founded in Williamsport, Pennsylvania, essentially to find a niche for boys too small to play sandlot baseball. While the recreational mania stimulated participatory ball and drew those customers with a dime to spend on softball, professional baseball gate receipts dropped from $17 million in 1929 to $11 million in 1933.

The President's Team

Then there was President Roosevelt himself, who loved sports—loved to watch them and loved to play them. At the age of 39 he contracted polio while on vacation at Campobello Island, New Brunswick, and never walked again. Even that did not diminish his love of games, but it did make things harder: A special ramp had to be erected at Griffith Stadium in Washington, D.C., to allow him to reach the presidential box.

Friends said he was happiest at the ball park and had a great love of high-scoring slug fests. "Roosevelt enjoys himself at a ball game as much as a kid on Christmas morning," wrote Harold C. Burr, in the June 1939 *Baseball Magazine*, adding, "Once in his field box the present President believes again that there is a Santa Claus. He gets right into the spirit of the game, munches peanuts, applauds good plays and chuckles over bad ones."

It was therefore only natural that he would have his own softball team. F.D.R.'s teams were composed of those around his summer White House, including members of his cabinet, his sons, members of the Secret Service and members of the White House press corps. F.D.R. acted as captain and manager and, because of his inability to walk, led the team from the back of an open touring car. The President's favorite and most famous opponent was a team fielded by newsman and world traveler Lowell Thomas.

Thomas was one of the most famous news-men of his time and became an enormous booster of the game, writing about it and playing it. The battles between F.D.R.'s team and Thomas's held on Quaker Hill, on the opposite corner of Dutchess County, New York, from F.D.R.'s Hyde Park were such a novelty that the *New York Times* sent reporters to cover them. In their own way they marked the beginning of a tradition that remains to this day: the celebrity softball game.

Thomas loaded his teams with some of the most well-known people of his day: athletes, actors, news people and, above all, comedians. Dale Carnegie played, as did Babe Ruth, Edward R. Murrow and cartoonist Rube Goldberg, who became something of a legend by pitching for five innings with a lit cigar clenched between his teeth. Thomas's teams also boasted the likes of Hay-

The President's Game The original caption on this 1938 photograph was: "THE PRESIDENT IS SERENADED." It was accompanied by this account:

PAWLING, N.Y.—A feature of the soft ball game here, August 21, between Lowell Thomas' "Nine Old Men" and the "White House Purgers," consisting of correspondents, cameramen and secret service operatives, was this hillbilly band. They are shown here demonstrating their talents for President Roosevelt who also witnessed the ball game. Standing by in bathing suit is Lowell Thomas.

(Cleveland Public Library)

wood Broun, Franklin P. Adams and Gene Sarazen. They called themselves the "Nine Old Men," an allusion to F.D.R.'s Supreme Court.

It was a jolly time for the game. So jolly that attempts were made to ban beer and other alcohol from the playing field, gaving rise to critic Alexander Woollcott's question, "Why . . . softball, when there is highball?"

Thomas went on to write a book about the game with Ted Shane entitled *Softball! So What?* Franklin D. Roosevelt's personal copy of the book, which is now at the Roosevelt Library in Hyde Park, New York, was inscribed by Thomas: "To President Roosevelt who helped start all this."

At one point Thomas was asked by *This Week* magazine to explain how he had become softball's most stalwart promoter, and he told this story:

My first experience with softball happened when it was comparatively little known in the East. Our Methodist Church needed a new pipe organ and a lot of us in the neighborhood needed exercise. So somebody suggested that we promote a softball game and turn over the gate money to the church.

We did—but we made one mistake. In our neighborhood we have two distinct communities, the Hill and the Town—Quaker Hill and Pawling, N.Y. In the old days, I am told there was no love lost between the two communities. But, having only recently moved there, I was blissfully ignorant about this feeling and, indeed, everybody thought it had died down.

So I organized a team of farmers and farm owners from the Hill to meet a team from the Town. And we all were set for plenty of fun with possibly a good haul for the organ fund.

But—

It was a blazing hot day and the game was hotter. Rooting became acrimonious. All of a sudden tempers flared and the ancient animosities of Town vs. Hill boiled to the surface. And before we knew it, that eminently well-intentioned sporting contest for the benefit of the church organ almost became as pretty a free-for-all as you ever saw—the same sort of rumpus as usually occurs between enlightened nations at the Olympic Games. Whereupon I announced that, so far as I was concerned, I never would play ball again in those parts unless the two teams were combined. That we have done ever since.

We call ourselves the Quaker Hill-Pawling Debtors and Creditors. The "debtors" are those who live on the Hill; the "creditors" are the doughty merchants of Pawling.

World War II ended the great contests between Roosevelt and Thomas; but in a relatively short time these two figures had done a great deal to promote the game. If Roosevelt helped softball then dominated by the fast pitch version, it would be another Democratic president, Jimmy Carter, who would boost the slow pitch version some 40 years later.

Pre-War Mania

As a rule sportswriters take care not to mention softball to a big league star. Baseball attracts the attention of the ordinary citizen and draws the fans to the ballpark; but softball gets him off his fanny.

—John R. Tunis, *Sport for the Fun of It*, 1940

By 1939 *Time* magazine was able to report, "A product of the Depression, softball has grown into a major U.S. mania."

That same year *Look* magazine deemed it the "girl's national game" (after the head of the ASA claimed that more women played the game than any other sport). It was also determined that 11 million Americans of both sexes played the game on 8,696 diamondettes (as softball fields were often called).

For girls and women, softball had indeed become a haven much to the surprise of those who felt that members of that sex had no interest in team play. There was still concern that women might overdo it. Even a force as friendly to female participation as the Amateur Softball Association felt it necessary to run this warning in its 1940 rule book: "It is the consensus of the Amateur Softball

Association Commissioners that, for health's sake, girls should not engage in more than three softball games in any one week, and that girls under the age of 15 years should not be used in any major softball competition." Apparently few felt strongly about the warning and it was soon dropped.

Everyone was getting into the act and the folks running the sport were boasting that at least one major leaguer, Tommy "Old Reliable" Heinrich, had gotten his start in sandlot softball.

In the late 1930s softball had become such a power that its effect on baseball developed into an issue. Major League team owners suggested that softball was cutting into their market and John R. Tunis, author of classic baseball novels including *The Kid From Tomkinsville*, wrote that

the softball threat was such that professional ball players themselves were worried.

No less a figure than Judge Kenesaw Mountain Landis, the all-powerful Commissioner of

Garden Stars   Players of the New York Roverettes, the New York Champion Softball Team, warmed up in this July 22, 1938, picture, preparing for the opening game of the season in Madison Square Garden on July 27. The Roverettes were the home team at the Garden in the late 1930s. Left to right, members of the starting team: Marguerite Taylor, Lillian Settanni, Minnie Pelletteri, Lee Ordine, Julia Perry, Ruth Murdock, Rose Oea, Billy Youpa and Rose de Rosa. (Cleveland Public Library)

Baseball, became involved and declared that the fear—and the use of the word "menace" to describe softball—was "stupid." He explained, "Any sport that attracts crowds is a help to every other sport. Baseball and softball are mutually helpful. You don't suppose people sit back and wait for wrestling matches, baseball games and other events. They are educated by going to sports events, and if softball brings out the crowds the same fans will attend other sports too."

It would seem that even Landis had his reservations when it came to the top male athletes being siphoned off for the game. In his foreward to the 1938 *Official Rules for Girls and Women* he wrote:

It is significant that baseball has retained the place it has in the hearts of sport-loving Americans throughout the half century and more of its existence as a competitive sport. Millions of our young men have played it and the spirit of sportsmanship it inculcates as well as the physical and mental alertness it develops have been no small factor in promoting good citizenship. It is indeed a wonderful thing that these benefits may now be enjoyed by our girls and young women under the supervision of properly constituted authorities on women's athletics. As a sport for women the softball version of the game should adapt itself admirably to the athletic programs of playgrounds, schools and colleges everywhere. It is easy to learn and enjoyment and practical benefits may be derived from playing it regardless of the player's skill.

Organized softball kept the issue alive and began making claims. "Call it treason if you like," wrote Leo Fischer in the *Reader's Digest*, "but in this year of 1939, when organized baseball is celebrating its centennial with much fanfare, baseball is no longer the leading sport of American youth."

Fischer claimed that softball had eclipsed baseball in all departments, that it had "stepped out in front" and had, in fact, "succeeded baseball as America's national pastime." He added, "Only in gate receipts does the new game lag behind baseball, and since softball is played mainly for amateur recreation, this doesn't mean much."

Speed Demons

This was also a time during which the game was changing and losing some of its loose and goofy informality. People—especially younger men and women—were taking it seriously, playing for keeps.

As Lowell Thomas put it in his book, *Softball: So What?*: "Youth streamlined the game . . . Young pitchers got the knack of burning it in so fast that poor paunchy Pop never saw it from the moment it left the pitcher's hand until it passed under his paunch and plopped into the catcher's mitt behind."

In the late 1930s, the game of softball seemed to have its own special niche as a spectator sport. It seemed to have so much going for it that made it different and, in some ways, more colorful than baseball. One thing that made it more colorful—literally—was that softball eschewed the traditional gray flannels of baseball for flashy satin colors with plenty of frills. Women wore shorts and the newspapers and picture magazines had a field day. Harry's Girls, a dominant team in New Mexico, dressed in uniforms inspired by Southwest Indian costumes, and the crowd-pleasing Red Jackets of Wichita Falls, Texas, went to the 1936 softball World Series in Chicago, played in bare feet and sung Texas songs between innings.

Then there was Joe "Two Gun" Hunt of the Arizona Lettuce Kings who by 1940 was a big enough name in the Southwest, with a team known as the Joe Hunt All Stars, to run for Arizona state treasurer. In California a teenage pitcher named Wilma "Willie" Turner, was able to post more than 100 straight victories over several seasons in the late 1930s.

Every town seemed to want to have its own lighted field and one of the major concerns was keeping the fans happy. "Make your entire program fast and snappy and everyone will want to come back the next night for more," advised the increasingly fan-conscious organ of the ASA, *Balls and Strikes*.

The fan reactions were overwhelming. Unknown softball teams with little newspaper attention were outdrawing some Major League baseball teams. Every time a softball team drew a few thousand the comparison was made to the

hapless St. Louis Browns, a pro team that, on one dreadful day in 1933, had entertained a mere 34 faithful fans.

The comparisons appeared everywhere. When, for example, an unheralded black softball crew known as the Sioux City Ghosts drew 2,000 *paying* spectators to Roberts Field, San Francisco, on July 14, 1939, the local press urged the Browns, the Washington Senators and others to take note.

Then there was the hoopla that went along with the speed demons of softball and their ability to strike out just about anyone—even the greatest hitter of all time. In 1937, Babe Ruth agreed to umpire a championship game in New York after which he would give a batting demonstration. The pitcher Johnny "Cannonball" Baker, got Ruth to take three swings and the Sultan of Swat never touched the ball.

Ruth turned to the catcher, retrieved the last ball from the catcher's mitt, and said, "Next time I'm up you might as well catch those pitches in front of the plate. I can't see them long enough to get the bat around."

Ruth then tossed it up and slammed it into the bleachers. As he walked away he said that he just wanted to see if the big ball could be hit.

Remarkably, Ruth came back for more. In 1938 Lowell Thomas took his celebrity team to Oyster Bay, Long Island, to play against two teams managed by Colonel Theodore Roosevelt.

With the score at 21–10 against his team, Roosevelt yanked columnist Westbrook Pegler, a miserable hitter, and installed the Bambino as a surprise pinch-hitter.

The pitcher for the Thomas team at this point was Dale (*How to Win Friends and Influence People*) Carnegie, whose softball trademark was pitching in a soft crush hat and an overcoat. Thomas yanked Carnegie and inserted a Pawling, New York, farm boy named Hardy Brownell.

The account of what happened next appeared in the ASA's *Balls and Strikes*:

Brownell looked the Babe over calmly, then deliberately threw three bad balls wide of the plate, reminiscent of the Babe's big-league days, when he was purposely passed on many occasions. Babe looked disgusted. Brownell then wound up, and let loose his cannon ball right over the pan. The Babe blinked, heard the ball plunk in the glove behind. That is, it might have landed in the glove, except that Lew Lehr, the newsreel comedian was doing the catching—that is, up to that moment. That ball surprised him as much as it did Ruth. Lehr took to his heels.

With a new battery mate installed, Brownell threw another fireball. This time Ruth swung

mightily, but too late. So Brownell pulled the string and humbled the mightly Sultan of Swat on three straight pitches. Babe admitted he hadn't hit, not because he hadn't tried, but because he hadn't been able to see the ball. Just to convince himself and the spectators that there really was a ball, he fungoed it across the field and into the stands.

The Ruth stories and others relating to stymied sluggers unable to hit the bigger ball helped popularize the game and may have been at the root of that old schoolyard credo that says that softball ruins one's "eye" for baseball.

Something was out of synch, however. Softball was beginning to look and feel more like baseball in every way, beginning with the comparisons as to how many people were coming through the turnstiles. Men's and women's uniforms suddenly started to look like baseball uniforms, and many teams moved away from the shorts that had

Distinguished Gentlemen *The Kids and Kubs in 1951. The title "Three-Quarters Century Club" alludes to the fact that they must be at least 75 years of age to play. (Ron Menchine Collection)*

1951 --- THREE-QUARTER CENTURY SOFTBALL CLUB ST. PETERSBURG FLORIDA --- 1951

been *de rigeur* a few years earlier. Barnstorming teams and out-of-town ringers had to be restricted, as the Amateur Softball Association worked hard to keep the "amateur" in its name protected.

George Sisler, the former St. Louis Browns baseball star, founded and became the head of a group called the American Softball Association in 1933—a local organization not to be confused with the other ASA, the Amateur Softball Association, which it was a part of until 1941. It was a strong force in promoting softball in the 1930s but finally was disbanded in 1945 as Sisler began devoting all of his time to his role as a scout for the Brooklyn Dodgers baseball club.

But while the American Softball Association was active president Sisler helped build softball stadiums, promoted the sport and delivered the message: "The only thing soft about the game is its name." Sisler starred in a series of comic strip–style Camel cigarette ads entitled "Softball is tough" that tell the story of a "nerve-straining, exhausting sport" in which good hitters are few. Sisler had this to say in the last panel of the ad:

'Course softballers go for Camels. It's a hard, tough sport that takes all the nerves you've got— and good, healthy nerves too. Camels don't get the nerves shaky. When you're dog-tired, a Camel gives a lift in energy. I smoke Camels regularly. Most champion softballers I know smoke Camels. They say "Camels set you right."

Also consider the following: The intensity of the game was such that injuries were becoming more and more common and serious. As writer for the *Coast*, a California magazine, described in 1939 "The 'soft' ball is hard, the base paths are short, and it has become a game of such intense speed that sprained ankles are looked upon as a minor injury." The writer pointed out that on July 31, 1939, a benefit game was going to be played at San Francisco Seals Stadium to aid injured softball players.

All of this came to a head at the end of 1939, when a group of promoters got together to recreate indoor baseball—with a clear emphasis on *baseball*—employing paid softball players. It was created with major publicity flurry and was billed, as *Time* termed it in its preview, "as a big time winter sport." Patterned after Major League baseball, franchises were sold to major cities and a 102-game schedule was created, with a World Series planned at the end of the season in mid-March between the Eastern and Western champions. Softball was about to become big business, like baseball.

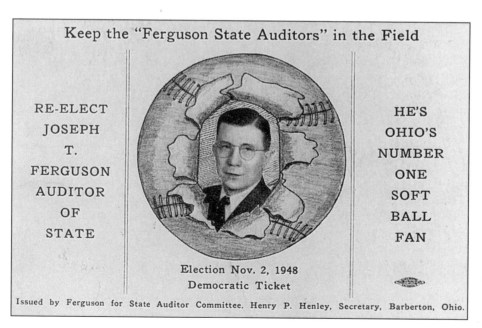

Keep the "Ferguson State Auditors" in the Field

RE-ELECT JOSEPH T. FERGUSON AUDITOR OF STATE

HE'S OHIO'S NUMBER ONE SOFT BALL FAN

Election Nov. 2, 1948
Democratic Ticket

Issued by Ferguson for State Auditor Committee. Henry P. Henley, Secretary, Barberton, Ohio.

Campaign Post Card
More than one politician of the 1930s and early 1940s used a softball team as a promotional vehicle. Ferguson's teams— known as the Auditors— won three Ohio State championships in the men's fast pitch. (Ron Menchine Collection)

The president of the league was baseball immortal Tris Speaker (salaried at a princely Depression sum of $7,500 a year). With one or two exceptions the clubs were managed by hardballers—locally admired baseball men. At the helm in Cleveland was Bill Wambsganss, the only player ever to make an unassisted triple play in a World Series game (against the Dodgers in 1920). Cincinnati had 1926 National League Batting Champion Bubbles Hargrave, and St. Louis hired peppery Gabby Street, who had led the Cardinals to two pennants and a World Series.

The Professional Indoor Softball League of 1939 was ill-advised, undercapitalized and short-lived, folding after only a few games. It would be the first of a number of failed attempts to professionalize softball.

It also created headaches for the amateur game. A number of players were suspended from ASA play when they signed with the Professional Indoor Softball League in 1939, and long lists of male and female players, managers and coaches who had signed with teams such as the

Landing Hard *Softball player Linda McConkey takes to the air with the greatest of ease as she dives into third base during an exhibition game in 1955 between the Lorelei Ladies and the Tomboys at Atlanta, Georgia. Linda is a Lorelei mainstay. The legs belong to Jerrie Rainey of the Tomboys.*
(Library of Congress, Prints and Photographs Division)

Chicago Downdraft Girls and the St. Louis Pandas were distributed, to keep them out of amateur play.

In early 1940, as the lists of suspended players were being published, a major men's team, the St. Joseph, Michigan, Autos converted to baseball from softball. Its sponsor maintained that it was due to what they termed the "decline of softball," but others claimed that it was because of tougher rules on paid and nonresident players; still others pointed to the fact that the team was never able to win a national championship. In 1939 they had won 63 of 69 games but lost the state title to *Big Six* of Pontiac, Michigan, who had been the World's Negro Softball Champions in 1937. Besides the Michigan title, the Big Six took the 1939 Central Championship.

In July, 1940, an unsigned article appeared in *Balls and Strikes* under the title "Spectators Urged to Become Players." It argued that baseball had begun as a participant sport but got better and better until it was "harder to play and easier to watch." The same thing was happening to softball, and was still speeding up even at this late date.

Skilled pitchers have learned to toss a ball underhand so fast and so accurately that it is necessary, in play under lights, to prescribe a dark uniform for the pitcher so that the batter can at least see the ball if he can't hit it. Effort is also made to prevent attempts by infielders to screen the pitcher by providing a light background against which it is difficult to see the ball. What is a legal pitch, has to be described in detail. Finally, the pitcher is now obliged to toss the ball three feet further than formerly. The harder the ball is thrown the harder and further it can be hit, and the harder it is to handle. So the base lines have been lengthened.

The telling point in the article was when its anonymous author wrote, "It is up to us to watch softball closely. If too many people prefer watching to playing, then we should find out why. Already there are the 'Slow Pitching Rules' adopted by the Joint Rules Committee."

While softball developed in the years between the world wars, not everyone was playing the game that the Canadians called "fastball." Some folks were content with a high level of competition and dazzling pitching for a little fun—for a chance to clobber the ball, even if one was a little out of shape. Facetiously termed the "Cripple A League," the slow pitch game was played under the same basic rules as the regulation game but pitchers were required to toss the ball "at a moderate speed, and it must have a perceptible arch on its way to the plate."

Chicago was a special case in point. The fast game was played but so was an oddity known then and now as "16 inch," which was played with a ball that seemed like a caricature of the standard 12-inch ball. By the summer of 1938 there were 2,500 teams playing this game.

The modern game of softball had clearly been created in the 1930s, and on the eve of World War II it was seen as a major American institution. In 1940 the ASA reported that 5 million people were playing the game. More astonishing was the fact that it had become a spectator sport: Between 80 million and 100 million people watched the game annually between the years 1938 and 1940, according to an ASA estimate.

A defining moment in all of this came at the Amateur Softball Association's annual meeting on March 9, 1940, when talk of the game's bright future was rampant. Keynote speaker L.H. Wier, director of planning for the National Recreation Association, very much set the tone for the whole affair.

He talked of softball as a major factor tending toward the continuation of American democracy and building a more virile America, and as a means of curbing crime. "Softball fields," he noted, "are cheaper to build and maintain and will build stronger character than penal institutions." Weir, a former circuit court judge in Cincinnati, was old enough to recall a day when that city had no public athletic facilities, and it was unlawful for children to play in the streets and swim in the canal.

Meanwhile, the game was moving out—heading off to those places where people were looking for a game to play. In August, 1937, a man named W.H. Wilson with the Ford Motor Company imported some bats and balls into New Zealand which later became one of the sport's strongest enclaves.

But war news was beginning to intrude on the nascent world of softball. Dudley Stilton, ASA Commissioner for England, wrote to the head office: "Conscription has indeed played the devil with our teams over here, but as you can see it is all for our own good. Even as I write now, if I glance out of the window I can see anti-aircraft guns and machine guns in the field at the back, the field, that ironically enough, we used to play on."

Softball Goes to the Front

The war clouds were gathering and Pearl Harbor was but three months away when the 1941 tournament was held in Detroit for the second year. World War II eventually changed the softball picture considerably, but the Amateur Softball Association weathered these changes well.

Although the war continued to dominate the national scene in 1943, the manpower authorities in Washington, D.C., gave full sanction to both baseball and softball on the home front, because they considered these activities vital to civilian morale and health. The manpower shortage caused the disbanding of thousands of civilian teams, but this gap was made up by hundreds of defense plant teams and 67,000 service teams that engaged in the active playing of the game.

The game received another boost during World War II. The military embraced the game, and it was played avidly at army installations around the world as had an earlier form of the game in the First World War.

The Amateur Softball Association was able to report that there were "... softball diamonds being built and games being played right up to the fighting fronts." The ASA supported a major U.S. Service Camp program with help from Coca-Cola as a sponsor. By the end of 1942 there was not an American camp or base of any size in the world where the game was not being played.

M. J. Pauley loved to tell reporters about the degree to which softball had become the game of the American fighting man. On Guadalcanal, after the beachhead was established and the enemy Japanese were driven back, the troops had cleared an area and built 20 softball diamonds within a matter of days.

There were stellar military baseball teams—many with major and minor league players in uniform—but the game of the average G.I. was softball.

Pauley was quick with numbers, which seemed to show that almost everyone involved with the war was spending his or her off-duty hours playing softball. In what must have been a remarkable session he presented his numbers to Paul Hennessey, sports writer for the International News Service in the summer of 1943. He began: "There are 67,000 U.S. Service Camp teams. With 15 men on a team that makes a total of 1,005,000 service men playing the game."

Pauley continued: "Assuming that each team plays only one game a week—although most of them play two or three games— and that only 100 service men watch a game, you face a total of 7,735,000 servicemen playing or watching the game."

War Effort

Major Moses Cohen, commander of the Army Aviation Station Hospital at Willow Run, is quite pleased on receiving softball equipment from Mrs. Charles Gitlin, representing the Amateur Softball Association. The presentation was made on September 3, 1943. (Amateur Softball Association)

By this time Pauley had really wound up and came in with the final number. "Each camp program extends over a 20-week period. Further multiplication reveals a total of 154,000,000 players and spectators during a season in camps alone."

A very direct effect of the war on the game was that it literally knocked the stuffing out of the ball. Kapok, the fine, silky fiber, a product of Java and the Galapagos Islands in the South Pacific, had become the standard ball stuffing. It was compressed into a sphere and covered in horsehide. But the Japanese captured those nations and the supply was cut off. Right after Pearl Harbor the U.S. Government requisitioned every pound of the substance to make, among other things, life preservers.

This cautionary notice ran in the 1943 ASA Guide:

IMPORTANT
For the Duration of the War

U.S. Government restrictions, because of shortage of certain component materials entering into softballs, may necessitate changing present specifications.

The Amateur Softball Association recommends—

MORE THAN EVER, FOR YOUR OWN PROTECTION to use exclusively only manufacturers' trade marked products as are advertised by the respective manufacturers in this, your *Official 1943 Softball Guide*. Your cooperation, please.

Raymond Johnson
President Amateur Softball Assn.

For the duration, the balls had to be made from reclaimed kapok and whatever else was at hand. After the war kapok came back into use.

Then there was the matter of the World Series. Prior to 1942, all state and metropolitan areas that desired to send their champions to the National Tournament were welcome, but when the total reached 83 men's and women's teams, it became too unwieldy. There was also the desire to make the event a bit more dependent upon skill than upon luck, which was often the deciding factor in a competition in which a team could be eliminated with one loss. It was, in the parlance of the game, a "single knockout" tournament.

In 1942, when transportation difficulties necessitated curtailed travel, the plan of admitting only regional winners was instituted. The United States was divided into 15 regions, and each region held tournaments in places that required a minimum of travel. This emergency greatly decreased the entry lists and made it possible for a "double knockout" or "double round robin" tournament to be held, thus eliminating the ever-present possibility of an inferior team winning the championship by a stroke of fortune instead of superior playing ability. This war-time innovation proved so popular that it has been followed down to the present day.

During World War II, two professional women's leagues sprung up in the Chicago area. One league, the All-American Girls Professional Baseball League, called its game baseball and was the one depicted in the 1992 hit motion picture *A League of Their Own*. It was created by Philip K. Wrigley, owner of the Chicago Cubs, and Branch Rickey of the National Baseball League, who were among the incorporators. The All-American Girls Professional Baseball League (A.A.G.P.B.L.) opened with six teams at the beginning of the 1943 season. Staffed primarily by women who had been top softball players, the teams were mostly managed by former major leaguers, including Jimmy Foxx and Max Carey.

Infused with Wrigley's own brand of showmanship, the league attracted great attention. He dressed his players in shorts and very short twirling skirts (designed by Mrs. Wrigley), ordered them all to wear pony tails and sent them all to Helena Rubenstein's Studio to learn to apply makeup and to brush up on their charm.

The game played was a hybrid between softball and baseball. The ball itself was 10½ inches in circumference, making it an exact split between the baseball and softball, and pitchers could throw overhand or underhand. The All-American Girls Professional Baseball League lasted 11 years, and in 1953 the Fort Wayne Daisies won the last championship.

The other wartime professional league was the Chicago Metropolitan Woman's Softball League, which had begun the war years as an amateur league but turned pro as the A.A.G.P.B.L. shanghaied players. At first the softball league tried to stop Wrigley and even appealed to baseball Commissioner Judge K. M. Landis to get Wrigley to behave. It was argued that some of these women had defense jobs by day and that Wrigley's moving these women around the Midwest for games might be hampering the war effort. Landis replied that the A.A.G.P.B.L. was Wrigley's business and had nothing to do with organized Major League baseball.

Baseball The All-American Girls Professional Baseball League (A.A.G.P.B.L.) was in force from 1943 to 1954. It combined elements of baseball with fast pitch softball for a rugged and demanding game. This photo from April 14, 1948, shows the Kenosha Comets playing the Muskegon Lassies in Miami during spring championship play. Left to right: Dorothy Naum (Lassie third baseman) chases Helen Filarski of the Comets, as Lassie catcher Charlene Pryer blocks the plate. The Lassies won the game.
(Cleveland State University)

Post-War Game

Softball came out of the war with a new intensity. The game continued to grow in popularity and the ASA's missionary work during the war created new converts who came home to an ever-expanding playing area. Leo Fischer reported to the ASA early in 1947:

At the end of 1946, it was estimated that there were approximately 2000 fenced-in fields through the United States, Canada, Mexico and other North American nations devoted exclusively to softball, with lighting equipment to permit night games. At a modest estimate of only 200 attendance per game during June to September, inclusive, and approximately five games per week in each of these parks, one arrives at the startling figure of more than thirty million paid admissions in these parks alone. The average admission fee is about fifty cents.

But the intense fascination with and ability to attract crowds was in decline, even though there was plenty of great softball to be seen. For one thing, in 1946 the National Fastball League came into being, uniting the nation's top male corporate teams. It was considered the top male fast pitch league ever put together. It would disband a few years later because of the onset of the Korean War.

It was in 1947 that softball got a long-range shot in the arm when Mr. Bill Simpson of the Raybestos Company of Stratford was instrumental in the erection of Memorial Field, built in

memory of and dedicated to the employees of Raybestos who had lost their lives in World War II.

This field, on which the 1952 Men's World Softball Series was played, was considered a model one. The site was carved out of a rock-studded marshland filled in at spots. The lighting system was considered perfect and the fieldhouse excellent. The 4,000-seat plant was surrounded by a 10-foot wire fence, all points of which were exactly 250 feet from home plate. An electrically operated scoreboard, dugouts for teams and a modern press box completed the picture.

The International Softball Congress, founded by Larry Walker, began holding its own tournaments in the West in 1947 against direct competition with the Amateur Softball Association. It would be the first of several organizations that would challenge the ASA's control of the game.

The ASA continued to fight against member teams going—or appearing to go—pro. The dynamic Jax Maids of New Orleans were made ineligible for amateur play in 1948 because they had played against professional teams. The Maids had been the 1947 Women's World Champions.

The papers were full of softball news in the late 1940s. Consider a few of the events that captured the public's attention.

In May 1947 the Senate and House were to battle in a softball game. President Truman tossed out the first ball and 25,000 tickets were sold to benefit the D.C. Police Boys Club. For the first time the men and women had their tournaments in different cities. A handsome young man named Herb Dudley pitching for the Clearwater Bombers, from Clearwater, Florida, fanned 55 hapless batters in a 21-inning national championship game in September, 1949.

Later that year a one-armed lad named Hal Nelms tossed a no-hitter in San Pedro, California, which seemed to open the game for others with disabilities. In 1951 Eddie Dodge of St. Petersburg, Florida, achieved national attention as a one-armed outfielder who was termed one of the fastest throwing outfielders in the sport; he was able to nail just about anyone striving for that extra base. He told *Balls and Strikes* how it all worked: "If it's a fly ball I try to catch it around my stomach. After I do nab it, I slide it down the side of my leg, dropping my glove in the process and there is the ball in my hand. When it's a ground ball, I just flip it up, throw the glove off, catch the ball and chuck it on in."

Perhaps the most extraordinary was a Lexington, Virginia, boy, *born without arms*, who *pitched* with some regularity for his high school softball team. He did it by grasping the ball with his right foot—actually easing the toes of his right foot under the ball, positioning it with his toes—and hurling it at the batter. Unable to hold a bat, a special rule was created by which the ball would be rolled on the ground so he could kick it with his foot. In 1952, he was credited with pitching two no-hit games.

That same year a team of amputees—all veterans who had lost limbs in the Korean War—began playing in Spokane. There were 20 of them, including an amputee youngster who was their bat boy. Special rules were created as they took on teams of men without disabilities. For instance, the vets could post an extra outfielder, lead off bases and freely employ pinch runners.

Television seemed like the next logical step for the game. "Eventually," wrote Jimmy Powers of the *New York Daily News* in late 1949, "as the stars became established and acquired a following, the big contests could be moved to the Garden." The front-page headline for the March 15, 1951, issue of *Balls and Strikes* blared "TV SOFTBALL BOOM SEEN OVER NATION" and, as plans seemed to be firming up for a softball game of the week in 1953, the same periodical told its readers "SOFTBALL STEPS INTO NATIONAL TV." An Amateur Softball Television Authority was created to handle it all and consultants were hired. Logic indicated that the game was ideally suited to television, as most softball games easily fit into an hour with time remaining for a few commercials.

There were a few network games but the concept of televised softball would never develop. Perhaps the top moment came in 1954 when Bertha Ragan, then of the Orange Lionettes, went on Groucho Marx's television show "You Bet Your Life." She rendered him speechless as she pointed to the fact that she had already thrown 107 no-hitters, a dozen of which were perfect games.

The Olympics were also part of the dream. In 1950 *Balls and Strikes* reported that softball

---

was "virtually assured for the 1956 games." This was, in fact, a time when the game began to develop as an international sport. Four countries played at this point, and the number would jump to more than 50 by 1965. In 1952 the International Softball Federation (ISF) was founded as the governing body of amateur softball with control over international competition, including the Pan-American Games. Even with the ISF and the tireless work of the ASA leadership, it would take 40 years longer than the 1956 date for the game to get to the Olympics.

Slow pitch moved out of the shadows and a separate national championship was added to the ASA finals in 1953. This event signified a major shift in the sport and brought to the fore a form of the game that had gotten scant attention up to this point. It was called "slow pitching" in its early years. Quoting from Leo H. Fischer's 1940 classic *Winning Softball*, it was "A type of softball which has attained popularity in many sections of the country and which is gaining in others is the variety known as 'slow-pitching.'" At this time, according to ASA founder Fischer, it was played with a 16-inch ball.

But it grew and grew and by 1960 had surpassed traditional fast-pitch softball—"original softball" in the terms of some partisans—and spread through today, where it totally dominates the game in terms of numbers. More than 90 percent of the softball played in America is slow pitch.

How and why this happened is a fascinating story.

Arizona Republicans *(Opposite) Senator Barry Goldwater (catching) and Senator Paul Fannin (at bat) in a Senate softball game. While younger and more athletic members of the House of Representatives still play baseball, the game of choice on Capitol Hill is softball. (Amateur Softball Association)*

5 Slowing

THE GAME THAT
TOOK OVER THE
GAME (BY MAKING
IT A TEAM SPORT)

In the Struggle

Any history of the game of softball is incomplete without acknowledging its long struggle with a basic imbalance. That imbalance has been the domination of pitching over batting.

Going all the way back to the Farragut Boat House in Chicago in 1887 and the first set of rules drafted by George Hancock, there was an attempt to make sure that the batter could get the ball into play. It stated: "Only straight arm pitching in which the arms and hands are parallel with the body will be allowed, and the ball is not to be curved."

It Down

The distinctive technique of softball was the underhand pitch, which was used at first to make sure the batters could hit the larger, mushier ball. But the people who were attracted to the game were athletes—male and female—who developed ways of achieving speed and a little something on the ball. These were corn-fed youngsters weaned on baseball who saw no reason to serve as a patsy to the batter.

By the early 1900s in Chicago, pitchers found that they could put a tremendous spin on the big 17-inch ball that was used in the high school gymnasiums and park field houses where indoor was played.

As the 19th century wore on, pitching got better and better, and the rule makers worked to put the bat back in the indoor game. As the indoor baseball rule makers met, they sat down to deal with an issue that would become a permanent tug-of-war in softball: the balance between dazzling pitching and the ability of the batter to get the ball into play.

The Spalding Indoor Base Ball Guide for 1903 addressed the issue:

Great wisdom has been displayed in the slight alterations made in the playing rules for this season. The powers that be figure that the public likes to see plenty of stick work and they are hedging in the poor pitcher, who finds his work growing harder and harder as the years roll by. The successful pitcher of the present day must need be a wonder, compared to the old-timer, who had easy marks in the days when the game was young. Increasing the size of the bat is something that will prove beneficial, while cutting out the clause which called a foul bunt a strike will give the shorts something to do to live up to their reputations and add interest to the game, for there is nothing so exciting as to see a good bunter drop a twister near the plate and then see the shorts, pitcher and catcher scramble to get it while the batter is digging for first.

The problem was a constant during the early days of the game. The pitcher became a one-man, or in many cases a one-woman, show and no-hit games were commonplace. Eighteen strikeouts per (seven-inning) game became the norm.

In the 1920s, with the further organization of the National Playground Ball Association and the National Diamond Ball Association and their various state and sectional tournaments, the competitive spirit began to develop in both the men's and women's form of the game. Pitchers found that they could generate great speed on the ball by swinging their pitching arms around in a complete vertical arc or circle before letting the ball go. This maneuver was called the "windmill pitch."

Fast Pitch *Janna Venice, pitcher for the Ocean Spray Blue Wave out of Plymouth, Massachusetts, in 1992, the year she was the Big East collegiate softball player of the year and the MVP at the Brakettes Invitational in Stratford, Connecticut.* (Russell Mott)

But it was not until 1934, after the 1933 Century of Progress, that the issue first had to be dealt with. The problem landed in the lap of the Joint Rules Committee of the National Recreational Congress in Washington, D.C. The Rules Committee was composed of such varied groups as the Amateur Softball Association, the National Collegiate Athletic Association, the Catholic Youth Organization, and the Young Men's Christian Association.

This began a period of much study into the domination of pitching, leading to changing and experimentation with the rules of the game. Deception was the issue. The pitchers used every legal trick in the book in coming up with faster and more bedazzling pitches. They were partially counteracted by increasing the pitching distance and eliminating some of the trick wind-ups.

The odds were against "reform," as good and diligent men and women worked for countless hours creating and refining deliveries and pitches that caused new headaches for the batters. They came up with spins, hooks, slants and drops. "Clam shells, twisting and turning, are said to have inspired Bill Cummings of Massachusetts to experiment for four years with curves until he finally developed the knack of pitching them," wrote Rosina M. Koetting in an essay on the early

Proud Papa (Above) Ron Parnell with two daughters, Dana, left, and Linsi, right, at the United States Slo-Pitch Softball Association World Series in Daytona Beach, Florida, Jackie Robinson Stadium.
(Russell Mott)

Gamer (Right) Tony Chavez, second baseman and a whirligig in the field, from the Albuquerque, New Mexico team named Our Place. They came all the way to Virginia to take part in the action of the ASA Class C Men's Fast Pitch National Championship.
(Russell Mott)

game. She added, "Paul 'Windmill' Watson of Arizona developed the circular wind-up and fast pitch. John 'Cannonball' Baker of Wisconsin invented the figure eight windup."

The pre-war softball career of Harold "Shifty" Gears reveals an interesting insight into just how dominant those pioneer pitchers could be. Gears, who was the first individual to be voted into the National Softball Hall of Fame, came onto the scene with both arms blazing. In his early years he could shift from right- to left-handed delivery, hence the nickname. He began in sandlot softball in 1922 and racked up one honor after another. In 1928 he attracted attention by winning 45 games in a row. In 1934, in his first year with Kodak Park of Rochester, New York, he won 86 games and lost only four. In 1935 he hurled 96 scoreless innings. His career record of 866–115 included 61 no-hitters and nine perfect games.

"They changed the rules because of Harold," said George "Hack" Krembel, a teammate of Gears, "They took away the windup he had—with both hands moving, then all of a sudden he'd come in with an underhand pitch."

Gears was the top vote-getter in that first Hall of Fame induction in 1957, which also saw the election of Sam Elliott, Amy Peralta May and M. Marie Wadlow—all pitchers; all were deserving of election and all served as testimony to the dominance of pitchers.

Elliott pitched 1,133 games and compiled a 1,046–87 won-lost record, striking out 13,396 batters in the process. Wadlow, the first woman elected, compiled a record of 341 wins and 51 defeats, including 42 no-hitters. Amy May was not only a domineering pitcher (447–79, including 300 shutouts, during a career that began in 1938 and ended in 1951), but a great hitter who led the 1945 ASA National Championships with a .577 average.

Shifty's Boys The first man to be elected to the National Softball Hall of Fame, Harold "Shifty" Gears, shown in his capacity of running the Kodak Park Athletic Association, for many years a major force in fast-pitch softball.
(Amateur Softball Association)

The news from the 1937 nationals, for instance, was little but pitching news. A team from Knoxville posted back-to-back no-hit, no-run victories using different pitchers. Mary Skorich of Cleveland became the first (but by no means the last) woman to toss two no-hitters in world championship play. A man threw two no-hitters but another man had beaten him to that record in 1936. The games were long too—a couple went on for 14 innings, another two continued for 15 innings and one lasted for 17 innings—and most of these were 0–0 or 1–1 marathons. Briggs Auto Body of Detroit, which won the men's title, had only two runs scored against them in six tough games.

Action at Home   *Plays like this were common at the ASA Men's Class A Fast Pitch National Championship in Salem, Virginia, in the summer of 1992, where players seemed willing to take a lot of chances. (Russell Mott)*

Tinker, Tinker . . .

As early as 1936 the tinkering with the rules had to do with giving the batter a better chance of putting the ball in play. In 1936 the distance to the pitcher from the plate was increased from 37 feet, 8½ inches to 40 feet and then to 43 feet in 1940. In 1946 a distance of 35 feet was created for women, keeping it 43 feet for men. In 1950 the men's distance was increased to 46 feet and the women's went up to 40 feet in 1965.

Eventually spikes were allowed (1936), the base runner was allowed to leave the bag as soon as the ball left the pitcher's hand instead of waiting until it crossed the plate (1937) and bunting was made legal (1939). Also, beginning in 1939 the batter was allowed to head for first base on a dropped third strike. Pitching still had the clear edge and the windmill delivery had batters fanning. And it was not just the speed of the ball. The rule makers always seemed to be a season behind the pitchers, who seized on every untested premise and loophole in the rules.

In Flight   Randy Boyle, shortstop for the Class A slow pitch power-house team Undercoverwear, based in Wilmington, Massachusetts. Action of this sort dispels the notion that the slow pitch game lacks defensive finesse. (Russell Mott)

In 1938 a new pitch—a balk in baseball—was very much in evidence. It was created for the sole purpose of getting a base runner to illegally leave his or her base before the ball left the pitcher's hand. The pitcher would start in motion—using the windmill—and take a step forward toward the batter. But instead of pitching the ball, the windmill would continue for several revolutions, confusing the batter and luring the base runner (or runners) off base.

Still more changes were made in an attempt to balance the scales—or, as the game's leaders liked to term it, "improving the offense." In 1940 the quick return pitch—that is, one thrown in an attempt to catch the batter off balance—was banned, the pitching distance was increased and the batter's box enlarged. In 1941 the rocking chair movement by the pitcher was eliminated.

Top pitchers were in great demand and were watched for infractions like contract jumping. A colorful gent named King Kong Kelly sat out most of the 1939 season because he left the Phillips 66 team for more lucrative pastures.

During all of this, attention was brought to bear on various aspects of equipment, including much deliberation on the hue of the pitcher's uniform, which was seen as an agent in pitching dominance. These ace fast ballers were playing under the lights and were using pure white uniforms and accessories to hide the big white ball zooming in on the batter from a short distance.

The astonishing sartorial rule making began in 1938 when pitchers for teams that wore light gray or white were forced to wear contrasting colors. Then, in 1939, a major loophole was closed when pitchers were barred from wearing light gray or white accessories—scarfs, socks, caps, etc. In 1940 these earlier rules were dropped for daylight play and only applied to pitchers playing under lights.

In 1941 a Draconian measure was adopted that became known as the "undertaker's rule." All

The Worth Book of Softball

Carpetman   (Opposite) Russell Bradley of the legendary Campbell's Carpets team as he appeared in 1979. (Washington Star Collection, Martin Luther King Library)

Perfection   (Below) Fast pitcher Clayton McGovern hurling for the Great Lakes Softball Club, the winners of the ASA Men's Class A Fast Pitch National Championship, at the Salem fields in Salem, Virginia. In the next-to-last game of the tournament, this gent pitched a perfect game. (Russell Mott)

pitchers, male and female, in both day and night games, were required to wear all black or all dark blue uniforms with no letters or trimming on the front of the uniform. The undertaker's rule was kept during the war years and was not repealed until 1947, also the year in which the tenth player—the rover or shortfielder—was eliminated.

The post-war game was fast and fascinating, but seemed to be losing some of its grassroots appeal; perhaps the constant rule changing had something to do with it.

What could not be overlooked was the fact that fine athletes—male and female—had come to dominate the game from one position, the pitching plate, and no matter how much tinkering was done with the rules, the game belonged to them. Underhand pitching allowed for great deception and motion, to which was added burning speed.

To demonstrate just how good the pitching was and how overwhelming one person could be, a man named Meryl King started a four-man softball team in 1946 to take on all comers. He changed his name to Eddie Feigner and the King and his Court was—and still is—off and running. Feigner, a barnstormer of the old school, would spend the rest of the 1940s, '50s, '60s, '70s, '80s and into the '90s taking on nine-man teams and beating most of them with his ever-changing cast of four. Aside from playing with a team five men short, Feigner would (and still does) pitch one inning blindfolded and another from second base.

Some people actually claimed that pitchers were throwing softballs faster than baseballs. Those who made the claim had all sorts of anecdotes to back them up, not the least of which was that, as we have learned earlier, the great Babe Ruth had whiffed in at least two public demonstrations.

But the demonstrations did not end with the Babe. Perhaps the most famous of these post-Ruthian showdowns took place in 1962 when Joan Joyce, considered by many to be the greatest female softball pitcher of all time, faced Ted Williams—considered by many to be the greatest hitter in baseball history—before 18,000 people in Waterbury, Connecticut. Forty pitches and 10 minutes later, Williams retired with one base hit and one foul ball. He did not touch another pitch.

Hit Men (Above) *The boys of summer getting ready to play. Three big guys from the 1992 Steele's Hit Men. The man with his back to the camera is Scott Virkus, a man of considerable presence both on and off the field. (Russell Mott)*

Showboat (Left) *Waterbury Transmissions player Joe Povinelli at the New Bedford, Massachusetts, slow pitch level "C's," in the rain.* (Russell Mott)

Joyce's career included over 100 no-hitters and 35 perfect games, plus numerous national and world championships. Her fast ball was reportedly clocked at over 100 miles per hour.

Then there were the informal pitch-offs in which softball pitchers and baseball pitchers went *mano a mano*. In the late 1940s a big kid from Long Island named Roy Stephenson seems to have thrown faster on a softball diamond than a very speedy future Hall of Famer named Bob Feller could pitch from a baseball mound.

Fans argued that there was no way that the big ball could be faster, but those who made their living with bat and ball knew otherwise. Frankie Frisch, the old Gas House Gang member, advocated that baseball batters face softball pitchers for the first week or two of spring training to sharpen up their reflexes.

One wonders whether something else is at work here and that baseball players aren't meant to take a poke at a softball, even if it is pitched slowly. Banned from baseball, Pete Rose returned to the batter's box in August, 1991, for a charity slow pitch softball game in West Hartford, Connecticut. In six at bats he managed a home run and a single playing for the Connecticut Kings in their 21–7 loss to the Peter Pan Cafe. Ironically, he told the *Hartford Courant* that he was thrown off by the slow pitch and would have done better against a fast ball.

In the spring of 1961 *This Week* magazine decided to settle the matter once and for all. They got Steve Barber of the Baltimore Orioles, who had proven to be the fastest pitcher in Major

Mushball Man   (Above) Pitcher Calvin Ammons at the 16-inch tournament in Wisconsin in 1992. (Russell Mott)

League Baseball in a 1960 testing by the magazine, and matched him against 24-year-old Bill Massey of the championship Clearwater Bombers. Using a 50-frame-per-second camera as a measuring device, the magazine determined that Barber's best fast ball crossed the plate at 95.55 miles per

Autograph Hounds   (Left) Rick Scheer signs autographs in Quebec in 1991. (Russell Mott)

Slowing It Down

hour at the end of its 60-foot trajectory. Massey's underhand pitch, which traveled 46 feet, crossed the plate at a stunning 98.8 m.p.h.

The magazine concluded: "It may be that the extra 14 feet the hard ball must travel reduces its overall average velocity. But whatever the explanation, there's no getting around the fact that foot for foot, the softball moves faster."

"The answer is in the wider sweep of the arm," said Gene Martin, an ASA official, "This generates greater thrust and also picks up body drive. By comparison, with the underhand delivery a pitcher throwing overhand or sidearm is almost awkward as far as speed is concerned."

A reporter asked Martin whether a softball would still travel faster over the same distance the baseball travels. "Probably not," Martin replied. "The extra 14 feet would have more spin and break sharper than a baseball over the longer route than it does at 46 feet, [so] it would be even tougher to hit."

The test was news and created enough interest in fast pitch softball that both CBS and NBC found space in their summer schedules for nationally televised games. The television people liked the idea of a sporting event that fit neatly into an hour. "There's a strong chance that in the space of two years softball will be just as popular on parlor screens as baseball," was a typical remark in a sports column of the era.

But it was not to be. Interest was booming in another form of the game, which had just become *more popular* among folks who played softball, and there were those who would soon start blaming television for the fall-off in interest in the slow pitch game. Folks, they reasoned, were home watching the boob tube when some of the best athletes in the nation were pitching their hearts out.

Flashback

Slow pitch, the "other game," had been around for many years, but seldom got attention or respect.

Going back in time for a moment, slow pitch was part of the picture as a separate game since the 1920s. To prevent strikeouts from making the game too lopsided and to put the ball back into play, some local leagues and associations made rules that the ball must be pitched slowly enough to display a visible vertical arc on the way to the plate. As the windmill pitch became common in the 1920s, more and more people realized that they could, at best, hope for a hit or two a season; and more people drifted into a game in which they might actually have a chance of scoring. When this change took place, the game went from being a pitcher's to a batter's paradise.

In 1932, when the National Diamond Ball Association assembled 40 teams for what is regarded as the first national tournament championship, it found all types of rules, distances, sizes of balls and pitching.

Slow pitching was not allowed for this tournament. Fast pitching was the norm, but a 14-inch ball preferred by the slow pitch partisans was used.

When the great softball tournament was created for the Century of Progress Exposition in 1933, the same question came up again: What can be done with those people who toss the ball high? The problem was solved by dividing the men's teams into two classes. Thirty of the 40 men's teams preferred fastball pitching. They were accommodated, while the ten who were accustomed to the slow pitch game played a tournament of

Backhanded   Rich Kolmetz pitching for Pace of Rochester, New York, in the United States Slo-Pitch Softball Association AA-level Slow Pitch Tournament in Agawam, Massachusetts. Pitching from behind one's back is permitted in U.S.S.S.A. play, but not in the ASA rules. (Russell Mott)

their own. It was the largest and most comprehensive tournament ever held in the sport that would sweep the country like wildfire. Champions were decided in three classes—fast pitching, slow pitching and women's softball. The assembled women's teams lacked a windmill pitcher, so there was no need to split up their division.

However, after 1933 the nascent Amateur Softball Association immediately dropped the slow pitch version, and it was not until 1953 that this governmental body again took up the slowball variety officially. In the meantime, most players in the city of Chicago had refused to substitute fast pitching for the slow variety. Chicago held on to a game that featured a 16-inch mushball and no gloves.

Ohio started a slow pitch movement in 1935 in Lakewood, a suburb of Cleveland, where the Amateur Softball Association championships were held from 1945 to 1948. The first such league was one composed of four teams of city employees operated by the Cleveland Recreation Department. At the end of the league's first season in Lakewood, Ohio, a tinsmith constructed a large tin cup, which was presented to the winners as a trophy. The cup was larger than any man on the team and had plenty of surface for suitable engraving. It was presented to the bewildered manager at an annual Trophy Night Banquet in Cleveland for all sports. The publicity this gag brought gave great impetus to the slow pitch game in the Cleveland area.

By 1953 slow pitch had become so popular that it came out of the shadows as a separate national championship for the ASA finals. The tournament was held in Cincinnati and the winners were the Cincinnati Fire Depart-

Turning the Double *(Right) Second baseman from Spectrum, based in the Twin Cities, Minnesota, turns a double play at the slow pitch tournament in Sherbrooke in 1991. With strike-outs very rare, one of the most effective and showy things that a slow pitch pitcher can do for his or her team is to get a batter to hit into a double play. (Russell Mott)*

ment, which went on to win it again for the next three years in a row. The program had started in the fire department a few years earlier when slow pitch had been introduced as part of a physical fitness plan for out-of-shape firefighters.

By 1958 an increasing number of industrial and recreation department leagues converted to the slower game and a headline in *Sporting Goods Dealer* magazine proclaimed that "SLOW PITCH SOFTBALL IS MOVING FAST IN SALES LEAGUE."

Firemen *(Below) The team that extinguished all opposition on its way to the first ASA Slow Pitch Industrial Championship in 1956. These guys started playing the game to get in shape.*
(Amateur Softball Association)

brought millions into the game. The numbers were stunning as slow pitch grew slowly into the 1970s when, suddenly, it took off. It hasn't come down yet. In 1970 some 15 million Americans were playing softball regularly but that total jumped to 25 million in 1980.

Fast pitch is alive and well, but mostly at the high school and college level. Fast pitch is a pitcher's game closer to baseball in tone and temperament and more likely to end with a score of 1–0 or 3–1. The rule of thumb for the fast version is that it is 80 percent pitching, 10 percent defense and 10 percent hitting. Good pitching—and a mound 46 feet from the plate—keeps a lot of good players with batting averages that are lower than their weight. The ball moves at 90 m.p.h., there are lots of bang-bang plays at first and bunts galore—great stuff requiring a high degree of athleticism.

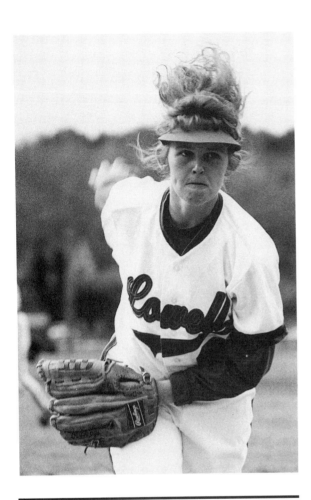

Bring It   *Kim Sullivan, a sophomore pitching for the University of Massachusetts, Lowell, an NCAA women's fast pitch team.*

(Russell Mott)

The Slow Pitch

Why the popularity of slow pitch? There's a play on almost every batter, and the ball can be used to scatter picnickers and sometimes lands in the parking lot. It is especially suited to the guy from accounting who can go three for four on a hot August night. The same for the *gal* from accounting, since over last few years co-ed slow pitch has started to take off and the male-only version seems to be standing still.

The opportunities to handle and hit the ball seem to be the key here. In the slow pitch game

The following year in Cleveland, already dominated by the slow pitch game, a new trend developed. The ASA Cleveland Metro Chief announced a "mixed couples" league to encourage co-ed participation. Thus co-ed softball got an official start. It was just like regular slow pitch softball, except that spikes were not allowed and that half of the players taking the field for each team must be male and the other half female at all times.

In 1960, the numbers were tallied and it was found that slow pitch eclipsed fast pitch softball in popularity for the first time. In terms of player popularity, fast pitch would never come back. But the slower game made softball more popular and

Fast Eddie

Eddie Foust, of Neuse Sand and Gravel, Kinston, North Carolina, at the United States Slo-Pitch Softball Association World Series in Daytona, Florida, in 1991.

(Russell Mott)

everyone gets into the act defensively, and not only are there more hits but there are more chances to get one. In a well-pitched fast pitch game a given batter will have two or three chances at the plate, while he or she will get four or five chances in a slow pitch game of the same number of innings.

But there is something more here, as evidenced by the case of McAdenville, a small town in North Carolina, where the slow pitch had never been heard of in 1950. It was a "hot bed" of fast pitch ball and the small town (population 750) had seen more than its share of players become All-State players. According to the town's recreation director, William L. West, Jr., who wrote about the town's experience in a 1962 issue of *Balls and Strikes*, the slow pitch came in 1951 as part of two new leagues to the state. Initially skeptical, players in the town had become fascinated by the game before the season was over.

West said there were four reasons for the quick acceptance of slow pitch. More players had a chance to participate, older players found they could be actually involved, the spectator was treated to a more action-packed game and a seven-inning game could be played in 30 to 40 minutes.

Within a few years the small town had become a powerhouse of the slow pitch game, as one by one they converted from one form of the game to another. By 1960 slow pitch was being played throughout North Carolina. A McAdenville company called Pharr Yarns sent a team to the National Championships seven times in a row in the late 1950s and early '60s.

Another difference between slow pitch and fast pitch is the rules. Rules call for a change in

Slow Baller *Mike Breen, pitcher for the Bushmasters team in Woburn, Massachusetts, directs the ball toward the plate in a men's municipal "B" slow pitch league. (Russell Mott)*

playing style and strategy. For starters, a fast pitch team fields nine players per team. A slow pitch team fields 10, the tenth player being known as the short fielder or rover who is free to roam the area but usually settles in left center field. You can bunt in fast pitch, but not so in slow pitch, which is constructed so that batters hit the ball, not tap it. Both leading off base and stealing are permitted in fast pitch; but a player can do neither in slow pitch. The batter can swing down or chop at the ball in fast pitch. The chop swing is not allowed in slow pitch, although it is often hard to call. In fast pitch the strike zone is over home plate between the top of a batter's knees and the line of

Seasoned Vet *Gary Lowell, of Hancock, New Hampshire, playing in a local co-ed slow pitch league during the summer of 1991. He plays for a restaurant-sponsored team and hit 22 home runs in 1991 and 28 in 1992. He had been playing for 16 years when this photograph was taken.* (Russell Mott)

his or her armpits. In slow pitch, the strike zone is over home plate between a batter's knees and shoulders. In slow pitch, every pitch must attain a perceptible arc (usually a height of between three

Dreamers Manchester North girls' softball team from Manchester, New Hampshire, appearing at the ASA 16 and under Field of Dreams Tournament in July, 1992. They went on to become the tournament champs. Left to right in the top row: Jennifer Velosky, Allison Lavoie, Samantha Scott and Andrea Paquin. In the bottom row, left to right: Kristy Gannon, Melissa Vincent, Karyn Kohler, Amy Dubois and Jennifer Koch.

(Russell Mott)

and 10 feet above the point of release, but this rule varies in different leagues) before reaching the plate. In fast pitch the pitcher can whip the ball over the plate with no arc.

In fast pitch the all-important pitcher must have both feet in contact with the pitcher's rubber before beginning his windup. In slow pitch the pitcher may touch the rubber with only one foot before beginning his windup. In fast pitch an illegal pitch results in a ball for the batter and advancement of a base for all runners on base. In slow pitch, an illegal pitch results in a ball for the batter, but the runners do not advance.

Perhaps the most common assumption in slow pitch is that there is no pitching to speak of.

It might seem so, but there are those who argue otherwise. Mike Ivankovich makes this compelling case in his book *The Strategy of Pitching Slow Pitch Softball*:

How do you strike a batter out? You don't. Occasionally you may have a strike out but don't flatter yourself into thinking you did something right. You probably didn't. More than likely, it was the batter's inexperience or lack of ability that should take the credit (or blame).

From a pitcher's perspective Slow Pitch is a game of defense, not a game of strike outs. The primary objective of any pitcher is to get the ball over the plate. Don't walk anyone unintentionally. Let the batter hit the ball so your defense can make the plays, get three outs, and go in and score some runs.

But a good pitcher takes it a step further. A good pitcher not only knows how to get the ball over the plate, he also knows how to get the batter to hit the ball *where he wants it to be hit*, i.e. to his defensive strengths and away from his defensive weaknesses.

Slow pitch softball would have its own history and one major schism. In 1968 in a Pittsburgh motel room a group of disenchanted slow pitch enthusiasts created a new group, the United States Slo-Pitch Softball Association (U.S.S.S.A.—or U-triple-S.A.) was thus formed, beginning with a handful of teams.

The upstart group argued that the Amateur Softball Association was in charge of both fast and slow pitch, yet was primarily interested in the faster game and was unwilling to consider improvements in slow pitch. Almost immediately the new group adopted 65-foot baselines and a smaller batter's box. As U.S.S.S.A. literature of the time put it, "The Amateur Softball Association did not greet the newly formed slow pitch organization with enthusiasm."

By 1992 the U.S.S.S.A. boasted a membership of over 100,000 teams.

Like fast pitch, which had tried to establish professional leagues, slow pitch organized its own in 1977. The American Professional Slo-Pitch League (A.P.S.P.L.) began with attendance aver-

aging around two thousand people in such cities as Baltimore, Cincinnati, Pittsburgh, Chicago, Columbus and Detroit. The Detroit Caesars won the first World Series in four straight games from the Baltimore Monuments. Jimmy Galloway, known as "Mr. Softball," joined the A.P.S.P.L. after being selected to the amateur All-American slow pitch team eight times. The league soon lost steam and died out.

But the game would have its heroes, mostly big tough guys who could clobber the ball with regularity. They emerged in the 1980s as a force of their own with strong personalities and stunning feats. In 1987, for instance, Mike Macenko, with a national record of 844 home runs in a single season, led Steele's Silver Bullets, of Grafton, Ohio, to its third consecutive ASA Supernational Slow-Pitch Title. In that same year Bruce Meade, the man with the handlebar moustache also called

Father and Son
Mike DeVita Jr. (dad) and Mike DeVita III (son) at the tournament in Sherbrooke, Canada in 1991. He is the manager and sometimes player of the Undercoverwear Softball Club of Burlington, Massachusetts, a very successful franchise. Mike III is the team bat boy. (Russell Mott)

Mr. Meade

Bruce Meade on a homerun trot. With his trademark handlebar moustache, Meade is one of the true legends of the slow-pitch game—and one of the game's most respected athletes. When he is not playing in tournaments he is deputy sheriff in Bradenton, Florida.

(Russell Mott)

"Mr. Softball"—and the only player to ever hit a softball out of the Houston Astrodome (460 feet)—led the Smythe Sox (Houston, Texas) to victory in the U.S.S.S.A. World Series.

Carl Rose, Jim Fuller and a handful of other players would follow as dominant figures as the game moved into the 1990s.

Still the President's Game

Jimmy Carter did for slow pitch softball what Lyndon Johnson did for chili con carne and what Calvin Coolidge did for the Indian headress.

Slow pitch did not actually need a boost when the president picked up a bat—but it got one. Pictures of the president as a softball player appeared in newspapers and magazines throughout the world. All sorts of people got into those pictures, ranging from brother Billy to Ralph Nader, who umpired on at least one occasion.

The president's infatuation even created a need for the world's press to explain the game to its readers. One of the most engaging descriptions appeared in the left-wing Paris daily *Le Matin* in August, 1977, when President Carter was in France. The newspaper wanted to let its readers in on the game that Carter said he was going to play as soon as he returned to Plains. As translated by the Associated Press:

Softball—literally soft ball—is played in Georgia at the end of the afternoon when the burning sun begins to go down. One person placed in the middle of the field, the pitcher, throws the ball at the player from an opposing team, the catcher, who, armed with a bat, a long piece of cylindrical wood, must try to project the ball beyond the reach of the pitcher's team-mates while they are trying to recuperate the ball, the catcher runs round the field with the opportunity of stopping at five or six bases. If he doesn't reach the base before his opponents get the ball he is eliminated. And that's just what regularly happens to President Carter.

Softball became Carter's great private and public indulgence, and even when others talked about him they often invoked his country boy penchant for the game. "They may play softball down in Plains, but they play hardball in the country," was Richard M. Nixon's 1980 comment on the Carter White House.

Jimmy Carter's particular spin on softball was not that he played the game, but that he played to win—for keeps.

It all began when Carter became involved with the Plains Church League, where he took the game seriously from the start. In 1976, during the presidential campaign after the Democratic Convention, the pack of journalists following Carter found themselves in Plains, Georgia, where the candidate had gone to relax for a few days before starting his campaign in earnest. A series of softball games were then begun, pitting Carter and his crew of unarmed Secret Service agents, who called themselves the News Makers, against a group of reporters who called themselves "The News Twisters." The media team quickly adopted the slogan "The Grin Will Not Win." Carter was "The Grin."

The games were loose at first—Carter's running mate Senator Walter Mondale played for the media on at least one occasion—but became increasingly competitive and slick. At first Carter showed up in black socks and cut-off jeans. Then on July 31 the Associated Press showed a picture displaying Carter's navel as he went up for a fly ball.

By all accounts, Jimmy Carter took his slow pitch softball even more seriously as president and had more than passing interest in the power he could assemble from the trim, fit Secret Service detail that accompanied him. He always positioned himself as captain of the team he was on. Reporters who played with him noted, for example, that Carter knew immediately which base to throw to for the force and never, ever had to ask what the score was or who was up next.

How did he celebrate a visit back to Plains, Georgia on August 20, 1978, which was billed as a folksy presidential reunion with hometown folks and friends? He and his Secret Service team beat a local team led by his brother Billy, 6–5.

If softball served Carter before and during the presidency, it has also served him as former

Observing

Jackie Brown of the
Local 265 Ladies Team
at the Black National
Invitational Tournament in
Cleveland, Ohio, in the
summer of 1992.
(Russell Mott)

president. On August 31, 1985, a game was set up between Carter and his former White House staff and a media team captained by Sam Donaldson, then of NBC.

"You may think that this is for fun, but this is a grudge match," said Donaldson. "In 1976 Jimmy Carter got the Secret Service on his team and they consistently beat the media but today he has just bums like us."

The game was a rough one. An attempt to push Donaldson off second base so that he could be tagged out was foiled when, according to the UPI reporter on the scene, "Donaldson pushed back and then deftly reached down and picked up the base, clutching it in his arms."

Carter's team was able to prevail, but only with the help of a ringer. With the former president's team down by a score of 5–4 he went to his bench for a ringer who produced a game-winning home run. The player in question was 19-year old DeAnn Young, who had grown up in Plains. Earlier in the year she had hit 23 homers for Georgia Southwestern College.

As president, Carter was a player and not much of a spectator, which infuriated some of

those who felt that part of the presidential job description is tossing out the first ball for a baseball game. One incident drove home the point. When Carter, as president, finally got around to attending a Major League game it was for game seven of the 1979 World Series between the Pirates and the Orioles; he was helicoptered to the game in Baltimore. On seeing the president in the edgy Orioles clubhouse just before the deciding game, the irrepressible Rick Dempsey said in a voice that could be heard by his teammates and a few reporters, "Next time, get your ass here before the 7th game."

Carter put his finger on it as he watched the game from his box with Speaker of the House Thomas P. "Tip" O'Neill and baseball commissioner Bowie Kuhn. As Kuhn put it in his memoir *Hardball*, Carter told him that he was more interested in participatory sports than in observing team sports. All in all, this was a heck of a thing to say to the Commissioner in the Commissioner's box in the midst of the seventh game of the World Series; but, as Kuhn wrote, "Since one of those participatory sports was softball, I could be forgiving."

Like Franklin D. Roosevelt before him, Jimmy Carter helped promote the game. Carter played a different game than the one that F.D.R. coached; so fast and slow pitch each had its own friend in the White House.

Presidential Form   (Opposite) President Jimmy Carter shows 'em how to hit the ball in Plains, Georgia. (Carter Library)

⁶ More Than

SOFTBALL IS, IN FACT,

COMPOSED OF A

NUMBER OF GAMES . . .

AND, FOR THAT MATTER,

A NUMBER OF TEAMS,

TOURNEYS AND

TECHNIQUES

Games People Play

"What people fail to realize," says Don Porter of the Amateur Softball Association, "is that softball is a sport of many games."

The point borders on understatement as the history and present state of the game is studded with unexpected and unusual variations. In fact, one can name almost any odd possibility and there has probably been a serious version of softball that encompassed it.

Overhand pitching?   In the 1950s an overhand-pitch version first cropped up in Kansas City, and by the late 1960s more than 100 teams were playing what amounted to a cross between baseball and fast pitch softball.

How about Overhand Slow Pitch?   This is done enough so that the United States Slo-Pitch Softball

a Game

Association has developed and publishes rules for this variation. It calls for throwing the ball overhand with an arc (not to exceed 10 feet off the ground) and a delivery that does not allow the elbow to bend. It is played here and there, including some parts of Louisiana where they still play an overhanded slow pitch game called "jungleball."

On the Ice?   Such a version was played in Cleveland beginning as early as 1926 in Wade Park. It was played on skates and grew to be a scheduled sport in the 1930s that, according to *Balls and Strikes*, drew large crowds.

With the Rules of Golf?   It was called "barnyard golf" and emerged as a small fad in the early 1960s. A softball was hit with a softball bat and ultimately driven into an oversized cup. It appears to have been created in West Virginia in a vacant

area between a golf driving range and a complex of softball fields.

In the Snow?   There are several snow tournaments in places such as Nebraska, Alaska and Maine. In Portland, Maine, they play by the regular rules to benefit the March of Dimes. It allows the *Portland Press Herald* the opportunity to run sports page leads that read like this one from 1990: "Softball players braved near blizzard conditions Sunday to raise about $4,200 in the 8th

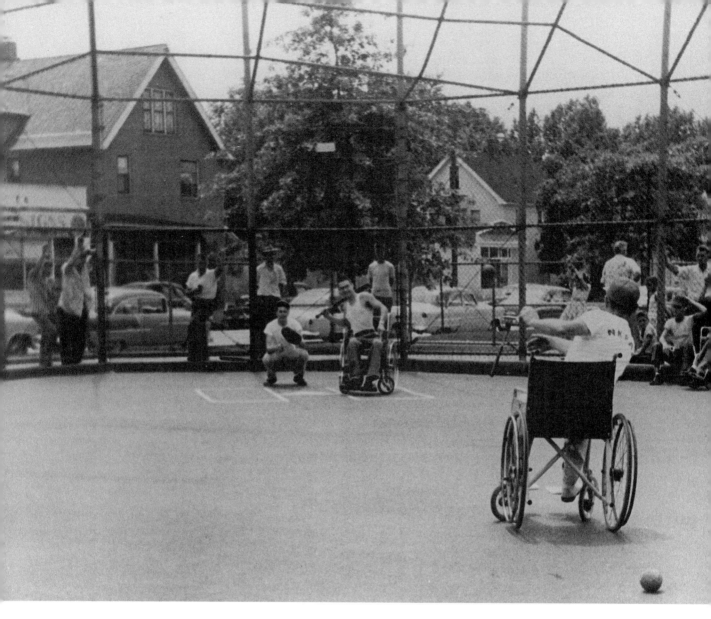

annual March of Dimes Snowball Softball Tournament."

On Snowshoes? Winthrop, Washington, and Priest Lake, Idaho, are places where they hold tournaments for folks who play the game so attired. At the Priest Lake tourney, which has been running for more than 20 years, games have been played with temperatures as low as 25 degrees below zero. Baselines in the snow? Red spray paint. Bases? Day-Glo traffic cones. Softballs? Several manufacturers make bright-colored balls for this market. The action? In 1989 the *New York Times* sent a reporter to Priest Lake in February and reported that ". . . the action on the diamond borrows more from Chevy Chase than Ozzie Smith." A pitcher winds up, steps on his snowshoe and takes a nose dive into the snow.

With a Ball that Behaves Outrageously? In the Akron-Canton area some folks play "fumbleball," using a 12-inch ball with a thick rib of an outseam that causes the ball to go in every direction but straight.

A Slow Pitch Version That Requires an Even Quicker Turn Around at the Plate?   Say, one in which the batter begins his or her at-bat with a count of three balls, two strikes and one foul? It is called one-pitch and it is all over the place. The U.S.S.S.A. Rule Book carries a set of rules for it.

Slow Pitch in Which There Is an Unlimited High Arc? A Marathon College Weekend Game That Lasts 150 Innings? A Game That Is Played Indoors?   Anybody can do it. Just because the Amateur Softball Association, the United States Slo-Pitch Softball Association or the National Softball Association has not sanctioned it doesn't mean it cannot be part of the game.

These variations are fascinating—and there are more—but they are not forces to be reckoned with, unlike fast pitch and slow pitch, which are the two major forces in softball. There are three more that also most be reckoned with, modified pitch, 16 inch and Over the Line. The first two are newcomers that are growing, while the third seems eternal.

Family Time   Shneka Whaley and Yakema Davis, two of the Cleveland, Tennessee, Pantherettes, women's slo-pitch, at the United States Slo-Pitch Softball Association Black National Invitational Tournament, in Cleveland, Ohio, in the summer of 1992. Their grandmother Evelyn Davis drove 24 hours from Tennessee to see their game. (Russell Mott)

Slow Fast Pitch or Fast Slow Pitch?

Modified pitch is what they call a fast, action-packed softball game that is neither modified fast pitch, nor modified slow pitch, but a game unto its own known by devotees simply as modified pitch. In some places it bore the oxymoronic name of "slow fast pitch" before modified became the name of choice.

It is a hybrid only in that it combines the rules of fast pitch with the hitting and defense of slow pitch. The pitch is key and was recently described this way by Merle Butler, the ASA Director of Umpires: "It's not lobbed and it's not a slingshot. There is no arc and there is no windmill. The pitch does have speed. The ball can drop, curve, or go straight and fast." Eddie Andrews,

Slider *Shortstop Kevin Starkey of the Miniature Precision Bearing softball team sliding into home. He is playing in a Keene, New Hampshire, modified pitch league.* (Russell Mott)

ASA Commissioner for South Florida and a member of the Modified Rules Committee added, "It is much like the original fast pitch. The pitcher just rears back and throws the ball. The motion is that of a bowler." A pitcher can achieve speeds of 60 to 70 miles per hour and the ball is hittable.

It is a full athletic game with bunting, stealing, hit-and-run plays and sacrifices—a game of speed and strategy but with plenty of runs. A well-played game of modified pitch will see 10 to 20 runs scored with just about everybody getting the bat on the ball.

Bill Plummer of the Amateur Softball Association says that there are those who predict that it may be "the game of the future" and compare it to slow pitch when it started to make its move on fast pitch. Eddie Andrews says he is convinced that it is the game of the future and that it will grow rapidly in the next few years. It is now a game of two coasts, having put down strong roots in such far-flung places as Florida, Atlanta, Boston, Spokane and Staten Island, New York. It is also gaining converts in Latin America. Andrews adds that the reason that it is not yet strong in the Midwest is because people there haven't been exposed to it thus far.

In 1991 3.1 percent of all teams registered with the ASA were modified teams; in 1992 that percentage had risen to 3.3 percent. More dramatic, in fact, is the rise in co-ed softball, which became part of the ASA stable of games in 1981 and had jumped to 13 percent of the teams in 1992.

For those who believe that softball does a good job of adapting itself to what players want, the co-ed and modified games are perfect examples of how that process has worked. It is as softball says through its liberal attitude: Decide how you want to play the game and softball will accommodate you. Both the Amateur Softball Association and United States Slo-Pitch Softball Association sanction this game as they do 16 inch or mushball, a very old form of the game.

__Bare Handed__ A stalwart for Chicago's California Gold—named for a street, not the state—demonstrates how the real way to approach the 16-inch ball is without a glove. (Russell Mott)

Mushball in the Windy City

On the small, urban fields in and around Chicago, they play softball with a 16-inch Clincher ball—a huge, mushy grapefruit of a sphere, a not-so-distant descendant of the balled-up boxing glove first batted around in a Chicago yacht club at the sport's birth.

"Chicago was," to quote the oft-stated softball honorific, "the cradle of softball." It was not only the place where the game began, it was also the site of the first world tournament held by the founders of the Amateur Softball Association. It

SOBIES

was the headquarters of this dominant organization the first 12 years of its existence.

The fast game bloomed in Chicago and in about 1937 it spread to downstate Illinois with, according to one historic account, "Litchfield, Peoria, Springfield, Danville, and Rock Island leading the parade." The state went crazy for the game and Illinois is still a place where there is a lot of intense fast pitch softball being played. Aurora, Bloomington and other sites are among the most dynamic in the game.

However, in the early 1940s an unusual apathy developed in Chicago, the city that had seen the development of a game that at one point

in the 1930s looked as if it could be one of the greatest of all spectator sports. Beginning in 1940 the fast pitch variety of softball began to wane in popularity and these teams almost disappeared completely after 1944, with the exception of the National Fastball League, which came after the war.

What took over was the neighborhood game of—as they called it in those days—"slow pitching." It was a game that evolved more from indoor baseball than from fast pitch and seemed a perfect fit for the many vest-pocket fields carved out of vacant lots in the city during the Depression. Nobody bothered to track its growth, but thousands of teams emerged and more than 1,000 leagues sprang up to accommodate them.

It has emerged as a game of its own: The Chicago-style, bare-knuckles, high-scoring variant (15 runs is not a great showing and will often put a team in the losing column) uses a ball that is a full 30 percent larger than the normal 12-inch ball. Because of its juiciness as a target and the mauling that the ball gets during a game, it is often called mushball or pillowball, the latter referring to how it loses some of its crispness as the game progresses and becomes more and more pillow-like.

Most people call the game 16 inch based on the size of the large ball used in play. They call it other things too, such as cabbageball and Windy City softball.

As the major nonconforming site in the soft-ball universe, Chicago is where most of the 16-inch softballs produced today are consumed, although the game is showing up farther and farther outside the city limits with pockets of play as far away as Iowa and Wisconsin.

This Chicago game is one of lore and color and gives one an excuse to invoke names such as George Hallas (an early devotee), "Machine Gun" Jack McGurn (who allegedly had a team), Mike Royko (who hired a lawyer to prevent the parks people from allowing gloves) and Michael Jordan, who popped two doubles in a 1992 charity game. It has its own heroes with names such as Ted "Skeets" Skadell, Whitey Maytag and Eggs Bromley. Then there are the great modern stars of the game such as Ed Zolna and Eddie Surma, and a guy named Moose Skowron who played this game before he diverted to Major League Base-ball. One of the game's early field announcers was Frank Reynolds, who went on to become a major figure in television news.

It may have also been the setting for the corrupt encore to baseball's 1919 Black Sox scan-dal. In 1969 no less a scribe than J. Anthony Lukas wrote about the game during the Depression in a rare New York Times mushball article: ". . . then the mobsters and gamblers moved in. Huge sums were bet on games, players were bribed to throw them. It is said in the folklore of the Windy City that the sport got so crooked that in one game there were six of the country's 10 'most wanted' men in the stands."

It is a world of deep tradition and if that tradition is threatened, controversy starts. In Chi-cago the game is played without gloves, even though 16-inch tournaments in places such as Iowa and Wisconsin allow them. In the late 1970s the city's park department decreed that one could wear a glove within the legal limits of the Windy City if one so desired, but an individual was not required to wear it. Boom! The city went crazy. Players wailed to the papers that the city was trying to ruin the game they loved; Chicago Daily News columnist Mike Royko sued the city and the Wall Street Journal came in to cover the issue with a feature.

The Royko suit was resolved by letting leagues vote on whether to permit the gloves. All 24 teams in Royko's orbit voted to outlaw them. Until he retired from the game a few years ago, Royko was one of the 16 inch game's staunchest supporters and testimonial givers: "Chicago-style softball is one of the most heroic, challenging and satisfying athletic activities ever devised by man, with the possible exception of procreation."

The gloveless tradition is said to date back to the Depression when few could afford such a luxury; but there is also a practical reason. Players find that the pockets of traditional baseball and softball mitts are not big enough.

What makes the Chicago game distinctive is what the players like to call finesse—the kind of thing that older guys have—and it is different from speed or strength. The common advice is: try to power the big ball over the fence and you're dead, especially with a tenth man in the outfield. The players with the good averages meet the big ball, chop it and send it among the five players in or close to the infield.

Defensive shifts are a major part of the game and it takes finesse to put the ball in one of those holes. Chopped balls, bloopers that fall, balls hit down the line—these are all part of the game. Base runners can lead off but cannot steal, insuring a lot of close plays.

Pitching is also different in this game, begin-ning with the distance from the mound to the plate, which is 38 feet. It is slow pitch with a capital S; but each real pitch of the ball can be accompanied by two deceptive moves known as "hesitations." A hesitation is a bluff set to deceive and throw off the timing of the batter. Despite this, strikeouts are still rare.

It has been said that 16 inch is to the culture of Chicago what stickball is to the culture of New York. It is seen as a nice local antidote to the increasingly national, standardized, subsidized and corporate realm of sport—a big-time neigh-

Going Over the Line

In the sun-drenched beaches of Southern California and Nevada's Sin City, bikini-clad participants play the hip, on-the-edge game called Over the Line. It is an outrageous game of spectacular

borhood game with more leagues and tournaments than can be easily counted.

Both the Amateur Softball Association and the United States Slo-Pitch Softball Association actively compete to affiliate teams and 16 inch tournaments, and there is strong competition between the two organizations. The next form of the game does not attract those atop the softball establishment.

dives and kicked-up sand.

Some take it most seriously and talk about it in the same breath as beach softball. Others see it as an instrument for a great big beach party in which the only thing that is serious is the effort to see who can come up with the most outrageous X- (or R-) rated team name.

In any event, the game is exciting and has a long playing season. In 1992, for example, it had a tournament schedule that began on March 7th in Paradise Valley, Arizona, and ended on December 5th in Yuma.

Over the Line (OTL) is a contest of abbreviated softball played between two teams of three players each. Although it's predominantly played on sand, OTL is not limited to beaches and deserts. Any flat surface can be used, from Astroturf to asphalt.

The key to the game is the line itself. Start with home plate and from that point mark off 55 feet. This is the distance to the all-important front line. Foul line to foul line should be 54 feet across.

The batter stands next to the plate while a teammate, usually kneeling opposite, gently tosses a regulation softball straight up so he can swing at it. Hitters bat from the front point of the triangle.

There are only two kinds of hits: singles and homeruns. Any ball falling safely past the last fielder is a homerun and clears the bases. This is what sets beach Over the Line apart from the basic sandlot version of Over the Line. Scoring is easy: A batted ball is a hit if it strikes the ground on the fly in fair territory. Two hits load the imaginary bases, and every one after that drives in a run. In other words, three hits to score a run and every hit after that scores another run, unless a home run clears the bases and the team starts over again. One other important detail: There's no base running in this game.

Fielders may play anywhere behind "the line" or its extensions; if they cross it in attempting a catch, the ball is ruled a hit. There is no end to how far back a defender can play or how far a hitter can hit the ball; in other words, there is no fence.

Men play barehanded, while women wear fielder's gloves. Spectacular diving catches are part of the character of the game and players are forever jamming their fingers in the sand. With this in mind, the taping of one's hands and fingers is permissible, if no padding is used. Golf gloves may be used for hitting only.

Each side gets three outs per inning. A batter is out if he swings and misses once, hits two foul balls, hits to a fielder who catches the ball on the fly or hits a ball that strikes the ground inside the triangle, the front line or lines around the triangle. Batting out of turn is also an out.

Games last four or five innings, depending on the rules of the tournament being played. If the score is tied, play can continue through seven innings if necessary; if there is still a tie, the team with the most hits wins. Any team leading by eleven or more runs at the end of an inning wins "by a skunk."

In most tournament play a substitute must be someone who hasn't yet participated in the tournament.

Over the Line is a *bona fide* California/Arizona phenomenon—which has made inroads elsewhere (26 states according to one count) with some toeholds on the East Coast—and has all the attributes of a full-blown subculture. OTL has its own slang. For instance, the proper name for home plate is the "can"; a "claw" is a one-handed catch; and a "dink" is a short placement shot. To be on the losing end of a big inning is to be "drilled," "blitzed" or "schooled." "Dome" is an important word usually preceded by the words "I'm in your," meaning that defense is getting a good read on the hitter. "Heat" is a hard-hit ball; a "worm burner" is a low hard shot; a "purse" is a soft hitting stroke and a "floater" is a ball that stays in the air for a long time, appearing to float.

Over the Line exists in several forms, including wheelchair OTL and junior OTL which offers a co-ed pee wee version for kids as young as five. Its traditional focal point is a hedonistic world championship in San Diego in July sponsored and run by the Old Mission Beach Athletic Club. This event is rowdy, bawdy, boozy and brash. Jack Williams, a writer for the *San Diego Union/Tribune*, put it in context with a series of rhetorical questions starting with these two:

- Where else do teams invent names imaginative enough to make the inside of a latrine read like a Sunday school etiquette manual?
- Where else do young ladies whose endowments sometimes outstrip their modesty . . .

And so forth. The programs from the San Diego championships have become institutions in themselves. They are full-color celebrations of the game that look more like *Penthouse* than *Sports Illustrated*.

Diver *(Above) This is why they wear band-aids in Over the Line play. This moment of daring was captured in La Jolla, California, during the spring of 1992.*

(Russell Mott)

Badge of Honor *(Left) Bandaged fingers are the "badge of honor" and protection for the true Over the Line player. These are important if one makes OTL hand-first dives into the same substance they use to make sandpaper.*

(Russell Mott)

Ready for Action *(Right)*
Over the Line fielder
Steve de la Cruz, ready to receive.
Note the obligatory finger bandages
for a man who within moments will be
jamming his digits into the sand.
(Russell Mott)

Ready to Roll *(Below)*
Over the Line daredevil fielder
Jerry Cooper in California
tournament play
in the spring of 1992.
(Russell Mott)

Diversity, Thy Name Is Softball

Where do these odd ballgames come from? Who knows?

Where do the balls to play these odd ballgames come from? West Albany, New York.

The diversity of softball as it is played today is nowhere better exemplified than by a visit to the J. deBeer & Sons Inc. offices and plant in West Albany, New York, and listening to Jim Muhlfelder—the grandson of the man who founded the company—talk about the many balls that are called softballs.

Other fine companies make softballs, but no other caters to the regional fancies and traditions like this one. It has been called a "one-of-a-kind" operation because it does things that nobody else does. It still works with horsehide—abandoned by the Major Leagues in 1973 when they switched to cowhide—and is, for example, the company they call when film producers need authentic period baseballs for movies such as *The Natural* and *The Babe*.

Softballs, now hand-stitched overseas, are the company's lifeblood. If America has become homogenized, as some have said, you could not prove it at deBeer. A recent catalog contained 78 different softballs and carried this indisputable claim, "If you need a particular size or style softball, deBeer makes it."

The deBeer softball possibilities seem endless. The centers? They come in poly core, cork and kapok. The seams? There are flat seam balls, outseams and specially designed seams that allow the stitching to stay on the inside. This latter seam is the key to the Clincher, perhaps the most distinctively different ball in the game. It is made of horsehide and kapok.

The special hidden seam was invented in 1931 (and subsequently patented) by Frederick deBeer. The first versions were created for the New York area in 12-inch and 14-inch sizes and in a 16-inch version for the streets and sidewalks

---

Connecting Point *Over the Line, pitching and batting.*

Left to right are Al Hamilton and Dale Olsen. (Russell Mott)

of Chicago. Since then, the 16-inch ball has totally dominated the Chicago game and, according to Jim Muhlfelder, constitutes 98 percent of the market. Clinchers are hardly ever seen outside the nation's two largest cities. DeBeer also has been a major presence in Southern California. Their "Official Over-the-Line" ball is seven ounces, has a kapok center and a rubber cover.

In a reception room with glass cases loaded with baseballs and softballs, Jim Muhlfelder points to the diversity of his line—and, by extension, the diversity of softball. There is the 212, a favorite of the fast pitch crew in Southern California (a very traditional market), to his line of XF balls: limited flight "softies" for indoor and handicapped play. There is a neon orange Corker (i.e., cork center ball) for play in the snow. They even make a plastic softball for batting ranges.

Stitch in Time *Stella McEwin works on a softball at Worth, Inc., Tullahoma, Tennessee. Softballs, like baseballs, must be hand sewn, as the stitching of such spheres has long defied even a hint of automation. Most of the hand-stitching is done offshore. When she began stitching balls in 1945, there were about 500 stitchers working in their homes in and around Tullahoma.*

(Russell Mott)

How local does local preference and custom get? Jim Muhlfelder answers, "The deBeer DB-212 is a gray high-seam ball demanded for high-school ball in Nevada." It is just this simple. The tradition there is for a gray softball and he is most eager to accommodate them.

More Than a Game

Star System

"The game has become more sophisticated as America has," says Worth's John Parish, whose company's active involvement in the game is long established. He sees something quite basic in the game beyond the diversity: "Softball today is high-tech equipment, fashion colors and health-inspired warmups. But at the heart of the game, there is still the kid in all of us who just wants to play . . . That part survives all of the new rules and equipment and fees and organizations and hype. It's the real reason we play the game."

Parish also wonders if softball has now become so strong in its own right that it exists on its own, apart from baseball. He thinks that it now stands alone.

Softball has certainly taken on a different evolutionary path from baseball and continues to do so. For instance, the idea of a baseball star and

Clobberer   (Above) Carl Rose pokes one out of Knoxville's Bill Meyer Stadium, home of the Knoxville Blue Jays, the AA baseball affiliation of the Toronto Blue Jays. Rose demonstrated his homerun prowess to members of the Knoxville media by hitting softballs that cleared the triple-deck outfield fence and landed on top of a warehouse roof some 450 feet away, beyond left-center field.

(Russell Mott)

Slugger   (Opposite) Carl Rose in 1992 in the uniform of Williams-Worth. He is one of the most well-known sluggers in slow pitch softball. Rose, who routinely hits the ball over 400 feet, has plans to hit a softball out of every Major League stadium in North America. (Russell Mott)

a softball star are a far cry from one another. There are softball stars but few big names outside the game itself. This could be changing.

The first and foremost factor will be the Olympics: 1996, 2000 and beyond. Without question these events will be epochal for a sport that has striven for medal status since the 1950s. It

Mike *(Below) Mike Macenko has served as a one man dynasty of slow pitch softball. This is how he looked during a pensive moment at the Sherbrooke, Quebec, tournament in 1991. (Russell Mott)*

promises to give the woman's game a once-in-a-century boost and, if the predictions hold, several women will doubtlessly emerge from the games with household-name status. If there is one who seems to have an early lead in this area it is Lisa Fernandez, formerly of UCLA and now playing with the Raybestos Brakettes.

As close as the men's slow pitch game has to a Babe Ruth or a Hank Aaron is a quiet power-house of a man named Carl Rose, who can routinely hit a ball over 400 feet. He gets good press, has a brisk-selling thin-walled aircraft aluminum bat named for him and has appeared in television commercials for it. He shows off on his travels by staging demonstrations in which he slams soft-balls out of Minor and Major League baseball parks. It is no secret that he eventually hopes to poke one out of every Major League park in North America. In team play in 1991 he had a .751 batting average, hit a home run every 2.2 times he came to bat and jacked one ball 480 feet. In 1992 the *Tennessean* of Nashville called him ". . . the most recognized slow pitch player in the world."

A former double-A level baseball player with the Pirates, Rose is studying physical education at Valdosta State College; he—along with Lisa Fernandez and Joan Joyce—is the exception rather than the rule.

After all, the immortals in the Softball Hall of Fame in Oklahoma City don't get much more famous than the first man inducted, pitcher Harold "Shifty" Gears (13,244 strikeouts and 61 no-hitters). But mighty Mike Macenko didn't get on the cover of any national magazine after he hit an amazing 844 homers in the 1987 season or when he ended 1989 with 3,143 homeruns over seven seasons.

In softballdom, the fame tends to go to the teams, the powerhouses and the occasional dy-

Former Red *(Opposite) Doug Flynn, shortstop of the Bell Corp. team, in 1992. Flynn had an 11-year Major League career, including being a member of the 1975–1976 World Champion Cincinnati Reds. Flynn is one of a handful of former Major Leaguers playing in the higher realms of slow pitch softball. Jim Fuller, formerly of the Baltimore Orioles, is another. (Russell Mott)*

The Worth Book of Softball

nasty—and even that fame is spread sparingly and tends to be local. The top women's fast pitch team is the Raybestos Brakettes, a dynasty of such proportions that they seem to redefine the term. They finished the 1992 regular season with an unblemished 55–0 record and then took the National Championship in August in Redding, California, with a 6–1 tournament record. It was the Brakettes' 24th National Championship. The Redding Rebels of Redding, California, who beat the Brakettes once in the 1992 championship tournament, and the Phoenix, Arizona, Sunbirds are among the other forces at the top of the fast pitch game.

Men's fast pitch has been dominated for the last several seasons by the Guanella Brothers of Rohnert Park, California; SeaFirst of Seattle, Washington; Larry H. Miller Toyota of Salt Lake City; and National Health Care Discount of Sioux City, Iowa, who won the championship in 1992.

In terms of national attention, the biggest thing going right now on the male side of the slower game is Super slow pitch, and the most popular teams are the re-emerging Steele's team, known as the Steele's/Sunbelt Hitmen, Bell Corp. of Tampa and the 1992 kings of the hill, Ritch's/Superior of Windsor Locks, Connecticut.

Steele's, whose full name was originally "The Men of Steele," gained its reputation as a band of barnstorming Ruthian monsters, including the aforementioned Macenko. They would go out and play up to 350 games in a season, during which they hit homeruns high over the heads of the hapless opposing slow pitch pitchers. In 1989 these guys hit 3,730 home runs, led by Dirk Androff of St. Louis, who poled 413 of them in 248 games. In the four seasons ending in 1989 the team hit 20,664 homers. Over the five

seasons from 1985 through 1990 they won 1,344 games and lost 100 and maintained a team batting average of .676. They played some 350 games in 1989, most of which were exhibition games played for show against lesser local teams ("church teams" says one admitted admirer who thinks the Men of Steele were hurt by too many easy games). They dominated the slow pitch world in 1990, disbanded before the 1991 season and came back as Steele's/Sun Belt Hit Men in 1992, when they looked like they were the team to beat, but were dominated by Ritch's/Superior.

At the end of the 1992 season the male slow pitch powerhouses include Ritch's/Superior, Bell Corp. and Starpath. The list of top teams changed in 1993 as loyalties, sponsorships and expenses took their toll. Before the 1993 season had gotten started, the very powerful Ritch's team had lost one of its strongest batters, Jim Fuller, who had signed with Williams-Worth.

Owner Woody Bell, who runs the Bell Corp. team, at the Smoky Mountain Classic in 1993, its 25th anniversary. (Russell Mott)

To understand this realm—and to some degree all other higher realms of softball—one must understand that these are amateur operations owned and operated by a band of mostly self-made individuals who bankroll their teams one season at a time.

In men's Super slow pitch, sponsors such as Woody Bell of Bell Corp. and Frank LaTeano of Ritch's/Superior are typical of those who work their way to the front of the pack. These are the owner/sponsors of the teams; they pump tens of thousands of dollars of their own money into their teams and pay all expenses. They travel all over the country, buy airline tickets in thick wads and take over large sections of good motels. Some get help from equipment manufacturers or a larger company and some don't. A top team costs close to $100,000 to maintain for a season and some have cost

Field of Dreams   Built for $2.5 million with local funds only, this four-field complex in Salem, Virginia, was the site of the Men's Amateur Softball Association "C" Fast Pitch National Championships in 1992. (Russell Mott)

$200,000 or more. The players are amateurs with regular weekday jobs as teachers, sales reps and body shop operators, but they expect expenses up to $1,000 for a weekend away from home.

The dominant forces in women's slow pitch in the late 1980s had been the Cannan's Illusion of San Antonio (led by a superior all-around athlete named Kathy Riley), the Busch Whiz Kids of Belleville, Illinois, and the Raiders of Farmington Hills, Michigan; but they have given way to new teams. The top two teams in the September, 1992, Women's National Slow Pitch Championships were UPI of Cookeville, Tennessee, and the Phoenix Ladies of Lawrenceville, Georgia.

Rankings and Venues

National softball ranking at the higher levels of the game can be a complicated affair with several publications using a series of regular season tournaments and various finales to determine the competing final rankings. A team's winning a major ASA slow pitch tournament will not show up in the final ranking by the U.S.S.S.A. and vice versa.

The season that produces those numbers and rankings is itself as diverse as the game. Consider just these three events from the 1992 season when softball showed off its best for the paying spectators.

May 21–25, 1992   In front of 13,940 fans in Oklahoma City, UCLA became the champion at the Women's College World Series by defeating defending national champion Arizona at the ASA's Hall of Fame Stadium. UCLA dominated in all departments, outscoring five opponents 31–

1 and batting .331 as a team. It was billed in advance as a pitching duel between Lisa Fernandez of UCLA and Michele Granger of the University of California, but the duel never materialized. Fernandez dominated with four shutouts and 26 scoreless innings. Granger, who came into the tournament leading the nation in strikeouts, was by her own admission "flat."

The tournament represents the ever-growing world of women's fast pitch and its dynamic future. At the time of this event there were more than 600 Division I, II and III teams with more

coming aboard each season. In 1993 there were two new Pac-10 Conference teams, the University of Washington and Stanford. As is proving true of basketball and volleyball for women, softball is being helped by tough state laws and regulations following the passage of Title IX to the Equal Rights Amendment, which first went into effect in 1979. One of the reasons that the University of Washington is creating a team is that Washington state law will require equal distribution of all financial aid—including athletic scholarships—by state colleges.

July 10–12, 1992 The Smoky—or the Smoky Mountain Classic—offer an atmosphere that the *Knoxville News-Sentinel* likened to "a county fair without the rides." These are rides of a different sort—those taken by Blue Dot Polycore softballs flying off the bat. Consider only three of the many records set at this tournament over the years:

1. "Most Runs Scored One Game, Both Teams," 115. This took place back in 1988 when Starpath Systems of Monticello, Kentucky, scored 59 in one game to defeat Marlton Trucking of Portland, Oregon, which had a measley 56 runs.
2. "Most Home Runs All Teams, Entire Tournament," 1,431 in 1977.
3. "Most Home Runs One Team, Entire Tournament," 152 by Steele's Sports, Grafton, Ohio, in 1987.

But perhaps the most remarkable record of all may be one set in 1974 when All Sports of Franklin, Ohio, beat Central States Painting of Kansas City, Missouri, by a score of 1–0. It was the lowest scoring game in the history of the Smoky and is not likely to be bested in this century.

Another top tournament held on July 10–12 in Maryville, Tennessee, outside of Knoxville routinely draws, according to its sponsors, 25,000 from beginning to end. Over this particular hot summer weekend more than 1,000 homeruns would land in Pistol Creek before Ritch's/Superior took home the trophy.

To watch this or any other super- or major-level slow pitch tournament is to be taken to an odd world in which play is continual and few people except for the teams themselves and a few spectators—who may have fallen asleep in the grass—are still in attendance when the Saturday schedule ends at 3 o'clock Sunday morning. Play on July 11 goes on for 18 hours non-stop, during which the only constant is the ringing of aluminum clobbering a polyurethane sphere. Only one person sees it all: Ray Molphy, the voice of softball, who announces every inning of every game played at the main diamond.

This tournament is representative of other slow pitch tournaments in which play is constant and many spectators have gone home hours before the winner is declared. Sometimes the ending is anti-climactic. Later in the year on the evening of August 23rd, Ritch's/Superior was declared champion of the ASA Super Nationals in Hendersonville, Tennessee, even though they only won the first game of the championship round and did not have to play the second. Heavy rains canceled the second game late Sunday night and most of the players had to get home for work on Monday morning.

September 11–19, 1992. The Mens National Championships were held in Bloomington, Illinois. This tournament is the grandson of the first national tournament in Chicago in 1933 and was held in a town where fast pitch softball still reigns in the 1990s (the hometown Bloomington Hearts would end up in seventh place). Known since 1933 as the National Championship, it is one of the few essentially American events in which dozens of New Zealanders play, along with a number of Canadians.

About one percent of the fast pitch teams make it to the men's or women's nationals, so the level of athleticism is high. The atmosphere is completely middle American. As Ronald A. Babb put it in *Balls and Strikes*, the "ASA nationals are about scrappy hometown teams that sell candy bars and magazines to raise money to travel out-of-town to qualifying tournaments, defying the odds, and perhaps common sense, that tells them that they are more likely to finish among the 99 percent who don't qualify than among the few who do."

As evidenced by the 1992 ASA tournament, this is an event for folks who love the fast ball game, and there are aficionados who have traveled hundreds of miles to watch 76 match-ups. In the end, the National Health Care Discount of Sioux City, Iowa, won in a final blaze of runs. The team, formerly known as Penn Corp. (under which name it was the 1989 and 1990 national championship winner), won by a score of 10–2 in a game shortened to five innings because of the tournament's seldom-invoked eight run "mercy" rule, which ends a game when one team is winning by eight runs.

Rivaling the ASA finals is the International Softball Congress's championship, which had

More Than a Game

been held a month earlier in Salt Lake City at the Big Cottonwood Regional Softball Complex; this is the other pinnacle for the fast pitch game—male division.

Even as the results of these major softball events are still being savored, thoughts turn to the next season and who will be back wearing what team name on their uniforms.

This is how it works at almost every level of the game, as players and spectators think about the season coming up. Is is time for Bill in accounting to move on to senior-level play? Isn't it about

time that our company fielded a co-ed team? I think it's time for a new glove.

No matter where they live or how well they play, most softball players agree on one point: winter is just too long.

Play ball!

Bringing It   *Michele Granger bringing in her fast ball in the NCAA women's championships in Oklahoma City in 1992. Here she pitches for the University of California at Berkeley. She has become a leading fast ball pitcher and should be a force in the game for years to come. (Russell Mott)*

7 The Softballer's

A COLLECTION OF
COMMANDMENTS,
LISTS, RULES, QUOTATIONS
AND OTHER MENTAL
SOFTBALL EQUIPMENT,
INCLUDING A THESIS ON
NAMING TEAMS

One of the things that makes softball softball and not simply an offshoot of baseball is that it has its own culture—customs and legends.

For starters, there are the team names.

Proper (and Improper) Softball Team Names
(Or, Penguins in Bondage Meet Braswell Metal Roofing Insulators)

Team names are important to softball. This has been true from an earlier time. When *Time* first wrote about the game in 1939 its writer was taken with the wonderful names ". . . ranging from Slapsie Maxie's Curvaceous Cuties to Bank of

Miscellany

America Bankerettes." The article noted that the national tourament was just over and had resulted in championships by Pohler's Cafe (sponsored by a beer garden) and the Num Num Girls of Cleveland.

Listed below are some of the other early names—teams with state titles—from the late 1930s: The Modesto Merchants, Tru-Blu Beer, Home Service Laundry, Bison Lassies (of Buffalo, New York), Briggs Beautyware, The Hollister Cowboys and Cincinnati Gas and Electric.

Why team names are important is more than suggested by Philip Roth in his memoir *My Life as a Boy*:

The *softball* and hardball teams we organized and reorganized obsessively throughout our grade school years—teams we called by unargu-

---

Bad *Team logo emblazoned on a T-shirt at the New England Slo-Pitch "C" Championships of New England in New Bedford, Massachusetts, in the summer of 1992. (Russell Mott)*

---

ably native names like the "Seabees" and the "Mohawks" and described as "social and athletic clubs"—aside from the opportunity they afforded to compete against one another in a game we loved, also operated as secret societies that separated us from the faint, residual foreignness still clinging to some of our parents' attitudes and that validated our own spotless credentials as American kids.

Also, team names are so important because they are often a major vehicle for sponsorship. For this reason, the big important nationally ranked power teams tend to have stunningly prosaic subsidized names such as Lab Petroleum Inc., Howard Furniture, Non-Ferrous Metals Fabricating, Seafirst, Bell Corp., United Surgical Steel, Beer Nuts and Tubbs and Sons Electric. These businesses deserve to get teams named for them because sponsorship may run up to $200,000 or more a season for a team with a national agenda.

Subsidies notwithstanding, team names are also varied, sometimes surrealistic, quintessentially American and meant to be savored. There is a certain pop poetry in names such as Fagan's Auto Parts, Elks Lodge #80, Twelfth Street Baptist, Local 638, Wendy's Wet Warriors, Morty's Avengers, Ferguson Trenching, Crisfield Crabs and Cecil's Roofing.

One also finds such an abundance of teams with tavern and restaurant names, that scanning lists of the regionally ranked teams, is enough to induce an appetite and a mighty thirst—OK Bar,

Idol *(Below) Fast baller Lisa Fernandez signs an autograph for a young fan at the NCAA tournament, Oklahoma City, 1992. (Russell Mott)*

Hitman? *(Above) This co-ed team name underscores the point that gender and team naming are often in conflict. (Russell Mott)*

Grand Theft   The name of a 16 inch softball club at the 16 inch tournament in Sturtevant, Wisconsin, in September 1992. (Russell Mott)

Angelo's Pizza, Stay's Bar & Cafe, Whiskey River and Climax Lounge. One of the earliest national champions (1939) was Pohler's Cafe, sponsored by the proprietor of a German beer garden.

Facts   (Opposite) A far cry from Fred's Auto Body, this curious cap is worn by Chris ("Chief") Walklet, one of the players for Facts On File, Inc., the publisher of this book. (Russell Mott)

Bowl of Red   (Below) The Chicago Chili Co. team from the 16 inch softball tournament in Sturdevant, Wisconsin in 1992. (Russell Mott)

Church teams add another element, especially when paired with secular opponents (Hilda's Grill vs. Central Christian, for example).

As is perhaps predictable, the names tend to get odder as one moves West. A V.D. Clinic in San Francisco, for instance, made the news a while back by fielding a softball team named the Burning Sensations. San Francisco columnist Herb Caen runs an unsanctioned team called Les Lapins Sauvages (The Wild Rabbits), which usually plays only two games a year (one home and one away) with away games in such places as Dublin and Moscow. It once played two away games in a season when it played in Boston's Fenway Park and Chicago's Wrigley Field in the same day.

But some of the oddest of the odd are the names attached to West Coast intramural college teams. What follows is a sampling of odd names culled in the sports pages of *The California Aggie* of the University of California at Davis during the 1980s. In no special order we have: The Moist Pits, Puking Peking Pygmies with Sticks, Penguins in Bondage, Mildew, Doomed to Win, Spam, The New York Hankies, Weenie Arms, The Libyan Hit Squad, Balls & Goils, Send in the Clones, Assault With a Friendly Weapon, Joy in Mudville, Don't Worry We Always Use Gloves for Protection, Toadsuckers, Well-Hung Jury, Glove Me Tender, Eve's Brain/Adam's Rib, The Yankems, The Pancake Batters, 3 Balls and You're Weird,

Patch *Emblem proudly displayed at the 1992 Broadway Show League Game in New York City's Central Park, in the summer of 1992.* (Russell Mott)

Nobaccos, Draught Picks, The Harrisburg Bubble, Same as Last Year's Team, Our Bats are Longer, On Any Given Day, Dr. Strangeglove, Vibrating Bats and Oh God It's Alive!

Hands down the most outlandish names in the business are affixed to the teams that play Over the Line softball. Many of those 1,000-plus teams that show up annually for the Old Mission Bay Athletic Club Annual World Championship Tournament in San Diego in July have names that are so nasty that the *Wall Street Journal* had this to say in an 1983 article on this renegade form of softball: ". . . the vast majority of team names are so tasteless and filthy that they cannot be printed." Putting another slant on the subject, it can be stated that roughly 91.234 percent of the names imply some form of *un*safe sex.

The *Journal* added, "About the only names that OMBAC censors are those that besmirch the memory of John Wayne." The Wayne Rule was explained by the Old Mission Bay Athletic Club "press lord" Bill Kronberger, Jr. "He was a macho, sexist chauvinist. Anything that reflected on him would diminish what we stand for. Dishonor your mother if you want, but don't mess

with the Duke." In 1992 an OTL tournament organizer told a reporter for *The Orange County Register* that the game was missing out on press coverage primarily because of, to quote the official, ". . . the names of the teams. Most are a little too risque to print in the paper or say on television."

Some of the men's teams of the last few years that can be printed include: Hung Like Hamsters; Low and Loose Full of Juice; Runaway Hormones; Tenacious Testicles I; Smash the State and Have a Nice Day; Crotch Potatoes; Frozen Organs from Minnesota; Love Handles; On Golden Blonde; Pure Perversion; Pickled Pig Farts; Sex and Free Beer; Driving Mr. Penis; Team Hooters; Throbbing Love Muscle; Cincinnati Obscenity

and Pete Rose Fan Club; and Amos, Get Out of the Can, the Plane's Landing.

The women's names are almost as bad and are largely unprintable outside of the Official Programs and *Penthouse*: 99% Virgin; Beat Me Whip Me Just Don't Mess My Hair; Jail Bait; Show Us Your Hot Rod; Menage A Trois; I Want to Have Your Baby So I Can Drown It; Crusty; Strawberry Sweet Cheeks; Sandwenches; Let's Pack Some Sand While We're Here; Lusty, Busty and Rusty; Down and Dirty; We're Not Getting Better; We're Getting Older; Death by Chocolate; Bun's O' Fun; Foxy Fossils; and We'll Do Anything Once.

Meanwhile, the team fielded by the *Atlanta Constitution* is known as the Bad News Bearers and a group of high-level Washington economists has a team known as The Invisible Hand. Wheelchair teams have apt names, as evidenced by meetings that pit the Rolling Gophers of Courage Center against the St. Paul Rolling Thunder (those two actually decided a national championship in 1987).

The best way to savor the names is to look at the teams showing up for any given tourney. Here are some of the male and female teams who, for example, participated in the August, 1992, Black N.I.T. in Cleveland: Our Rib House, Street Level Lounge, Ubiquity, Local 265, Dixie Automotive, Jimmy's Wildcats and The Prime Time All-Stars. Or, those who showed up to play at the 1991 Men's World 16 inch Tournament in Sturtevant, Wisconsin: Grand Theft, Unknown, Wisconsin #5, ICE, Rats, Pandas, Rebels, Bandits South, Dogs, Lords, Saints, California Gold, The Rage, Ron's Bar, Rockers, Stars, Overtime, Traffic, Longshots and VFW Post. For that matter, just grab any of the regional softball periodicals and look at the names in the standings. Here are a few picked from an issue of *Georgia U.S.S.S.A. Softball*: Butler Tire Bandits, Brookside Shopperette, Noonday Stars, Buck Wilson Used Cars and, if to prove that there are no rules here and that names can be neither too long or too short, Gnats.

Top Catcher   *Leslie Adams, as catcher for the 1992 Raybestos Brakettes. A native of Clover, South Carolina, she went on to play college softball at Florida State University. (Russell Mott)*

Baseball Compared to Softball

Softball

1. A regulation game lasts seven innings.
2. The distance between the bases is 60 feet; 65 feet in men's slow pitch.
3. Shorter distance to the fences.
4. The ball is either 12 inches, 14 inches or 16 inches in circumference (unless it is of some other circumference).
5. Regulation bats must be no longer than 34 inches in length and no thicker than 2¼ inches at the largest part.
6. The ball is pitched underhand only.
7. The pitching distance is closer to the plate.
8. Base runners may not leave a base until the ball leaves the pitcher's hand.

Baseball

1. A regulation game has nine innings. This may be more of a factor than it might seem at first. In 1940 newsman Lowell Thomas discussed the point in his book *Softball! So What?*: "You play only seven innings—can get a game in before breakfast or work or before supper or after. By playing seven innings you never seem to get enough. Softball addicts leave the game reluctantly. Hardballers always have had enough. Whoever heard of a hardball team playing a double-header willingly? Softballers often play triple-headers under pressure."
2. The distance between the bases is 90 feet.
3. Longer distance to the fences.
4. The ball has a 9-inch circumference.
5. Regulation bats must be no longer than 42 inches in length and no thicker than 2¾ inches at the largest part.
6. The ball is pitched overhand or sidearm.
7. The pitching distance is farther from the plate.
8. Base runners may leave a base at any time.

Danger Sign

Spotted on the fence of a softball complex in Brunswick, Maine.

(Russell Mott)

Baseball Players with Softball Roots

In 1952, when the ASA and others in the sport were pushing for a commemorative $.03 stamp for softball, some substantial hostility to the game came forth. George Case, a former New Jersey state coach and Rutger's University coach, threw caution to the wind and had this to say to a sportswriter: ". . . [To] play softball with an enlarged ball, on a shortened base path and on a diamond originally built for baseball is as far as I'm concerned sacreligious."

4. Tommy Henrich
5. Hank Borowey
6. Lou Boudreau
7. Lou Novikoff

Lou Novikoff? Known as "the Mad Russian" Novikoff (and playing under the name Louie Nova), Novikoff was one of fast pitch softball's greatest hitters, but was such an outstanding hitter that he was signed to a professional baseball contract in the Pacific Coast League. He played briefly for the Chicago Cubs in 1942 (in 128 games he hit an even .300) and the Philadelphia Phillies. He returned to softball and played

The line was repeated, forcing the ASA. to take action: to compile a list of the Major League ballplayers who "played softball before entering baseball."

The list, which amounts to an All-Star Softball-Baseball team, goes as follows:

1. Joe DiMaggio
2. Luke Easter
3. Hack Wilson

well into his 50s. He was the first inductee to the International Softball Congress Hall of Fame.

Tailgaters *Barbecue action during games at a tournament in East Providence, Rhode Island, in the summer of 1992. The smell of barbecue is as common to softball tournaments as are the sounds of dogs and little kids. (Russell Mott)*

Colonel Stoopnagle's Rules

Back in the 1930s when celebrity softball was all the rage, Colonel Lemuel Stoopnagle, the radio comedian and self-described survivor of "the Johnstown flood, several marriages, earthquakes and other major disasters," felt that standard softball rules were too rigid and proposed his own.

Softball, according to Stoopnagle, differs from regulation baseball mainly as follows:

1. It is not as interesting.
2. Base distances: They are not as great as in baseball, but they seem farther.
3. Bat: When bats are grown on the Connecticut Bat Farms, the softball bats are picked early before they mature. This makes them smaller than the regulation baseball bats, I guess.
4. Ball: Stings.
5. Style of pitching: The ball is supposed to be thrown underhand. This is done by experts. However, for the ordinary pouchy business man, playing his only game of the season, the Delayed Toss is very popular. Also the Roll-up and the Pardon Me.
6. Number of players: The game is started with four players—the guy who suggested the game, another guy who thinks he can hit as well as when he was eighteen, a third party who just happened by, and often Anna May Wong . . . As time goes on, there are six, eight, 10, or 12 players up until the second inning, when it becomes a free-for-all. The game usually ends in the first half of the fifth, with the team in the bleachers watching the audience play.
7. Scoring: On one side of the field there is a scoreboard, where the runs are totaled and exhibited. Here is a fairly accurate facsimile of the three-inning score of a recent game:

	1	2	3	4	5	6	7
Home Team	1	3	9				
Visitors	7	0	0				

According to the best softball traditions, the score, as I see it, is Home Team 13; Visitors 7. However, the wag who always accompanies the Visitors yells, "Look! We're ahead seven hundred to a hundred and thirty-nine!!"

Over the Fence   Left fielder Jeff Rice for Drinkwater Construction, going after a fly and over the fence. Rice was playing in a modified pitch game in a Putnum, Connecticut, tournament.

(Russell Mott)

Commandments of Softball

These are hardly original, but are distilled from hours of listening, reading and observation.

1. Do unto others as they do unto you, but do it in the early innings.
2. If you don't know the score, you can be pretty sure that you're behind. (Francis O. Walsh rule, which has been quoted for years in women's softball publications.)
3. If you don't know what kind of softball you're playing, ask the coach.
4. In true amateur softball there is no such thing as a "routine play."
5. Don't take it too seriously ("it" being anything but softball—work, one's reputation, one's capacity for humility, and virtually any issue of life and death).
6. A ball will travel farther in the early innings of a game. A ball will travel farther on some days than others, depending on the weather conditions. (Both are true. It will travel 15 to 30 feet farther on a hot, dry, sunny day than it does on cold or cool damp days, or very humid days.)
7. Always beware of a team with a hard industrial/patriotic name. American Rivet or Eagle Masonry has a built-in two-run edge over Ed's Lounge or the Beerhunters.
8. Whomsoever shows the greatest bravado in a victory celebration is almost certainly the person who did the least to insure that victory.
9. In any given game, at almost any given level of play, a dog or a crying child will appear on the field to temporarily stop play. (In *Softball: So What?* Lowell Thomas and Ted Shane point out that back in the 1930s the extra rule they played with was "A dog on the field means a drink on the house, if you can find the house.")
10. If someone yells to a teammate that "A walk is as good as a hit" this means that there is a terrible fear that the batter might actually try to take a poke at the ball.

Crowd-Pleaser *(Opposite) Brad Edwards, United States Slo-Pitch Softball Association umpire working the teams and the crowd at the New England "C" Championships in New Bedford, Massachusetts, in the summer of 1992. (Russell Mott)*

The Softballer's Miscellany

Lists for Softballers

1. What to Pack.

An informal survey of players, coaches and league officials resulted in these items being voted "most likely to be overlooked but needed once you're at the park":

- Enough balls to allow pairs to play catch.
- Extra caps and sunglasses for players who fail to consider game time or field location in relation to sun conditions.
- Extra team schedules (particularly early in the season).
- Enough water to last through pre-game warmup.
- Extra shoelaces (for spikes or fast-fix on a glove).

—*Sportswise*/March-April 1984

2. Advice for the Beleaguered Pitcher in Slow Pitch Softball:

In his book *The Strategy of Pitching Slow Pitch Softball* Mike Ivankovich says that a successful pitcher is one who can throw off a batter's timing. These are his methods for doing such, entitled "Ways to Throw Off a Batter's Timing":

- vary the arc
- vary the spin
- vary the location
- vary the length of backswing
- vary the type of delivery
- vary the time between pitches
- quick pitch
- confer with the catcher, coach or some infielder to delay and make the batter wait
- make a great defensive play or turn a key double play, thereby demoralizing the batter and the opposing team
- as soon as it becomes evident that batters have zeroed in on a pitcher's timing, change pitchers.

3. How to Walk the Walk

Amy Wilson's important set of rules for the softball stylist, which originally appeared in the *Detroit Free Press*:

1. Don't throw your glove, hat or bat. Children may be watching.
2. The batting glove is a wonderful prop. Hang it out of your back pocket at all times, except when you bat. It belongs on the bottom hand—if you don't use two gloves. Put it on

---

Voice of the Game   *Ray Molphy of Pompano Beach, Florida, fills a unique role in the slow pitch game as the field announcer for most of the major slow pitch softball tournaments in the U.S. As these tournaments often go on from morning one day to early morning the next day, his voice is a pleasant constant. (Russell Mott)*

in the on-deck circle. You'll know how to find that when the batter before you hovers there.

3. Don't do all your running with your legs. Pump your knees and move your arms.

4. A single is not worth spitting about. The pitcher can spit after a strikeout.

5. When your team is in need of good hitting, turn your cap backwards if you're sitting on the bench, so the bill is resting on the back of your neck. This, we are assured, improves hitting.

6. Pay attention. If you are in the outfield and cannot get to the ball coming your way, get out of the way because other players will (supposedly) be in pursuit. Or wander around, looking up and kind of confused. Now say, "I lost it in the sun." (Prerequisite: It must be sunny.)

7. If you are not a starter and you're sitting on the bench, get up once in a while and spit. Be sure to move to the end of the bench so the starters can get to the bats. If they have to ask you to move, you look bad. Call the bench "the pine." Say, "I'm tired of riding the pine." Very smooth.

Softball's Greatest Bumperstickers

1. SOFTBALL PLAYERS ARE NEVER OFF BASE
2. PLAY SOFTBALL THE GAME FOR EV-ERYONE
3. SOFTBALL PLAYERS WIELD BIG BATS
4. SOFTBALL PLAYERS LIKE TO SCORE
5. SOFTBALL PLAYERS ARE SWINGERS
6. I'D RATHER BE PLAYING SOFTBALL
7. WHY JOG? HIT AND RUN! PLAY SOFT-BALL
8. IF SOFTBALL INTERFERES WITH WORK, QUIT YOUR JOB
9. HAVE SOME UNDERHANDED FUN PLAY SOFTBALL
10. I AM A SOFTBALL NUT HOW ABOUT YOU

In Uniform Here is a well-dressed designated hitter at a local slow pitch tournament in Putnam, Connecticut, in the summer of 1992. (Russell Mott)

Worst Softball Stories of All Time

1. Overcome with Emotion

When Louis DelMastro, a pitcher for Pittsburgh, won the award for Most Valuable Player in the ASA nationals at Parma, Ohio, in 1965, he was almost overcome with emotion. He took off his hat, his jersey, shoes, and glove, and gave them all to a crippled child who was sitting on the side lines. The only trouble was . . . the glove and shoes belonged to another player.

—Edward Claflin, *The Irresistible*
American Softball Book

2. The Senator's Most Difficult Decision

Over the years pressure has been exerted on members of the House and Senate from cluttering up the Congressional Record with news of their office softball teams. Philip A. Hart, U.S. Senator from Michigan, dealt with the problem thusly. Quoting from the *Congressional Record*:

Mr. President, as the President of the United States did on announcing his veto of the education appropriations bill last January 26, I wish to share with Senators one of the most difficult decisions I have made since I became a U.S. Senator.

I have on my desk a speech praising my *office softball team*.

Now let us clearly understand the issues. The issue is not whether some of us like softball and others are against it.

Softball Honeymoon   (Below) Bobby and Michelle Russell from Monterey, California, after winning fourth place in the Men's Class C Fast Pitch Championships in Salem, Virginia in 1992; they were married on the field just before the tournament began on Thursday. The custom of tying the knot on the softball diamond has become such that in October, 1989, Balls and Strikes ran a feature on the subject, which began with this line: "Softball bats will be raised by an honor guard as the bride and groom walk ceremoniously from second base to home plate where they will score a home run." (Russell Mott)

There *is no game* which I consider more important to the health and welfare of my office staff *than softball*.

So, why, in an election year, particularly, would a Senator hesitate for one moment to give a speech praising such a politically popular activity as this.

For this reason, a Senator has an obligation to consider all the ramifications of a speech with this principle in mind: What is best for all of the members of the team?

The team has one game remaining after which those members who are interns will be leaving Washington to return home.

At election time, it is tempting to place in the Record, a speech praising them for their efforts and then to send reprints to the parents of each.

However, I think this is wrong, for placing such a speech in the Record the day before the final game could jinx the team and cost it an undefeated season.

Therefore, my decision not to give the speech praising them for the six straight victories over the staffs of Senators Long, Mondale, Dominici, McCarthy, Brooke and Tower is painful but necessary if we are to give them every chance of winning tomorrow night.

However, I would like to thank the interns for the envelopes stuffed, letters folded, errands run, newspapers clipped, records kept, research accomplished, sound suggestions made and difficult questions asked between ball games.

3.   Nuclear Team

In 1953, members of the softball team representing the repair ship U.S.S. *Romulus* put ashore in Yokosuka, Japan, to play other teams, some local. On their jerseys the team had the letters ARL, which stood for Auxiliary Repair, Landing Ships, but they told everyone who would listen that it stood for Atomic Rocket Launcher, strongly implying that the nearby harbor was harboring nuclear weapons. International attention was focused on this very sensitive matter and the Navy had to issue broad denials: Not only were there no such weapons in the harbor, but there was no such thing as an Atomic Rocket Launcher.

Connecting   (Opposite) Kenny Carver rounding the bases in July, 1991, at Sherbrooke, Quebec. (Russell Mott)

4. Religious Zeal

"CHRISTIAN SPIRIT?" was the headline on this April 11, 1983, wire service story:

Double Play   (Above) Jül and Janel, the Gerrior twins, catcher and second base of Keene State. (Russell Mott)

Officials in Morehead City, N.C., have banned a church softball league from public fields because the league refused to admit a team from a local Mormon church, an action which officials termed "a clear-cut case of religious discrimination."

Representatives of eight of the 12 churches in the league turned thumbs down on the Mormons,

contending that allowing them to play would open the way for participation by other "extreme church groups." The league includes Baptist, Methodist, Pentecostal and Roman Catholic churches.

The church league said it would not challenge the official action and would play its season on private softball fields.

A Mormon spokesman said his group wanted to join the church league because the league did not allow cursing and had a Christian environment. He said his group didn't want to start a controversy.

"We just wanted to play some softball," he said.

Fan Act   (Opposite) Partisan at the New Hampshire Babe Ruth Girls Fast Pitch tournament in Barrington, New Hampshire, in 1992.

(Russell Mott)

The Softballer's Miscellany

8 The Official

SOFTBALL HAS

NEVER HAD A

RECORD BOOK—

NOW IT DOES

Records are made to be broken, and softball has certainly had its share of record makers since George Hancock invented the sport in 1887.

People such as Herb Dudley, Bob McClish, Ted Hicks, Greg Fuhrman, Stan Harvey, Rick (The Crusher) Scherr, Joan Joyce, Bertha Tickey, Dot Richardson, Michele Granger and a host of others have put their names into the Softball Record Book.

How long their records will remain is anyone's guess, but these people have gone above and beyond to excel in national championship play.

Part of the fun and excitement of attending a national championship is watching history being made when records are broken or tied. The records that have been established in the past are a legacy for the millions of softball players who'll play softball in the years ahead.

Record Book

(Compiled by Bill Plummer III, Director of Public Relations & Media, Amateur Softball Association with records verified through July 1, 1993)

Marge Dobson   *(Above) Hall of Famer Dr. Margaret Dobson—holder of a Ph.D. in educational administration—long held the record for the highest batting average in a women's national championship— .615. Her softball career began in 1944.*
(Amateur Softball Association)

Softball Hero   *(Right) The incomparable Herb Dudley is still devoted to the game and gives many clinics, turning out a new generation of women fast pitch pitchers.*
(Amateur Softball Association)

I. FAST PITCH RECORDS

ASA MEN'S MAJOR FAST PITCH NATIONAL CHAMPIONS		
Year	**Where Played**	**Champions**
1933	Chicago, Illinois	J.L. Friedman Boosters, Chicago, Illinois This championship provided a basis for a permanent national softball association—the Amateur Softball Association, now located in Oklahoma City, Oklahoma. The ASA is the recognized national governing body of softball in the United States with 101 state/metro associations in 15 regions.
1934	Chicago, Illinois	Ke Nash-A's, Kenosha, Wisconsin
1935	Chicago, Illinois	Crimson Coaches, Toledo, Ohio
1936	Chicago, Illinois	Kodak Park, Rochester, New York
1937	Chicago, Illinois	Briggs Mfg. Co., Detroit, Michigan
1938	Chicago, Illinois	Pohler's Cafe, Cincinnati, Ohio An estimated 72 million people watched softball games this season.
1939	Chicago, Illinois	Carr's Boosters, Covington, Kentucky
1940	Detroit, Michigan	Kodak Park, Rochester, New York The pitching distance for men was changed to 43 feet by the Joint Rules Committee on Softball. This was the third time the pitching distance for men was changed since the ASA was founded in 1933. There was much debate on this rule change. The distance of 43 feet was a compromise between those favoring 45 feet and others who wanted the distance to remain at 40 feet.
1941	Detroit, Michigan	Bendix Brakes, South Bend, Indiana
1942	Detroit, Michigan	Deep Rock Oilers, Tulsa, Oklahoma
1943	Detroit, Michigan	Hammer Field Army Base, Fresno, California
1944	Cleveland, Ohio	Hammer Field Army Base, Fresno, California
1945	Cleveland, Ohio	Fort Wayne Zollner Pistons, Ft. Wayne, Indiana
1946	Cleveland, Ohio	Fort Wayne Zollner Pistons, Ft. Wayne, Indiana
1947	Cleveland, Ohio	Fort Wayne Zollner Pistons, Ft. Wayne, Indiana
1948	Portland, Oregon	Briggs Beautyware, Detroit, Michigan Briggs compiles 42–1 record with 41 of the wins in succession.
1949	Little Rock, Arkansas	Tip-Top Clothiers, Toronto, Canada

All-World In 1961 these guys were selected as the top male fast pitch players. They were dominated by players of Burch Grinding in Detroit and the Aurora, Illinois, Sealmasters. (Amateur Softball Association)

Year	Where Played	Champions
1950	Austin, Texas	Clearwater Bombers, Clearwater, Florida This was the first of 10 national titles won by the Bombers, the most by an ASA men's major fast pitch team. This year also marked an increase of men's major fast pitch pitching distance from 43 feet to 46 feet—the fourth time this distance was changed since the Association's founding in 1933.
1951	Detroit, Michigan	Dow Chemical Co., Midland, Michigan
1952	Stratford, Connecticut	Briggs Beautyware, Detroit, Michigan

Year	Where Played	Champions
1953	Miami, Florida	Briggs Beautyware, Detroit, Michigan
1954	Minneapolis, Minnesota	Clearwater Bombers, Clearwater, Florida
1955	Clearwater, Florida	Raybestos Cardinals, Stratford, Connecticut
1956	Sacramento, California	Clearwater Bombers, Clearwater, Florida
1957	Clearwater, Florida	Clearwater Bombers, Clearwater, Florida
1958	Minneapolis, Minnesota	Raybestos Cardinals, Stratford, Connecticut
1959	Clearwater, Florida	Sealmasters, Aurora, Illinois
1960	Long Island, New York	Clearwater Bombers, Clearwater, Florida
1961	Clearwater, Florida	Sealmasters, Aurora, Illinois
1962	Stratford, Connecticut	Clearwater Bombers, Clearwater, Florida
1963	Clearwater, Florida	Clearwater Bombers, Clearwater, Florida
1964	Sunnyvale, California	Burch Tool & Die, Detroit, Michigan
1965	Clearwater, Florida	Sealmasters, Aurora, Illinois
1966	Indianapolis, Indiana	Clearwater Bombers, Clearwater, Florida
1967	Springfield, Missouri	Sealmasters, Aurora, Illinois
1968	Clearwater, Florida	Clearwater Bombers, Clearwater, Florida
1969	Springfield, Missouri	Raybestos Cardinals, Stratford, Connecticut
1970	Clearwater, Florida	Raybestos Cardinals, Stratford, Connecticut
1971	Springfield, Missouri	Welty Way, Cedar Rapids, Iowa
1972	Dallas, Texas	Raybestos Cardinals, Stratford, Connecticut
1973	Seattle, Washington	Clearwater Bombers, Clearwater, Florida
1974	Clearwater, Florida	Guanella Brothers, Santa Rosa, California
1975	Hayward, California	Rising Sun Hotel, Reading, Pennsylvania
1976	Allentown, Pennsylvania	Raybestos Cardinals, Stratford, Connecticut. The Raybestos Cardinals, behind pitching of future Hall of Famer Al Lewis, go through the tourney undefeated (5–0) and are flawless defensively with a fielding percentage of 1.000 with 111 putouts and 46 assists. It was the first time a team had compiled a fielding percentage of 1.000 in a Men's Major Fast Pitch National Tournament playing three or more games.

Year	Where Played	Champions
1977	Midland, Michigan	Billard Barbell, Reading, Pennsylvania
1978	Springfield, Missouri	Billard Barbell, Reading, Pennsylvania
1979	Midland, Michigan	McArdle Pontiac-Cadillac, Midland, Michigan
1980	Decatur, Illinois	Peterbilt Western, Seattle, Washington
1981	St. Joseph, Missouri	Archer Daniels Midland, Decatur, Illinois
1982	Midland, Michigan	Peterbilt Western, Seattle, Washington
1983	Decatur, Illinois	Franklin Cardinals, West Haven, Connecticut
1984	St. Joseph, Missouri	California Kings, Merced, California
1985	Salt Lake City, Utah	Pay 'n Pak, Seattle, Washington
1986	Seattle, Washington	Pay 'n Pak, Seattle, Washington
1987	Springfield, Missouri	Pay 'n Pak, Seattle, Washington The Pak thus equaled the record of the Fort Wayne, Indiana Zollner Pistons of winning three consecutive Major Fast Pitch National Championships. There was nothing easy about equaling the mark, as Pay 'n Pak lost its first game, then won a record 11 games in a row in the loser's bracket. Pak pitcher Grame Robertson equaled the record for most wins by a pitcher in a national championship with eight.
1988	Bloomington, Illinois	Trans-Aire, Elkhart, Indiana Southpaw hurler Mike Piechnik of Farm Tavern, Madison, Wisconsin, set a tourney strikeout record with 140 in seven games. Trans-Aire hurler Peter Meredith equaled the record for most wins with eight and set an innings-pitched mark with 88. The two hurlers shared the MVP Award.
1989	Midland, Michigan	Penn Corp., Sioux City, Iowa
1990	North Mankato, Minnesota	Penn Corp., Sioux City, Iowa
1991	Midland, Michigan	Guanella Brothers, Rohnert Park, California
1992	Bloomington, Illinois	National Health Care Discount, Sioux City, Iowa Jody Hennigar of the Clearwater Bombers equaled a single-game home run record with three against the Colonial Bakers, Aurora, Illinois.

Paymaster *Jimmy Moore, a former Pay 'n Pak standout hurler in men's fast pitch softball.*

(Amateur Softball Association)

ASA MEN'S MAJOR FAST PITCH NATIONAL TOURNAMENT

Pitching Leaders Through the 1992 Season

	Pitcher	W	L	Pct.
1.	Ty Stofflet	46	21	.687
*2.	John Spring	44	13	.772
*3.	Harvey Sterkel	43	24	.642
4.	Dave Scott	37	16	.698
5.	Peter Meredith	35	16	.686
*6.	Bonnie Jones	33	17	.660
7.	Jimmy Moore	32	9	.780
*8.	Herb Dudley	28	9	.757
9.	Chuck D'Arcy	26	11	.703
*10.	Weldon Haney	25	5	.833
*11.	Joe Lynch	24	9	.727
12.	Roy Burlison	23	14	.622
	*Roy Stephenson	23	16	.590
*14.	Charles Justice	21	16	.568
	Bobby Quinn	21	16	.568
*16.	John Hunter	20	3	.870
	*Harold Gears	20	6	.769
	*Al Lewis	20	11	.645
19.	Dick Brubaker	19	8	.704
	Al DeWall	19	13	.594
21.	Steve Padilla	18	4	.818
	*Eddie King	18	7	.720
	Graham Arnold	18	9	.667
	Owen Walford	18	12	.600
*25.	Bobby Spell	17	5	.773
	Chubb Tangaroa	17	6	.739
	Peter Brown	17	12	.586
*27.	Bill Massey	16	8	.667
	Peter Finn	16	9	.640
29.	Edmore Johnson	15	11	.577
30.	Metro Szeryk	14	3	.824
	Rich Balswick	14	6	.700

Best winning percentages (14 or more wins)

		W	L	Pct.
1.	John Hunter	20	3	.870
2.	Weldon Haney	25	5	.833
3.	Metro Szeryk	14	4	.824
4.	Steve Padilla	18	4	.818
5.	Jimmy Moore	32	9	.780

*Member of the National Softball Hall of Fame and Museum in Oklahoma City, Oklahoma.

ASA BATTING RECORDS —INDIVIDUAL

Most hits in a championship tournament

16—Curt Petersen, Larry Miller Toyota, Salt Lake City, Utah (1985)

Most hits in a game

4 each—Bob McClish, Springfield, Missouri (1973); John Chestnut, Clearwater, Florida (1949); Art Upper, Toronto, Canada (1949) and Myron Guthrie, Clearwater, Florida (1949)

Most triples in a championship tournament

4 each—Jim Henley, Chattanooga, Tennessee (1965), and John McEldowney, Trans-Aire, Elkhart, Indiana (1987)

Most doubles in a championship tournament

5 each—Steve Newell, Pay 'n Pak, Seattle, Washington (1985); George Bettineski, Peterbilt Western, Seattle, Washington (1977); Al Linde, Dow Chemical, Midland, Michigan (1951); and Mike Parnow, Guanella Brothers, Rohnert Park, California (1991)

Most RBI in a championship tournament

13—Bob McClish, Springfield, Missouri (1973); 11—Bruce Beard, Pay 'n Pak, Seattle, Washington (1987); and Steve DeFazio, Guanella Brothers, Rohnert Park, California (1990)

Most RBI in a game

7—Bob McClish, Springfield, Missouri (1973); four others are tied with 6: Joe Morecraft, Baltimore, Maryland (1953); Dennis Delorit, Madison, Wisconsin (1984); Randy Brown, Atlanta, Georgia (1984); and Mike Gomez, St. Paul, Minnesota (1992)

Most RBI in a national championship final game

5—Bill Wojie, Stratford, Connecticut (1956)

Most homeruns in a championship tournament

5—Bob McClish, Springfield, Missouri (1973); five others with 4 each: Randy Burnside, Sioux City, Iowa (1991); Steve Scott, Midland, Michigan (1991); Bill Stewart, Seattle, Washington (1980); Bill Roberson, Deep Rock Oilers, Tulsa, Oklahoma (1942); and George Kremble, Kodak Park, Rochester, New York (1935)

Most consecutive games hitting a homerun in a national championship

4 in 4 games—George Kremble, Kodak Park, Rochester, New York (1935)

Most homeruns in a game

3 each—Jody Hennigar, Clearwater Bombers, Clearwater, Florida (1992) and Bob McClish, Springfield, Missouri (1973)

Most runs scored in a championship tournament

11—Peter Turner, Guanella Brothers, Rohnert Park, California (1990)

Highest batting average

.632—Ted Hicks, CMI, Springfield, Missouri (1978)

PITCHING RECORDS—INDIVIDUAL

Most innings pitched in a national championship

88—Peter Meredith, Trans-Aire, Elkhart, Indiana (1988)

Most wins in a national championship

8 each—Peter Meredith, Tran-Aire, Elkhart, Indiana (1988); Grame Robertson, Pay 'n Pak, Seattle, Washington (1987); Harvey Sterkel, Aurora, Illinois (1959); and Bonnie Jones, Burch Grinders, Detroit, Michigan (1959)

Most games pitched in a national championship

10—Bonnie Jones, Burch Grinders, Detroit, Michigan (1961)

Most strikeouts in a national championship

140—Mike Piechnik, Farm Tavern, Madison, Wisconsin (1988)

Most strikeouts in a game

55 in 21 innings—Herb Dudley, Clearwater, Florida, Bombers (1949); 46 in 20 innings—Mike Piechnik, Farm Tavern, Madison, Wisconsin (1988)

Most strikeouts in a game by two pitchers

81—Herb Dudley, Clearwater, Florida, Bombers (1949), 55, and Arno Lamb, Phillips 66, Bartlesville, Oklahoma (1949), 26

Most strikeouts in a game by two pitchers same team

21—Shifty Gears and Joe Witzigman, Kodak Park, Rochester, New York (1936)

Most strikeouts in a seven-inning game by one pitcher

19—John Hunter, Clearwater, Florida (1951); Harvey Sterkel, Aurora, Illinois (1959); Richard Brubaker, Chicago, Illinois (1971); and Chubb Tangaroa, Guanella Brothers, Rohnert Park, California (1991)

Most hits allowed in a national championship

42—Kevin Herlihy, Lancaster, California (1984)

Most walks allowed in a national championship

24—Gil Weslowski, Baltimore, Maryland (1951)

Most consecutive wins in national championship play

14—Ty Stofflet, Reading, Pennsylvania (1977–79)

Most consecutive innings without allowing an earned run

74 2/3—Ty Stofflet, Reading, Pennsylvania (1974–1975)

TEAM FIELDING

Highest fielding percentage, tournament (at least three games)

1.000—Raybestos Cardinals, Stratford, Connecticut (1976)

Most errors in a tournament

13—Casper, Wyoming, and San Gabriel, California (1958); Bloomington, Illinois (1954)

Most errors in a game

9—San Bernardino, California (1985)

Most putouts in a tournament

261—Tie: Penn Corp., Sioux City, Iowa (1991); and Guanella Brothers, Rohnert Park, California (1990)

Most assists in a tournament

98—Pay 'n Pak, Seattle, Washington (1987)

Most games in a tournament

12 each—Guanella Brothers, Rohnert Park, California (1990); Penn Corp., Sioux City, Iowa (1991); and Pay 'n Pak, Seattle, Washington (1987)

Most assists in a tournament game

32—Clearwater Bombers, Clearwater, Florida (1963)

Most double plays in a tournament

12 (in eight games)—Clearwater Bombers, Clearwater, Florida (1955)

Most putouts in a tournament game

93 each—Clearwater Bombers, Clearwater, Florida (1963), and Portland, Oregon (1963)

Dominant Force (Opposite) Jim Fuller and his wife Gail with the MVP trophy at the Sherbrooke Tournament in 1991. At the time this picture was taken he was with Ritch's/Superior of Windsor Locks, Connecticut. He played baseball with the Baltimore Orioles. (Russell Mott)

TEAM BATTING

Highest batting average

.343 National Health Care Discount, Sioux City, Iowa (1992)

Most hits in a game

20—Miller Toyota, Salt Lake City, Utah (1985)

Most hits in a tournament

97—National Health Care Discount, Sioux City, Iowa (1992), and Guanella Brothers, Rohnert Park, California (1990)

Most runs in a tournament

73—Guanella Brothers, Rohnert Park, California (1990)

Most runs in a tournament game

18—Worcester, Massachusetts (1974)

Most stolen bases in a tournament

9 each—National Health Care Discount, Sioux City, Iowa (1992), and Strategic Air Command, Offutt AFB, Nebraska (1966)

Longest tournament games

31 innings—Portland, Oregon, vs. Clearwater Bombers, Clearwater, Florida (1963)

MOST VALUABLE PLAYER AWARD WINNERS

Men's Major Fast Pitch National Tourney

1955 John Hunter, Bombers, Clearwater, Florida
1956 Harvey Sterkel, Sealmasters, Aurora, Illinois
1957 Herb Dudley, Bombers, Clearwater, Florida
1958 Max Trahan, McDonald Scots, Lake Charles, Louisiana
1959 Harvey Sterkel, Sealmasters, Aurora, Illinois
1960 Bill Simoni, Delta Merchants, Stockton, California
1961 Bonnie Jones, Burch Grinders, Detroit, Michigan
1962 Weldon Haney, Bombers, Clearwater, Florida
1963 Weldon Haney, Bombers, Clearwater, Florida
1964 Bonnie Jones, Burch Gage & Tool, Detroit, Michigan
1965 Joe Lynch, Sealmasters, Aurora, Illinois
1966 Abe Baker, Local 57, Providence, Rhode Island
1967 Rich Balswick, Falcons, Mountain View, California
1968 Weldon Haney, Bombers, Clearwater, Florida
1969 Roy Burlison, Falcons, Mountain View, California
1970 John Anquillare, Raybestos Cardinals, Stratford, Connecticut
1971 Ty Stofflet, Rising Sun Hotel, Reading, Pennsylvania
1972 Metro Szeryk, Raybestos Cardinals, Stratford, Connecticut
1973 Bob McClish, Gaslight Realty, Springfield, Missouri
1974 Ty Stofflet, Rising Sun Hotel, Reading, Pennsylvania
1975 Ty Stofflet, Rising Sun Hotel, Reading, Pennsylvania
1976 Al Lewis, Raybestos Cardinals, Stratford, Connecticut
1977 Ty Stofflet, Billard Barbell, Reading, Pennsylvania
1978 Ty Stofflet, Billard Barbell, Reading, Pennsylvania, and Ted Hicks, CMI, Springfield, Missouri
1979 Jeff Peck, McArdle Pontiac, Midland, Michigan
1980 Graham Arnold, Peterbilt Western, Seattle, Washington
1981 Dave Scott, Archer Daniels Midland, Decatur, Illinois
1982 Butch Batt, Peterbilt Western, Seattle, Washington
1983 John Anquillare, Franklin Cardinals, West Haven, Connecticut
1984 Chuck Hamilton, Coors Kings, Merced, California
1985 Steve Newell, Pay 'n Pak, Seattle, Washington

1986 Jimmy Carrithers, Pay 'n Pak, Seattle, Washington
1987 Bruce Beard, Pay 'n Pak, Seattle, Washington
1988 Peter Meredith, Trans-Aire International, Elkhart, Indiana, and Mike Piechnik, Farm Tavern, Madison, Wisconsin
1989 Bill Boyer, Penn Corp., Sioux City, Iowa
1990 Mark Sorenson, Penn Corp., Sioux City, Iowa
1991 Chubb Tangaroa, Guanella Brothers, Rohnert Park, California
1992 Mark Sorenson, National Health Care, Sioux City, Iowa

NATIONAL CHAMPIONS

ASA men's major fast pitch batting leaders

1950 Ed Tyranski, Detroit, Michigan (.615)
1951 John Zula, Calumet City, Illinois (.535)
1952 Joe Overfield, Lackland AFB, Texas (.545)
1953 Joe Morecraft, Baltimore, Maryland (.375)
1954 Al Martin, Denver NAS, Colorado (.455)
1955 Marion Cook, Memphis, Tennessee (.500)
1956 Bob Forbes, Clearwater, Florida (.471)
1957 Al McCoy, Norristown, Pennsylvania (.467)
1958 Dominick Golio, Long Island, New York (.421)
1959 Clyde Miller, Canton, North Carolina (.500)
1960 Frank Doucette, Gardena, California (.600)
1961 LeRoy Hess, Aurora, Illinois (.462)
1962 Tom Moore, Clearwater, Florida (.444)
1963 Joe Higgens, Mesa, Arizona (.455)
1964 Ned Wickersham, Aurora, Illinois (.438)
1965 Ned Wickersham, Aurora, Illinois (.500)
1966 Ray Philips, Mountain View, California (.563)
1967 Bill Parker, Clearwater, Florida (.409)
1968 Weldon Haney, Clearwater, Florida (.412)
1969 Charles Acklin, Armed Forces (.353)
1970 John Anquillare, Stratford, Connecticut (.500)
1971 Al Yaeger, Stratford, Connecticut (.455)
1972 Vince Caserto, Poughkeepsie, New York (.444)
1973 Terry Muck, St. Paul, Minnesota (.467)
1974 Bob Quinn, Aurora, Illinois (.467)

Owner's Delight Frank La Teano holding the first place trophy from the slow pitch tournament in Sherbrooke, Quebec, in the summer of 1991. (Russell Mott)

1975 Tie between Larry Hale, Springfield, Missouri, and Abe Baker, Spencer, Massachusetts (.545)
1976 Scott Simmons, Salt Lake City, Utah (.476)
1977 George Bettineski, Seattle, Washington (.476)
1978 Ted Hicks, Springfield, Missouri (.632, national tourney record)
1979 Jim Brackin, Wilson Powell, Maryland (.533)
1980 Bill Stewart, Seattle, Washington (.524)
1981 Tie between Leon Wood, Clearwater, Florida, and Steve Moore, Reading, Pennsylvania (.400)

1982 Bruce Miller, Midland, Michigan (.417)
1983 Jeff Seip, Reading, Pennsylvania (.500)
1984 Jim Quick, Madison, Wisconsin (.522)
1985 Curt Peterson, Salt Lake City, Utah (.593)
1986 Jim Brackin, Allentown, Pennsylvania (.562)
1987 Cleon Young, Midland, Michigan (.529)
1988 Brian Rothrock, Decatur, Illinois (.458)
1989 John Melchiori, Ashland, Ohio (.400)
1990 Nick Genna, Rohnert Park, California (.538)
1991 Dave Johnson, Madison, Wisconsin (.500)
1992 Jody Hennigar, Clearwater, Florida (.538)

INTERNATIONAL SOFTBALL CONGRESS (ISC) WORLD CHAMPIONS
(Supplied by the International Softball Congress)

Year	Where Played	Champions
1947	Phoenix, Arizona	Farm Fresh Market, Phoenix, Arizona
1948	Oklahoma City, Oklahoma	Taft Merchants, Taft, California
1949	Greeley, Colorado	Hanford Kings, Hanford, California
1950	Greeley, Colorado	Hoak Packers, Fresno, California
1951	Greeley, Colorado	Hoak Packers, Fresno, California *NSC—Calvert, Texas
1952	Plainview, Texas	Hoak Packers, Fresno, California *NSC—Mary Star, San Pedro, California
1953	Selma, California	Long Beach Nitehawks, Long Beach, California *NSC—Mary Star, San Pedro, California
1954	Selma, California	Hoak Packers, Fresno, California *NSC—Mary Star, San Pedro, California
1955	New Bedford, Illinois	Long Beach Nitehawks, Long Beach, California *NSC—Sapulpa Brick & Tile, Sapulpa, Oklahoma
1956	New Bedford, Illinois	Long Beach Nitehawks, Long Beach, California *NSC—Mary Star, San Pedro, California
1957	New Bedford, Illinois	Long Beach Nitehawks, Long Beach, California *NSC—Mary Star, San Pedro, California
1958	Long Beach, California	Long Beach Nitehawks, Long Beach, California
1959	Long Beach California	Long Beach Nitehawks, Long Beach, California
1960	Long Beach California	Long Beach Nitehawks, Long Beach, California
1961	Rock Island, Illinois	Dautrich Realty, El Paso, Texas

Year	Where Played	Champions
1962	Rock Island, Illinois	Dautrich Realty, El Paso, Texas
1963	Rock Island, Illinois	Gardena Merchants, Gardena, California
1964	Rock Island, Illinois	Paramount Chevrolet Impalas, Downey, California
1965	Rock Island, Illinois	Pomona Bombers, Pomona, California
1966	Rock Island, Illinois	Gardena Merchants, Gardena, California
1967	Rock Island, Illinois	Harrelson Motors, Moline, Illinois
1968	Rock Island, Illinois	Long Beach Nitehawks, Long Beach, California
1969	Rock Island, Illinois	Sal's Lunch, Philadelphia, Pennsylvania
1970	Kerman, California	Schaefer-Smith Insurance, Phoenix, Arizona
1971	Tulsa, Oklahoma	Long Beach Nitehawks, Long Beach, California
1972	Kimberly, Wisconsin	Burbank Comets, Burbank, California
1973	Rock Island, Illinois	Lakewood Jets, Lakewood, California
1974	Sun City, Arizona	Page's Raiders, Sun City, Arizona
1975	Kimberly, Wisconsin	Long Beach Nitehawks, Long Beach, California
1976	Long Beach, California	All-American Bar, St. Paul, Minnesota
1977	Phoeniz, Arizona	Reno Toyota, Reno, Nevada
1978	Kimberly, Wisconsin	Atlee's Carpet Co., Oklahoma City, Oklahoma
1979	Bakersfield, California	Saginaw Bolters, Saginaw, Michigan
1980	Tempe, Arizona	Home Savings, Aurora, Illinois
1981	Saginaw, Michigan	Camarillo Kings, Camarillo, California
1982	Kimberly, Wisconsin	Camarillo Kings, Camarillo, California
1983	Bakersfield, California	Lancaster Chameleons, Lancaster, California
1984	Allentown, Pennsylvania	Archer Daniels Midland (ADM), Decatur, Illinois
1985	Kimberly, Wisconsin	Pay 'n Pak, Seattle, Washington
1986	Sioux City, Iowa	Pay 'n Pak, Seattle, Washington
1987	Saskatoon, Saskatchewan, Canada	Teleconnect, Cedar Rapids, Iowa
1988	Decatur, Illinois	Penn Corp., Sioux City, Iowa
1989	Kimberly, Wisconsin	Penn Corp., Sioux City, Iowa
1990	Victoria, B.C., Canada	Seafirst Bank, Bellevue, Washington
1991	Sioux City, Iowa	Penn Corp., Sioux City, Iowa

*The ISC and the NSC (National Softball Congress) merged in 1958.

ASA WOMEN'S MAJOR FAST PITCH NATIONAL CHAMPIONS

Year	Where Played	Champions
1933	Chicago, Illinois	Great Northerns, Chicago, Illinois
1934	Chicago, Illinois	Hart Motors, Chicago, Illinois
1935	Chicago, Illinois	Bloomer Girls, Cleveland, Ohio
1936	Chicago, Illinois	National Screw and Mfg. Co., Cleveland, Ohio
1937	Chicago, Illinois	National Screw and Mfg. Co., Cleveland, Ohio
1938	Chicago, Illinois	J.J. Kreig's, Alameda, California
1939	Chicago, Illinois	J.J. Kreig's, Alameda, California

Dynasty's Digs   The field in Stratford, Connecticut, that the Brakettes call home, and the site of the 1993 ASA Women's Major Fast Pitch National Championship. Built in 1966, it has been the home of the Brakettes dynasty since 1988. The official stadium name is the Textron Lycoming Field. (Russell Mott)

Year	Where Played	Champions
1940	Detroit, Michigan	Arizona Ramblers, Phoenix, Arizona
1941	Detroit, Michigan	Higgins "Midgets," Tulsa, Oklahoma
1942	Detroit, Michigan	Jax Maids, New Orleans, Louisiana
1943	Detroit, Michigan	Jax Maids, New Orleans, Louisiana
1944	Cleveland, Ohio	Lind & Pomeroy, Portland, Oregon
1945	Cleveland, Ohio	Jax Maids, New Orleans, Louisiana
1946	Cleveland, Ohio	Jax Maids, New Orleans, Louisiana
1947	Cleveland, Ohio	Jax Maids, New Orleans, Louisiana
1948	Portland, Oregon	Arizona Ramblers, Phoenix, Arizona
1949	Portland, Oregon	Arizona Ramblers, Phoenix, Arizona
1950	San Antonio, Texas	Orange Lionettes, Orange, California
1951	Detroit, Michigan	Orange Lionettes, Orange, California
1952	Toronto, Canada	Orange Lionettes, Orange, California
1953	Toronto, Canada	Betsy Ross Rockets, Fresno, California
1954	Orange, California	Leach Motor Rockets, Fresno, California
1955	Portland, Oregon	Orange Lionettes, Orange, California
1956	Clearwater, Florida	Orange Lionettes, Orange, California
1957	Buena Park, California	Hacienda Rockets, Fresno, California
1958	Stratford, Connecticut	Raybestos Brakettes, Stratford, Connecticut
1959	Stratford, Connecticut	Raybestos Brakettes, Stratford, Connecticut
1960	Stratford, Connecticut	Raybestos Brakettes, Stratford, Connecticut
1961	Portland, Oregon	Gold Sox, Whittier, California
1962	Stratford, Connecticut	Orange Lionettes, Orange, California
1963	Stratford, Connecticut	Raybestos Brakettes, Stratford, Connecticut
1964	Orlando, Florida	Erv Lind Florists, Portland, Oregon
1965	Stratford, Connecticut	Orange Lionettes, Orange, California
1966	Orlando, Florida	Raybestos Brakettes, Stratford, Connecticut

Year	Where Played	Champions
1967	Stratford, Connecticut	Raybestos Brakettes, Stratford, Connecticut
1968	Stratford, Connecticut	Raybestos Brakettes, Stratford, Connecticut
1969	Tucson, Arizona	Orange Lionettes, Orange, California
1970	Stratford, Connecticut	Orange Lionettes, Orange, California
1971	Orlando, Florida	Raybestos Brakettes, Stratford, Connecticut
1972	Tucson, Arizona	Raybestos Brakettes, Stratford, Connecticut
1973	Stratford, Connecticut	Raybestos Brakettes, Stratford, Connecticut
1974	Orlando, Florida	Raybestos Brakettes, Stratford, Connecticut
1975	Salt Lake City, Utah	Raybestos Brakettes, Stratford, Connecticut
1976	Stratford, Connecticut	Raybestos Brakettes, Stratford, Connecticut
1977	Hayward, California	Raybestos Brakettes, Stratford, Connecticut
1978	Allentown, Pennsylvania	Raybestos Brakettes, Stratford, Connecticut
1979	Springfield, Missouri	Sun City Saints, Sun City, Arizona
1980	Lansing, Michigan	Raybestos Brakettes, Stratford, Connecticut
1981	Houston, Texas	Orlando Rebels, Orlando, Florida
1982	Binghamton, New York	Raybestos Brakettes, Stratford, Connecticut
1983	Salt Lake City, Utah	Raybestos Brakettes, Stratford, Connecticut
1984	Buffalo, New York	Los Angeles Diamonds, Los Angeles, California
1985	Lansing, Michigan	Hi-Ho Brakettes, Stratford, Connecticut
1986	Pekin, Illinois	Southern California Invasion, Los Angeles, California
1987	Houston, Texas	Orange County Majestics, Orange California
1988	Pekin, Illinois	Hi-Ho Brakettes, Stratford, Connecticut
1989	Decatur, Illinois	Whittier Raiders, Whittier, California
1990	Redding, California	Raybestos Brakettes, Stratford, Connecticut
1991	Decatur, Illinois	Raybestos Brakettes, Stratford, Connecticut
1992	Redding, California	Raybestos Brakettes, Stratford, Connecticut

The Worth Book of Softball

Dynasty *The 1967 Raybestos Brakettes as defending national champions. Fabled pitchers Bertha Tickey (back row, third from left) and Joan Joyce (fifth from the left in the back row) were part of this team. (Amateur Softball Association)*

NCAA WOMEN'S COLLEGE WORLD SERIES PAST CHAMPIONSHIP RESULTS

Year	Champion	Coach	Score	Runner-up	Site
1982	UCLA*	Sharron Backus	2–0 (8 innings)	Fresno State	Omaha
1983	Texas A&M	Bob Brock	2–0 (12 innings)	Cal State–Fullerton	Omaha
1984	UCLA	Sharron Backus	1–0 (13 innings)	Texas A&M	Omaha
1985	UCLA	Sharron Backus	2–1 (9 innings)	Cal State–Fullerton#	Omaha
1986	Cal State–Fullerton*	Judi Garman	3–0	Texas A&M	Omaha
1987	Texas A&M	Bob Brock	4–1	UCLA	Omaha
1988	UCLA	Sharron Backus	3–0	Fresno State	Sunnyvale
1989	UCLA*	Sharron Backus	1–0	Fresno State	Sunnyvale
1990	UCLA	Sharron Backus	2–0	Fresno State	Oklahoma City
1991	Arizona	Mike Candera	5–1	UCLA	Oklahoma City
1992	UCLA	Sharron Backus	2–0	Arizona	Oklahoma City
1993	Arizona	Mike Candera	1–0	UCLA	Oklahoma City

(*) Indicates undefeated team through finals.
(#) Nebraska actually finished second on the field but its participation and standing in the tournament was vacated because of an NCAA rules violation. Cal State–Fullerton was awarded second place.

Star *Lisa Fernandez at the 1992 NCAA Championships in Oklahoma City where she starred as pitcher and offensive threat.* (Russell Mott)

BATTING—INDIVIDUAL

Most runs scored in a tournament

9 each—Pat Dufficy, Stratford, Connecticut (1983); Irene Shea, Stratford, Connecticut (1975); and Kris Peterson, Stratford, Connecticut (1987)

Most hits in a tournament

16—Pat Guenzler, Stratford, Connecticut (1983)

Most hits in a game

5—Kay Rich, Fresno, California (1955); and Tricia Popowski, Stratford, Connecticut (1992)

Most consecutive hits

9—Kris Peterson, Stratford, Connecticut (1987)

Most doubles in a national championship

6—Dot Richardson, Stratford, Connecticut (1989)

Most triples

3 each—Irene Huber, Fresno, California (1949); Marilyn Rau, Sun City, Arizona (1978 and 1981); Lu Flanagan, Seattle, Washington (1971); and Lana Svec, Ashland, Ohio (1977)

Most homeruns

4—Robbie Mulkey, Portland, Oregon (1949); 3 each—Sheila Cornell, Sepulveda, California (1982 and 1983) and Pat Dufficy, Stratford, Connecticut (1991)

Most RBI in a national championship

10 each—Pat Dufficy, Stratford, Connecticut (1983), and Kay Rich, Fresno, California (1955); 9—Dionna Harris, Stratford, Connecticut (1992)

Most RBI in a game

7—Dionna Harris, Stratford, Connecticut (1992); 6 each—Joan Joyce, Stratford, Connecticut (1975), and Kay Rich, Fresno, California (1955)

Most at-bats in a national championship

41—Jackie Gaw, Stratford, Connecticut (1983); 40—Irene Shea, Stratford, Connecticut (1974)

PITCHING—INDIVIDUAL

Most innings pitched in a national championship

70—Joan Joyce, Stratford, Connecticut (1973); 69 2/3—Joan Joyce, Stratford, Connecticut (1974)

Most strikeouts in a game

40—Joan Joyce, Stratford, Connecticut, in 19 innings (1961); 33—Tiffany Boyd, California Raiders, in 27 innings (1987); 32 each—Becky Duffin, Jefferson City, Missouri, in 27 innings (1987) and Leslie Partch, Hayward, California, in 17 innings (1984)

Most strikeouts in a tournament

134—Joan Joyce, Stratford, Connecticut (1973)

Most strikeouts in a seven-inning game

20—Bertha Tickey, Orange, California (1953); Michele Granger, Orange County Majestics, Orange, California (1988); 19—Bertha Tickey, Orange, California (1954)

Most strikeouts by two pitchers combined in one game

65—Becky Duffin, Jefferson City, Missouri, and Tiffany Boyd, California Raiders (1987)

Most consecutive strikeouts in a game

18—Michele Granger, Orange County Majestics (1988)

Most no-hitters in a national championship

3—Louise Mazzuca, Portland, Oregon (1960)

Most perfect games in a national championship

2—Bertha Tickey, Orange, California (1950–54) and Margie Law, Phoenix (1954–57)

Most wins in a national championship

8—Joan Joyce, Stratford, Connecticut (1973); 7—Joan Joyce, Stratford, Connecticut (1974)

TEAM FIELDING

Highest fielding percentage in a tournament (at least three games)

.996—Stratford, Connecticut (1965)

Most errors in a game

11—Houston, Texas (1958) and District of Columbia (1947)

Most errors in a tournament

18—Pekin, Illinois (1965) and District of Columbia (1947)

Most putouts in a game

81 each—California Raiders and Jefferson City, Missouri (1987)

Most putouts in a tournament

277—Stratford, Connecticut (1961)

Most assists in a tournament

124—Stratford, Connecticut (1983)

Most games in a tournament

11—Stratford, Connecticut (1983)

Most double plays in a tournament

7—Portland, Oregon (1949); 5 each—Fresno, California (1963), and Plainfield, New Jersey (1960)

Most consecutive wins out of the losers' bracket

9—Stratford, Connecticut (1983)

Good Sport   *University of Kansas Jayhawk player Shelly Sack enjoying the limelight at the NCAA 1992 championships.* (Russell Mott)

TEAM BATTING

Highest batting average in a tournament

.358—Stratford, Connecticut (1983)

Most hits in a game

27—Stratford, Connecticut (1992)

Most hits in a tournament

118—Stratford, Connecticut (1983)

Trophyland *Lebeau's Tavern in New Bedford, Massachusetts, where the windows are filled with softball trophies. The man in the photo posing with a new acquisition is Morris "Mo" Herbert, a customer of Lebeau's. (Russell Mott)*

Most homeruns in a tournament

10—Stratford, Connecticut (1992)

Most triples in a tournament

7—Phoenix, Arizona (1955) and Ashland, Ohio (1977)

Most doubles in a tournament

12 each—Stratford, Connecticut (1968 and 1983)

Most runs in a game

30—Raybestos Brakettes, Stratford, Connecticut (1992)

Most runs in an inning

12—Raybestos Brakettes, Stratford, Connecticut (1992)

Most runs in a tournament

58—Stratford, Connecticut (1992)
57—Stratford, Connecticut (1983)

Most stolen bases in a tournament

14—Portland, Oregon (1962)

Most RBI in a game

26—Stratford, Connecticut (1992)

Longest game

28 innings—California Commotion vs. Redding, CA Rebels (1993)

ERV LIND AWARD WINNERS

(Given to the Outstanding Defensive Player in the ASA Women's Major Fast Pitch National Championship)

1965 Nera White, Nashville, Tennessee
1966 Gladys Crespo, Stratford, Connecticut
1967 Margaret Propst, Topeka, Kansas
1968 Carol Spanks, Orange, California
1969 Carol Spanks, Orange, California
1970 Carol Spanks, Orange, California

1971	No award given
1972	Chris Miner, Fresno, California
1973	Kathy Fraser, Bloomington, Minnesota
1974	Jamie Smith, Lansing, Michigan
1975	Bethel Stout, St. Louis, Missouri
1976	Dori Anderson, Orlando, Florida
1977	Kathy Strahan, Stratford, Connecticut
1978	Mary Faure, Greeley, Colorado
1979	Dot Richardson, Orlando, Florida
1980	Suzy Brazney, Long Beach, California
1981	Dot Richardson, Orlando, Florida
1982	Helen Andrade, Sun City, Arizona
1983	Jonelle Johnson, Sacramento, California
1984	Dot Richardson, Stratford, Connecticut
1985	Allyson Rioux, Stratford, Connecticut
1986	Dot Richardson, Stratford, Connecticut
1987	Dot Richardson, Stratford, Connecticut
1988	Julie Standering, SSK Invasion, Southern California
1989	Kris Peterson, Stratford, Connecticut
1990	Dot Richardson, Stratford, Connecticut
1991	Julie Smith, Redding, California
1992	Ann Rowan, Phoenix, Arizona

BERTHA TICKEY AWARD WINNERS

(Given to the Outstanding Pitcher in the ASA Women's Major Fast Pitch National Championship)

1968	Bertha Tickey, Stratford, Connecticut
1969	Nancy Welborn, Orange, California
1970	Nancy Welborn, Orange, California
1971	Nancy Welborn, Orange, California
1972	Nancy Welborn, Orange, California
1973	Joan Joyce, Stratford, Connecticut
1974	Joan Joyce, Stratford, Connecticut
1975	Joan Joyce, Stratford, Connecticut
1976	Barbara Reinalda, Stratford, Connecticut

Lionette Pitching great Bertha Tickey, in the uniform of the Orange Lionettes, is lifted aloft by members of the team after one of her many victories. Her record with the Lionettes and Raybestos Brakettes was 757–88. A major ASA pitching award, the Bertha Tickey Outstanding Pitcher Award, is named for her. (Amateur Softball Association)

1977	Barbara Reinalda, Stratford, Connecticut		1973	National Champions
1978	Kathy Arendsen, Stratford, Connecticut		1974	World Champions
1979	Michele Thomas, Sun City, Arizona			National Champions
1980	Kathy Arendsen, Stratford, Connecticut		1975	National Champions
1981	Lou Piel, Orlando, Florida		1976	National Champions
1982	Kathy Arendsen, Stratford, Connecticut		1977	National Champions
1983	Barbara Reinalda, Stratford, Connecticut		1978	World Champions
1984	Kathy Van Wyk, Los Angeles, California			National Champions
1985	Susan Lefebvre, Long Beach, California		1979	National Sports Festival Champs
1986	Michele Granger, Orange County, California		1980	National Champions
1987	Michele Granger, Orange County, California		1981	World Games Champions
1988	Michele Granger, Orange County, California		1982	National Champions
1989	Lisa Longaker, Whittier, California		1983	National Champions
1990	Michele Smith, Redding, California		1984	International Cup Champions
1991	Kathy Arendsen, Stratford, Connecticut		1985	National Champions
1992	Lisa Fernandez, Stratford, Connecticut			World Games Champions

1985 World Games Champions
Women's International Champions

1986 World Champions
World Challenge Cup Champions
U.S. Olympic Festival Champions

1988 National Champions

1989 Olympic Festival Champions

1990 National Champions

1991 National Champions
Olympic Festival Champions

1992 National Champions

Total: 2,480 wins, 278 losses

RAYBESTOS BRAKETTES TEAM MILESTONES

They are probably the strongest dynasty in all of organized sport and have dominated women's softball since Eisenhower was in the White House. The team's record:

1958	National Champions
1959	National Champions
1960	National Champions
1963	National Champions
1966	National Champions
1967	National Champions
1968	National Champions
1971	National Champions
1972	National Champions

Trophy Hunter *Fran Pierce and his 152 trophies won in the name of the Pierce Construction Softball Team out of Tolland, Connecticut, the United States Slo-Pitch Softball Association B grand slam winners and world champs for 1991. (Russell Mott)*

II. SLOW PITCH RECORDS

ASA MEN'S SUPER SLOW PITCH NATIONAL CHAMPIONS

Year	Where Played	Champions
1981	Burlington, North Carolina	Howard's-Western Steer, Denver, North Carolina
1982	Burlington, North Carolina	Jerry's Catering, Miami, Florida
1983	Burlington, North Carolina	Howard's-Western Steer, Denver, North Carolina
1984	Burlington, North Carolina	Howard's-Western Steer, Denver, North Carolina
1985	Burlington, North Carolina	Steele's Sports, Grafton, Ohio
1986	Burlington, North Carolina	Steele's Sports, Grafton, Ohio
1987	Parma, Ohio	Steele's Sports, Grafton, Ohio
1988	Oklahoma City, Oklahoma	Starpath, Monticello, Kentucky
1989	Oklahoma City, Oklahoma	Ritch's Salvage, Harrisburg, North Carolina
1990	Oklahoma City, Oklahoma	Steele's Silver Bullets, Grafton, Ohio
1991	Little Rock, Arkansas	Worth/Sunbelt, Centerville, Georgia
1992	Hendersonville, Tennessee	Ritch's/Superior, Windsor Locks, Connecticut

SUPER SLOW PITCH RECORDS
BATTING—INDIVIDUAL

Batting average in a tournament

.900—Carl Rose, Lighthouse/Sunbelt, Stone Mountain, Georgia, and Wes Lord, Budweiser, San Francisco, California (1990)

Most homeruns in a game

8—Dirk Androff, Steele's Silver Bullets, Grafton, Ohio (1989)

Most homeruns in a tournament

20 each—Doug Roberson, Superior/Apollo, Windsor Locks, Connecticut (1990), and Rick (The Crusher) Scherr, Howard's-Western Steer, Denver, North Carolina (1984)

Most RBI in a game

11—Dirk Androff, Steele's Silver Bullets, Grafton, Ohio (1989)

Most RBI in a tournament

35—Doug Roberson, Superior/Apollo, Windsor Locks, Connecticut (1990)

Most hits in a game

8 each—Billy Blake and Dirk Androff, Steele's Silver Bullets, Grafton, Ohio (1989)

BATTING—TEAM

Highest batting average

.741—Steele's Silver Bullets, Grafton, Ohio (1990)

Most runs in a tournament

275—Superior/Apollo, Windsor Locks, Connecticut (1990)

Most runs in a game

75—Steele's Silver Bullets, Grafton, Ohio (1989)

Most homeruns in a game

56—Steele's Silver Bullets, Grafton, Ohio (1989)

Most homeruns in a tournament

148—Superior/Apollo, Windsor Locks, Connecticut (1989)

ASA NATIONAL SLOW PITCH CHAMPIONS
MEN'S MAJOR SLOW PITCH

Year	Where Played	Champions
1953	Cincinnati, Ohio	Shields Construction, Newport, Kentucky
1954	Louisville, Kentucky	Waldneck's Tavern, Cincinnati, Ohio
1955	Pittsburgh, Pennsylvania	Lang's Pet Shop, Covington, Kentucky
1956	Cleveland, Ohio	Gatliff Auto Sales, Newport, Kentucky
1957	Toledo, Ohio	Gatliff Auto Sales, Newport, Kentucky
1958	Cleveland, Ohio	East Side Sports, Detroit, Michigan
1959	Cleveland, Ohio	Yorkshire Restaurant, Newport, Kentucky
1960	Toledo, Ohio	Hamilton Tailoring, Cincinnati, Ohio
1961	Louisville, Kentucky	Hamilton Tailoring, Cincinnati, Ohio
1962	Cleveland, Ohio	Skip Hogan A.C., Pittsburgh, Pennsylvania
1963	Jones Beach, New York	Gatliff Auto Sales, Newport, Kentucky
1964	Springfield, Ohio	Skip A.C., Pittsburgh, Pennsylvania
1965	Maumee, Ohio	Skip A.C., Pittsburgh, Pennsylvania
1966	Parma, Ohio	Michael's Lounge, Detroit, Michigan
1967	Parma, Ohio	Skip Hogan A.C./Jim's Sport Shop, Pittsburgh, Pennsylvania
1968	Jones Beach, New York	County Sports, Levittown, New York
1969	Parma, Ohio	Copper Hearth, Milwaukee, Wisconsin

Year	Where Played	Champions
1970	Southgate, Michigan	Little Caesar's, Southgate, Michigan
1971	Parma, Ohio	Pile Drivers, Virginia Beach, Virginia
1972	Jacksonville, Florida	Jiffy Club, Louisville, Kentucky
1973	Cleveland, Ohio	Howard's Furniture, Denver, North Carolina
1974	York, Pennsylvania	Howard's Furniture, Denver, North Carolina
1975	Cleveland, Ohio	Pyramid Cafe, Lakewood, Ohio
1976	Jacksonville, Florida	Warren Motors, Jacksonville, Florida Warren Motors, led by Mike Nye, Ronnie Ford and Bruce Meade, compile 94–2 record en route to title.
1977	Parma, Ohio	Nelson Painting, Oklahoma City, Oklahoma
1978	Elk Grove, California	Campbell's Carpets, Concord, California
1979	York, Pennsylvania	Nelco Manufacturing, Oklahoma City, Oklahoma
1980	Montgomery, Alabama	Campbell's Carpets, Concord, California
1981	Burlington, North Carolina	Elite Coatings, Gordon, Georgia
1982	Parma, Ohio	Triangle Sports, Minneapolis, Minnesota
1983	Parma, Ohio	No. 1 Electric, Charlotte, North Carolina
1984	Garland, Texas	Lilly Air, Chicago, Illinois
1985	Burlington, North Carolina	Blanton's, Fayetteville, North Carolina
1986	Maumee, Ohio	Non-Ferrous, Cleveland, Ohio
1987	Parma, Ohio	Starpath, Monticello, Kentucky
1988	Gadsden, Alabama	Bell Corp., Tampa, Florida
1989	Burlington, North Carolina	Ritch's Salvage, Harrisburg, North Carolina Ritch's also won the ASA Super National title. It was the first time a team won both the Super and Major Championships in the same year.
1990	Maumee, Ohio	Riverside Paving, Lexington, Kentucky
1991	Decatur, Alabama	New Construction, Shelbyville, Indiana
1992	Jacksonville, Florida	Vernon's, Jacksonville, Florida

Slow Pitcher Tippy Larson, U.S.S.S.A. Hall of Fame slow pitcher for Cassidy and Lee, showing his stuff in 1992 in Hopkinton, Massachusetts. (Russell Mott)

MAJOR SLOW PITCH RECORDS
BATTING—INDIVIDUAL

Highest Batting Average

.944—Greg Fuhrman, York Barbell, York, Pennsylvania

Most homers in a tournament

23—Stan Harvey, Howard's-Western Steer, Denver, North Carolina (1978)

Most homers in one inning

3—Craig Elliott, Ken Sanders, Phenix City, Alabama (1989)

Most consecutive homers in a tournament

9—Craig Elliott, Ken Sanders, Phenix City, Alabama (1979)

Most RBI in a tournament

45—Stan Harvey, Howard's-Western Steer, Denver, North Carolina (1978)

TEAM—BATTING

Most homers in a game

29—Dave Carroll Sports, Sherrills Ford, North Carolina (1979)

Most runs in a game

86—Campbell's Carpets, Concord, California (1978)

Largest margin of victory

84 Runs—Campbell's Carpets, Concord, California (1978); Won 86–2.

ASA MEN'S MAJOR SLOW PITCH NATIONAL CHAMPIONSHIP MVP'S

1953–1957
No information available
1958 Joe Gauci, Detroit, Michigan
1959 Walt Wherry, Yorkshire Restaurant, Newport, Kentucky
1960 No information available
1961 Jim Harper, Ready Mix, Knoxville, Tennessee
1962 Bill Cole, East Side Sporting Goods, Detroit, Michigan
1963 Myron Reinhardt, Gatliff Auto, Covington, Kentucky
1964 Paul Tomasovich, Skip A.C., Pittsburgh, Pennsylvania
1965 Lou Del Mastro, Skip A.C., Pittsburgh, Pennsylvania
1966 Mike Axelson, Michael's Lounge, Detroit, Michigan
1967 Miller Adams, Jim's Sports Shop/Skip Hogan A.C., Pittsburgh, Pennsylvania
1968 Bert Smith, County Sports, Levittown, Long Island
1969 H.T. Waller, Joe's Pizza, Milton, Florida
1970 Mike Gouin, Little Caesar's, Southgate, Michigan

1971 Bert Smith, Piledrivers, Virginia Beach, Virginia

1972 Don Arndt, Howard's Furniture, Denver, North Carolina

1973 Bert Smith, Howard's Furniture, Denver, North Carolina

1974 Roger Brown, Howard's Furniture, Denver, North Carolina

1975 Steve Loya, Pyramid Cafe, Lakewood, Ohio

1976 Ronnie Ford and Mike Nye, Warren Motors, Jacksonville, Florida

1977 Craig Elliott, Ken Sanders Ford, Phenix City, Alabama, and Bruce Meade, Nelson Painting, Oklahoma City, Oklahoma

1978 Denny Jones, Campbell's Carpets, Concord, California

1979 Joe Young, Nelco Manufacturing, Oklahoma City, Oklahoma

1980 Buddy Slater, Campbell's Carpets, Concord, California

1981 Ricky Huggins, Elite Coatings, Gordon, Georgia

1982 Glenn Bourquin, Triangle Sports, Minneapolis, Minnesota

1983 Tim White, No. 1 Electric/Heating and Air Conditioning, Charlotte, North Carolina

1984 Phil Higgins, Lilly Air, Chicago, Illinois

1985 Andy Cook, Blanton's, Fayetteville, North Carolina

1986 Ron Wood, Non-Ferrous, Cleveland, Ohio

1987 Gary Jones, Starpath, Monticello, Kentucky

1988 Mike Ambers, Bell Corporation, Tampa, Florida

1989 Bill Gatti, Ritch's Salvage, Harrisburg, North Carolina

1990 Greg Pyle, New Construction, Shelbyville, Indiana

1991 Donnie Rardin, Riverside Paving, Lexington, Kentucky

1992 Ricky Huggins, Vernon's, Jacksonville, Florida

Victors *Ritch's/Superior team photo from the Yvon Pif Depatie tournament in Sherbrooke, Quebec, Canada in July, 1991. Over three days and nights they drew over 60,000 people—the highest attendance anywhere for a slow pitch softball event. (Russell Mott)*

ASA MEN'S MAJOR SLOW PITCH NATIONAL CHAMPIONSHIP HOMERUN CHAMPIONS

1953–
1955 No information available
1956 Lenny Roth, Helf Builders, Cleveland, Ohio; 5 homeruns
1957 No information available
1958 Ron Annotico, Sheffield Bronze, Cleveland, Ohio; 6
1959 George Rosewicz, Grande Caruso, Columbus, Ohio; 4
1960 Denny Braun, Cleveland, Ohio; 6
1961 No information available
1962 John Stone, Milwaukee Enterprise Bar, Milwaukee, Wisconsin; 11
1963 Lou Russo, Musicaro's, Massapequa Park, New York; 6
1964 Don Arndt, TWUA, Leaksville, North Carolina; 10
1965 Jack Goodrich, Swing Inn, Cleveland, Ohio; Dan Hansen, Meriden, Connecticut; Paul Tomasovich, Skip A.C., Pittsburgh, Pennsylvania; Bob Auten, Monroe, Michigan; and George Siford, Skip A.C., Pittsburgh, Pennsylvania; all 5 each
*1966 Jim Galloway, County Sports, Levittown, New York; 11
*1967 Carl (Tex) Collins, Michael's Lounge, Detroit, Michigan; 13
1968 Bert Smith, County Sports, Levittown, New York; 11
1969 H.T. Waller, Joe's Pizza, Milton, Florida; 16
1970 Jay Justice, Worthington Steel, Columbus, Ohio; 11
1971 Jim Puckett, Little Caesar's, Detroit, Michigan; 13
1972 Bill Gattie, Jiffy Club, Louisville, Kentucky, and Al White, Warren Motors, Jacksonville, Florida; 14 each
1973 Bert Smith, Howard's Furniture, Denver, North Carolina; 21
1974 Al White, Jerry's Catering, Miami, Florida; 10
1975 Stan Harvey and *Don Arndt, Howard's Furniture, Denver, North Carolina; 7 each
1976 Ken Carlton, Green Machine, Starke, Florida; 13

1977 Herman Rathman, Nelson's Painting, and Bruce Meade, Nelson's Painting, Oklahoma City, Oklahoma; 22 each
1978 Stan Harvey, Howard's Furniture, Denver, North Carolina; 23 (RECORD)
1979 David Beaird, Ken Sanders Ford, Phenix City, Alabama; 14
*1980 Tom Beall, Howard's Western Steer, Denver, North Carolina; 17
1981 Cecil Whitehead, Elite Coatings, Gordon, Georgia; 9
1982 Glenn Bourquin, Triangle Sports, Minneapolis, Minnesota; 14
1983 Tim Clemmons, Carroll Marathon, Columbus, Ohio; 16
1984 Dennis Crawford, Ray's Metal Works, Alachua, Florida; 16
1985 Gary Robertson, Larry Jacobs, Modesto, California; 10
1986 Jim Fuller, Shubin's Softball Club, Los Angeles, California; 11
1987 Dave Allen, Starpath, Lexington, Kentucky, and Don Clatterbough, Blanton's, Fayetteville, North Carolina; 15 each
1988 Scott Jones, Starpath, Monticello, Kentucky; 14
1989 Clyde Guy, Superior/Apollo, Windsor Locks, Connecticut; 11
1990 F.A. Martin, SETA Corporation, Charlotte, North Carolina; 12
1991 Dewayne Nevitt, Wildcat Fence, Lexington, Kentucky; 17
1992 Ricky Huggins, Vernon's, Jacksonville, Florida; 18

*Member of the National Softball Hall of Fame and Museum, Oklahoma City.

ASA MEN'S MAJOR INDUSTRIAL SLOW PITCH NATIONAL CHAMPIONS

1957 Turbine Jets, Cincinnati, Ohio
1958 Turbine Jets, Cincinnati, Ohio
1959 Turbine Jets, Cincinnati, Ohio
1960 Pharr Yarn, McAdenville, North Carolina
1961 Pharr Yarn, McAdenville, North Carolina
1962 Tirabassi Excavation, Kenosha, Wisconsin
1963 Pharr Yarn, McAdenville, North Carolina
1964 Pabst/International Harvester, Springfield, Ohio

1965	Wiegand Company, Pittsburgh, Pennsylvania
1966	IBM, Lexington, Kentucky
1967	Grumman Aircraft, Bethpage, New York
1968	Avco Lycoming, Stratford, Connecticut
1969	Avco Lycoming, Stratford, Connecticut
1970	Pharr Yarn, McAdenville, North Carolina
1971	Pharr Yarn, McAdenville, North Carolina
1972	Pharr Yarn, McAdenville, North Carolina
1973	Pabst/International Harvester, Springfield, Ohio
1974	Aetna Life & Casualty, Charlotte, North Carolina
1975	Nassau County Police Dept., Mineola, New York
1976	Armco Triangles, Middletown, Ohio
1977	Armco Triangles, Middletown, Ohio
1978	GE Wacos, Louisville, Kentucky
1979	Sikorsky Aircraft, Stratford, Connecticut
1980	Sikorsky Aircraft, Stratford, Connecticut
1981	Raffield Fisheries, Port St. Joseph, Florida
1982	Sikorsky Aircraft, Stratford, Connecticut
1983	Russell Southern, Alexander City, Alabama
1984	Sikorsky Aircraft, Stratford, Connecticut
1985	Grumman Aerospace, Bayshore, New York
1986	Landrum & Son, Atlanta, Georgia
1987	Sikorsky Aircraft, Stratford, Connecticut
1988	Publix, Lakeland, Florida
1989	Delta All-Stars, Atlanta, Georgia
1990	Sikorsky Aircraft, Stratford, Connecticut
1991	County Fed Meats, Riverdale, Georgia
1992	Sikorsky Aircraft, Stratford, Connecticut

MAJOR INDUSTRIAL SLOW PITCH RECORDS

Highest batting average

.933—Bob Hurd, Sikorsky Aircraft, Stratford, Connecticut (1974)

Most homeruns

15 each—Bobby Height, Aeta, Charlotte, North Carolina (1978), and Chris Cammack, Aeta, Charlotte, North Carolina (1974)

Most major industrial titles won

7—Sikorsky Aircraft, Stratford, Connecticut

ASA MEN'S CLASS A SLOW PITCH CHAMPIONS

1974	Piedmont Sheet Metal, Winston-Salem, North Carolina
1975	Levittown American Legion, Levittown, New York
1976	Reed's Nuts, Macon, Georgia
1977	Higgins Cycle, Greensboro, North Carolina
1978	Port City Ford, Houston, Texas
1979	Clark & Sons, Providence, Rhode Island
1980	Houston Wreckers, Houston, Texas
1981	Ray Sears & Son, Gambrills, Maryland
1982	Lawson Auto Parts, Orlando, Florida
1983	Lawson Auto Parts, Orlando, Florida
1984	Bender Plumbing, New Haven, Connecticut
1985	Thompson's Sporting Goods, Savannah, Georgia
1986	Vernon's, Jacksonville, Florida
1987	Minneapolis Merchants, Minneapolis, Minnesota
1988	Smith's Transport, Roaring Springs, Pennsylvania
1989	Vernon's, Jacksonville, Florida
1990	Vernon's, Jacksonville, Florida
1991	Lee Roy's Framing, Claremont, North Carolina
1992	Medina Body Shop, Cleveland, Ohio

ASA MEN'S MASTERS (45 AND OVER) SLOW PITCH CHAMPIONS

1987	John Hanson Savings & Loan, Beltsville, Maryland
1988	Lithoplates North, Charlotte, North Carolina
1989	Capital Oil, Columbus, Indiana
1990	Capital Oil, Columbus, Indiana
1991	Nothdurft, Clinton Township, Michigan
1992	Country's Cable TV, Monroe, Washington

ASA MEN'S MASTERS (55 AND OVER) SLOW PITCH NATIONAL CHAMPIONS

1988	Southern California Braves, San Marcos, California

1989 Masters 12, Harrison, Ohio
1990 Miami Sawaia's, Miami, Florida
1991 Wiggins Iron Works, Savannah, Georgia
1992 Joseph Chevrolet, Cincinnati, Ohio

ASA MEN'S MAJOR MODIFIED PITCH NATIONAL CHAMPIONS

1975 Silvestri's, Staten Island, New York
1976 Clinica, Miami, Florida
1977 Clinica, Miami, Florida
1978 Mariano, Miami Beach, Florida
1979 Clinica, Miami, Florida
1980 Cadillacs, Atlanta, Georgia
1981 Clinica, Miami, Florida
1982 Silvestri's, Staten Island, New York
1983 Silvestri's, Staten Island, New York
1984 Tighe Club, Wilmington, Delaware
1985 Piefer Pest Control, Miami, Florida
1986 Don Swann Sales, Atlanta, Georgia
1987 WTB Broadway, Spokane, Washington
1988 Sullivan Roofing, Athens, Georgia
1989 Don Swann Sales, Atlanta, Georgia
1990 CBS, Huntington, New York
1991 Stings, Hialeah, Florida
1992 Stafford Tires, Monmouth, New Jersey

ASA MEN'S MAJOR CHURCH SLOW PITCH NATIONAL CHAMPIONS

1974 St. Martin's, St. Louis, Missouri
1975 Hickory Hammock, Milton, Florida
1976 Hickory Hammock, Milton, Florida
1977 Hickory Hammock, Milton, Florida
1978 Grace Methodist, Oklahoma City, Oklahoma
1979 Grace Methodist, Oklahoma City, Oklahoma
1980 West End Baptist, Houston, Texas
1981 Lewisville First Methodist, Lewisville, Texas
1982 Grace Methodist, Oklahoma City, Oklahoma
1983 Northside Baptist, Arlington, Virginia
1984 First Baptist, Palatka, Florida
1985 Hickory Hammock, Milton, Florida

1986 New Covenant, Oklahoma City, Oklahoma
1987 12th Street Baptist, Gadsden, Alabama
1988 Choto, Nashville, Tennessee
1989 Choto, Nashville, Tennessee
1990 Mt. Zion Methodist, Rainbow City, Alabama
1991 Oakview Presbyterian, Burlington, North Carolina
1992 Rehoboth Presbyterian, Tucker, Georgia

Barbara Reinalda   A key pitcher with the Raybestos Brakettes since 1976, she has posted more than 400 victories with the team. In one four-year period her record was 100–3. (Russell Mott)

ASA NATIONAL MAJOR SLOW PITCH CHAMPIONS (WOMEN'S DIVISION)

Year	Where Played	Champions
1959	Richmond, Virginia	Pearl Laundry, Richmond, Virginia
1960	Richmond, Virginia	Carolina Rockets, High Point, North Carolina
1961	Cincinnati, Ohio	Dairy Cottage, Covington, Kentucky
1962	Cincinnati, Ohio	Dana Gardens, Cincinnati, Ohio
1963	Cincinnati, Ohio	Dana Gardens, Cincinnati, Ohio
1964	Omaha, Nebraska	Dana Gardens, Cincinnati, Ohio
1965	Omaha, Nebraska	Art's Acres, Omaha, Nebraska
1966	Burlington, North Carolina	Dana Gardens, Cincinnati, Ohio
1967	Sheboygan, Wisconsin	Ridge Maintenance, Cleveland, Ohio
1968	Cincinnati, Ohio	Escue Pontiac, Cincinnati, Ohio
1969	Chattanooga, Tennessee	Converse Dots, Hialeah, Florida
1970	Parma, Ohio	Rutenschroer Floral, Cincinnati, Ohio
1971	Satellite Beach, Florida	Gators, Ft. Lauderdale, Florida
1972	York, Pennsylvania	Riverside Ford, Cincinnati, Ohio
1973	Chattanooga, Tennessee	Sweeney Chevrolet, Cincinnati, Ohio
1974	Elk Grove, California	N. Miami Dots, Miami, Florida
1975	Jacksonville, Florida	N. Miami Dots, Miami, Florida
1976	Chattanooga, Tennessee	Sorrento's Pizza, Cincinnati, Ohio
1977	Graham, North Carolina	Fox Valley Lassies, St. Charles, Illinois
1978	Jacksonville, Florida	Bob Hoffman's Dots, Miami, Florida
1979	Nashville, Tennessee	Bob Hoffman's Dots, Miami, Florida
1980	York, Pennsylvania	Howard's Rubi-Otts, Graham, North Carolina
1981	Seattle, Washington	Tifton Tomboys, Tifton, Georgia
1982	Marietta, Georgia	Richmond Stompers, Richmond, Virginia
1983	Montgomery, Alabama	Spooks, Anoka, Minnesota
1984	Marietta, Georgia	Spooks, Anoka, Minnesota
1985	Springfield, Missouri	Key Ford Mustangs, Pensacola, Florida
1986	Parma, Ohio	Sur-Way Tomboys, Tifton, Georgia

Year	Where Played	Champions
1987	Pensacola, Florida	Key Ford Mustangs, Pensacola, Florida
1988	Bloomington, Minnesota	Spooks, Anoka, Minnesota
1989	Marietta, Georgia	Cannan's Illusion, San Antonio, Texas
1990	Bloomington, Minnesota	Spooks, Anoka, Minnesota
1991	Novi, Michigan	Cannan's Illusion, San Antonio, Texas
1992	Gadsden, Alabama	UPI, Cookeville, Tennessee

ASA WOMEN'S MAJOR SLOW PITCH NATIONAL CHAMPIONSHIP BATTING CHAMPIONS

Year	Champions	Pct
1969	Emma Pope, Bill's Restaurant, Virginia Beach, Virginia and Kay Smith, One-Eyed Jacks, Little Rock, Arkansas; both	.600
1970	Ida Jean Hopkins, Raney Tire, Cleveland, Ohio	.704
1971	Sue Taylor, The Mice, Huntington, New York	.722
1972	Susan Smith, Acme Rebellettes, Montgomery, Alabama	.579
1973	Princess Carpenter, Rutenschroer Floral, Cincinnati, Ohio (National Record)	.857
1974	Tiera Edwards, Rebels, Jacksonville, Florida	.737
1975	Sandra Russum, Gremlins, Tampa, Florida	.588
1976	Sue Malcolm, Sorrento's Pizza, Cincinnati, Ohio	.529
1977	Marylyss Runestead, Fox Valley Lassies, St. Charles, Illinois	.680
1978	Kristy Boston, Dots, Miami, Florida	.652
1979	Pam Nelson, McLaughlin Oil, Columbus, Ohio	.733
1980	Inga Lees, McLaughlin Oil, Columbus, Ohio	.813
1981	Debbie Bregler, P.D.S. Sunshriners, Jacksonville Beach, Florida	.523
1982	Shelly Vick, Spooks, Anoka, Minnesota and Paula Christalwa, JEA Awards, Seattle, Washington	.560
1983	Kathy Riley, Silver Streak, Denton, Texas	.636
1984	Debbie Krebs, Jenelle Kathan, Sellbergs, Vancouver, Washington	.619
1985	Lorraine Hudson, Key Ford Mustangs, Pensacola, Florida	.640
1986	Caryl Moehring, Coors, Champaign, Illinois	.840

Year	Champions	Pct
1987	Joanne Zayac, W.W. Gay Rebels, Jacksonville, Florida	.640
1988	Tricia Hartzos, Key Ford Mustangs, Pensacola, Florida	.775
1989	Joanna Zayac, W.W. Gay Rebels, Jacksonville, Florida	.666
1990	Karen Murphy, Wilson Softball, Wichita, KS	.526
1991	Kathy Dyer, Raiders, Farmington Hills, Michigan	.640
1992	Laura Elmore, York Pacers, York, Pennsylvania	.722

ASA WOMEN'S MAJOR SLOW PITCH RECORDS

Highest batting average

.857—Princess Carpenter, Rutenschroer Floral, Cincinnati, Ohio (1973)

Most homeruns

5 each—Patsy Danson, Carter's Rebel, Jacksonville, Florida (1970), and Sue Taylor, Huntington YMCA, New York (1970)

ASA WOMEN'S CLASS A SLOW PITCH

1973 Redford Stingers, Detroit, Michigan
1974 Seaman's IGA, Athens, Ohio
1975 Shamrocks, Winston-Salem, North Carolina
1976 Rustic Bar, Duluth, Minnesota
1977 Cotter's Penn Hill, Penn Hills, Pennsylvania
1978 Stillwater A's, Stillwater, Oklahoma
1979 Northside Knights of Columbus, Cincinnati, Ohio
1980 Encore, Prince George's County, Virginia
1981 Orlando Stars, Orlando, Florida
1982 Circle K Roadrunners, Tempe, Arizona
1983 Somerset, Sacramento, California
1984 Mr. A's Express, Sacramento, California
1985 Tuffie's, Bloomington, Minnesota
1986 Comfort Inn, Raleigh, North Carolina
1987 Stompers, Richmond, Virginia
1987 Stompers, Richmond, Virginia
1988 Bally, Orlando, Florida
1989 Bally, Orlando, Florida

1990 Vernon's, Jacksonville, Florida
1991 Destin Roofing, Destin, Florida
1992 Drug Free All-Stars, Millersville, Maryland

ASA WOMEN'S MAJOR CHURCH SLOW PITCH

1979 Mt. Herman Methodist, Graham, North Carolina
1980 Rock Creek Methodist, Snow Camp, North Carolina
1981 South Main Baptist, Houston, Texas
1982 First Baptist, Tallahassee, Florida
1983 First Baptist, Tallahassee, Florida
1984 CME Crushettes, Warner Robins, Georgia
1985 Faith Baptist, Wichita Falls, Texas
1986 Rock Creek, Graham, North Carolina
1987 North Cleveland Church of God, Cleveland, Tennessee
1988 First Baptist of Houston, Houston, Texas
1989 First Baptist of Houston, Texas
1990 Westside Baptist, Jasper, Alabama
1991 First Baptist Red, Milton, Florida
1992 Immaculate Conception, Tyler, Texas

ASA WOMEN'S CLASS A CHURCH SLOW PITCH

1988 First Baptist, Muskogee, Oklahoma
1989 First Baptist, Muskogee, Oklahoma
1990 First Baptist, Muskogee, Oklahoma
1991 Mount Olive, Cleveland, Tennessee
1992 Hillcrest, Jacksonville, Florida

UNITED STATES SLO-PITCH SOFTBALL ASSOCIATION MEN'S MAJOR WORLD SERIES CHAMPIONS		
Year	Champion	Location of Series
1971	Accurate Welding of Milwaukee, Wisconsin	Las Vegas, Nevada
1972	Marasco's Variety Faire of Milwaukee, Wisconsin	Oak Creek, Wisconsin
1973	Bay Area Merchants of Richmond, California	Southgate, Michigan
1974	Dino's Pizza of Detroit Michigan	Pinole, California
1975	Snyder's Softball Club of Detroit, Michigan	Rochester, New York
1976	Snyder's Softball Club of Detroit, Michigan	Wyandotte, Michigan
1977	Mazzola Castle of Rochester, New York	Petersburg, Virginia
1978	Howard's Furniture of Denver, North Carolina	Petersburg, Virginia
1979	Nelson's Painting Service of Oklahoma	Kinston, North Carolina
1980	Campbell's Carpet of Concord, California	Concord, California
1981	Howard's Western Steer of Denver, North Carolina	Winston-Salem, North Carolina
1982	Jerry's Caterers of Miami, Florida	Greensboro, North Carolina
1983	Jerry's Caterers of Miami, Florida	Greensboro, North Carolina
1984	Elite Coating of Gordon, Georgia	Indianapolis, Indiana
1985	Elite Coating of Gordon, Georgia	Greensboro, North Carolina
1986	Smythe Sox of Houston, Texas	Greensboro, North Carolina
1987	Smythe Sox of Houston, Texas	Waterloo, Iowa
1988	Steele's Silver Bullets of Grafton, Ohio	Long Beach, California
1989	Superior-Apollo Softball of Windsor Locks, Connecticut	Omaha, Nebraska
1990	Ritch's-Kirks of Harrisburg, North Carolina	Greensboro, North Carolina
1991	Ritch's/Superior of Windsor Locks, Connecticut	Daytona Beach, Florida
1992	Ritch's/Superior of Windsor Locks, Connecticut	Daytona Beach, Florida

UNITED STATES SLO-PITCH SOFTBALL ASSOCIATION MEN'S MAJOR WORLD SERIES MOST VALUABLE PLAYERS

Oddly enough, no player has ever won this prestigious award more than once. Listed below are the recipients of this coveted award.

1971 James Mortl, Accurate Welding of Milwaukee, Wisconsin
1972 Dick Polgar, Marasco's Variety Faire of Milwaukee, Wisconsin
1973 Charles Pierce, Bay Area Merchants of Richmond, California
1974 Joe Patti, Dino's Pizza of Detroit, Michigan
1975 Doug Gerdes, Snyders Softball Club of Detroit, Michigan

1976	Rick Pinto, Snyders Softball Club of Detroit, Michigan
1977	Jerry Laspanara, Mazzola Castle of Rochester, New York
1978	Denny Hogan, Howard's Furniture of Denver, North Carolina
1979	Chick Downing, Nelson's Painting Serv. of Oklahoma City, Oklahoma
1980	Buddy Slater, Campbell's Carpets of Concord, California
1981	Rick Scherr, Howard's Western Steer of Denver, North Carolina
1982	Greg Fuhrman, Jerry's Caterers of Miami, Florida
1983	Bruce Meade, Jerry's Caterers of Miami, Florida
1984	Craig Elliott, Elite Coating of Gordon, Georgia
1985	Rick Wheeler, Elite Coating of Gordon, Georgia
1986	Doug Brown, Smythe Sox of Houston, Texas
1987	Billy Blake, Smythe Sox of Houston, Texas
1988	Rick Weiterman, Steele's Silver Bullets of Grafton, Ohio
1989	Clyde Guy, Superior-Apollo Softball of Windsor Locks, Connecticut
1990	Cecil Whitehead, Ritch's-Kirks of Harrisburg, North Carolina
1991	Dirk Androff, Ritch's/Superior of Windsor Locks, Connecticut
1992	Dave Steffen, Ritch's/Superior of Windsor Locks, Connecticut

Fins and Females *This is one of the ways they got publicity for the women's game in the late 1950s.*

(Amateur Softball Association)

III. ASSORTED RECORDS

ASA MEN'S MAJOR 16 INCH SLOW PITCH NATIONAL CHAMPIONS

1964	Bobcats, Chicago, Illinois
1965	Bobcats, Chicago, Illinois
1966	Sobies, Chicago, Illinois
1967	Sobies, Chicago, Illinois
1968	Sobies, Chicago, Illinois
1969	Dr. Carlucci Bobcats, Chicago, Illinois
1970	Dr. Carlucci Bobcats, Chicago, Illinois
1971	Dr. Carlucci Bobcats, Chicago, Illinois
1972	Dr. Carlucci Bobcats, Chicago, Illinois
1973	Dr. Carlucci Bobcats, Chicago, Illinois
1974	Strikers, Chicago, Illinois
1975	Josef's, Chicago, Illinois
1976	Dr. Carlucci Bobcats, Chicago, Illinois
1977	Bobcats, Chicago, Illinois
1978	Bobcats, Chicago, Illinois
1979	Bobcats, Chicago, Illinois
1980	Har Crest Whips, Chicago, Illinois
1981	C&K Roller-Bobcats, Harvey, Illinois
1982	Park Avenue Spats, Chicago, Illinois
1983	Budweiser Whips, Chicago, Illinois
1984	Budweiser Whips, Chicago, Illinois
1985	Touch, Chicago, Illinois
1986	Ducks, Oak Lawn, Illinois
1987	Sports Station, Blue Island, Illinois
1988	Whips, Chicago, Illinois
1989	Whips, Chicago, Illinois
1990	Pete's Hideaway Whips, Chicago, Illinois
1991	Splinter Sporting Goods, Mt. Prospect, Illinois
1992	Lettuce, Chicago, Illinois

ASA MEN'S 16 INCH CLASS A SLOW PITCH CHAMPIONS

1984	Golden Q, Mishawaka, Indiana
1985	Last Chance, Aberdeen, South Dakota

1986	Edison Park Inn, Chicago, Illinois
1987	Aces, Chicago, Illinois
1988	Doctors, Chicago, Illinois
1989	Aces, Chicago, Illinois
1990	Chicago Gamblers, Chicago, Illinois
1991	Stickmen, Chicago, Illinois
1992	Ice, Cicero, Illinois

ASA WOMEN'S MAJOR MODIFIED NATIONAL CHAMPIONS

1984	Alibi Inn, Staten Island, New York
1985	Alibi Inn, Staten Island, New York
1986	Zerbo's Hellbenders, Staten Island, New York
1987	Talk of the Town, Staten Island, New York
1988	Dennis' Islanders, Staten Island, New York
1989	Kulick's, Keene, New Hampshire
1990	Dennis' Islanders, Staten Island, New York
1991	The House That Jack Built, Buffalo, New York
1992	Guaynabo Mets, Puerto Rico

ASA MEN'S CLASS A MODIFIED PITCH NATIONAL CHAMPIONS

1987	LSI-Triangle, Delano, Minnesota
1988	Hurley's, Albany, New York
1989	All-Star Chevrolet, Milford, Delaware
1990	Green Oak Cannons, Indianapolis, Indiana
1991	Hawks, Roxbury, Massachusetts
1992	Warriors, Chapel Hill, North Carolina

ASA CO-ED SLOW PITCH NATIONAL CHAMPIONS

1982	C.E. Zumstein, Englewood, Ohio
1983	Microlights, Coon Rapids, Minnesota

1984 Video Box Office, Coon Rapids, Minnesota
1985 Green Oak Cannons, Indianapolis, Indiana
1986 Lab Petroleum, San Antonio, Texas
1987 SA Cannan's, San Antonio, Texas
1988 South Florida Softball Club, Harbor Island, Florida
1989 Braves, Jacksonville, Florida
1990 Steffe's Sports, Celestine, Indiana
1991 South Florida Softball Club, Hollywood, Florida
1992 Lewis Drywall, Orlando, Florida

ASA CO-ED CLASS A SLOW PITCH NATIONAL CHAMPIONS

1991 Chick's Crew, Ardmore, Oklahoma
1992 Tharaldson's, Fargo, North Dakota

ASA MEN'S 35-AND-OVER SLOW PITCH NATIONAL CHAMPIONS

1987 Budweiser, Detroit, Michigan
1988 Nothdurft Tool & Die, Mt. Clemens, Michigan
1989 Nothdurft Tool & Die, Mt. Clemens, Michigan
1990 Nothdruft Tool & Die, Mt. Clemens, Michigan

1991 Virginia Pets, Annandale, Virginia
1992 Nothdurft Tool & Die, Mt. Clemens, Michigan

ASA MEN'S SENIOR 50-AND-OVER SLOW PITCH CHAMPIONS

1992 Great Lakes UAW #1112, Youngstown, Ohio

ASA WOMEN'S MAJOR INDUSTRIAL SLOW PITCH NATIONAL CHAMPIONS

1979 Philip Morris, Richmond, Virginia
1980 Provident Vets, Chattanooga, Tennessee
1981 Provident Vets, Chattanooga, Tennessee
1982 Provident Vets, Chattanooga, Tennessee
1983 Provident Vets, Chattanooga, Tennessee
1984 Cargill Hold, Mount, Minnesota
1985 Sheriff's Stars, Pensacola, Florida
1986 Sheriff's Stars, Pensacola, Florida
1987 Provident Vets, Chattanooga, Tennessee
1988 Provident Vets, Chattanooga, Tennessee
1989 Provident Vets, Chattanooga, Tennessee
1990 Shaw Industries, Dalton, Georgia
1991 TI Express, Dallas, Texas
1992 Provident, East Ridge, Tennessee

IV. NATIONAL SOFTBALL HALL OF FAME

* Deceased

HALL OF FAME MEN'S FAST PITCH

*1957	Harold (Shifty) Gears	Pitcher
*1957	Sam (Sambo) Elliott	Pitcher
1958	Al Linde	Pitcher
1959	Bernie Kampschmidt, Fort Wayne, Indiana	Catcher
*1959	Clyde (Dizzy) Kirkendall	Pitcher
*1960	Warren (Fireball) Gerber	Pitcher
1960	Clarence (Buck) Miller, Memphis, Tennessee	Pitcher
1960	Jim Ramage, Fort Wayne, Indiana	Shortstop
1961	John (Cannonball) Baker, Stanford, Connecticut	Pitcher
*1961	Ben Crain	Pitcher
1961	Hugh Johnston, Ft. Wayne, Indiana	First Base
1963	John Hunter, Clearwater, Florida	Pitcher
*1963	B.E. (Gene) Martin	ASA Executive Secretary, Treasurer
*1963	Bill West	Pitcher
1964	Tom Castle, Rochester, New York	First Base
1965	Roy Stephenson, Muttontown, New York	Pitcher
1966	Jim Chambers, Oshkosh, Wisconsin	Pitcher
*1966	Robert Forbes	Outfielder
*1967	Noland Whitlock	Shortstop
*1967	Bill Wojie	Third Base
1967	Ronald Kronwitter, Mishawaka, Indiana	Pitcher
*1968	Leroy Hess	Catcher
1968	Bob Sprentall, Clearwater, Florida	Outfielder
1970	John Spring, Aurora, Illinois	Pitcher
1970	Frankie Williams, Stratford, Connecticut	Second Base
1970	John (Buster) Ziegler, Miami, Florida	Outfielder
1971	Ray (Ned) Wickersham, Palestine, Illinois	Outfielder

1972	Don Ropp, Aurora, Illinois	Third Base
1972	Jerry Curtis, Clearwater, Florida	Outfielder
*1973	Richard Tomlinson	Shortstop
*1974	Charles Justice	Pitcher
1976	Bobby Spell, Lake Charles, Louisiana	Pitcher
1978	Tom Moore, Clearwater, Florida	Infielder
1978	Doug Mason, Clearwater, Florida	Infielder
1979	Bill Massey, Houston, Texas	Pitcher
*1979	Weldon Haney	Pitcher
1980	Ron Weathersby, Clearwater, Florida	Outfielder
1981	Harvey Sterkel, Aurora, Illinois	Pitcher
1981	Bill Parker, Clearwater, Florida	Infielder
1981	George Adam, Branford, Connecticut	First Base
*1983	Bonnie Jones	Pitcher
1983	Robert Kyukendall, Clearwater, Florida	Catcher
1984	Bob Barron, Aurora, Illinois	Second Base
1986	Herb Dudley, Clearwater, Florida	Pitcher
1988	John Anquillare, New Haven, Connecticut	Shortstop
1988	Vinnie Caserto, Marlboro, New York	First Base-Outfielder
1988	Al Lewis, Milford, Connecticut	Pitcher
1989	Joe Lynch, Nashville, Tennessee	Pitcher
1989	Carl Walker, Providence, Rhode Island	Outfielder-First Base
1990	Harry (Coon) Rosen, Las Vegas, Nevada	Pitcher
1990	Abe Baker, Cranston, Rhode Island	Outfield
*1991	Eddie King	Pitcher
1991	Sam Lombardo, Detroit, Michigan	First Base-Outfield
*1992	Elmer Rohrs	Pitcher
1993	Leo Kuken, Deerfield Beach, Florida	Pitcher

The Official Record Book

MEN'S SLOW PITCH

1973	Myron Reinhardt, Alexandria, Kentucky	Catcher-Outfielder
1974	Frank De Luca, Stratford, Connecticut	Pitcher
1975	Donald Rardin, Lexington, Kentucky	Pitcher-Infielder
1982	Bill Cole, Sterling Heights, Michigan	Third Base
*1984	J.D. McDonald	Shortstop
1985	James Galloway, Westbury, New York	Infielder
1986	Hal Wiggins, Ft. Thomas, Kentucky	Outfielder
*1987	Carl (Tex) Collins	Catcher
1988	Eugene Fisher, Denver, North Carolina	Catcher
1989	Raymond Brown, Covington, Kentucky	Third Base
1989	Mike Gouin, Detroit, Michigan	Outfield
1989	Eddie Zolna, Chicago, Illinois	Pitcher
1990	Dick Bartel, San Antonio, Texas	Outfield
1990	Tom Beall, Monticello, Georgia	Outfield
1990	Ken Clark, Stratford, Connecticut	Pitcher
1992	Lou Del Mastro, Pittsburgh, Pennsylvania	Pitcher
1992	Paul Tomasovich, Pittsburgh, Pennsylvania	Third Base
1993	Don Arndt, Sherrills Ford, North Carolina	Pitcher
1993	Eddie Finnegan, Stratford, Connecticut	Shortstop
*1993	Steve Loya, Pyramid Cafe, Cleveland, Ohio	Catcher

WOMEN'S FAST PITCH

*1957	Amy Peralta Shelton	Pitcher
*1957	Marie Wadlow	Pitcher
*1959	Betty Evans Grayson	Pitcher
1960	Nina Korgan, New Orleans, Louisiana	Pitcher
1960	Ruth Sears, Santa Ana, California	First Base
1963	Kay Rich, Fresno, California	Shortstop
1964	Margaret Dobson, Portland, Oregon	Third Base
1965	Marjorie Law, Chandler, Arizona	Pitcher, Outfielder, Infielder
1966	Carolyn Thome Hart, Pekin, Illinois	Outfielder
1969	Jeanne Contel, Fresno, California	Infielder
1969	Mickey Stratton, Stratford, Connecticut	Catcher
1970	Dot Wilkinson, Phoeniz, Arizona	Catcher
*1971	Virginia Busick	Pitcher
1972	Bertha Tickey, Stratford, Connecticut	Pitcher

1973	Estelle (Ricki) Caito, Phoenix, Arizona	Second Base
1973	Gloria May, Kerman, California	First Base
1975	Kathryn (Sis) King, Shelton, Connecticut	Catcher
1976	Pat Harrison, Stratford, Connecticut	Outfielder
1976	Pat Walker, Orlando, Florida	Outfielder
1980	Jean Daves, Orlando, Florida	Pitcher
1981	Shirley Topley, Tustin, California	First Base
1981	Carol Spanks, Tustin, California	Infielder-Pitcher
1982	Nancy Welborn, Tustin, California	Pitcher
*1982	Nance Ito	Catcher
1982	Billie Harris, Phoenix, Arizona	Pitcher-Infielder
1983	Donna Lopiano, Austin, Texas	Pitcher-First Base
1983	Joan Joyce, Stratford, Connecticut	Pitcher
1984	Mickey Davis, Sunset Beach, California	Outfielder
1984	Jackie Rice, Monmouth, Oregon	Pitcher
1984	Diane Kalliam, San Francisco, California	Outfield-Shortstop
1985	Sharron Backus, Fullerton, California	Shortstop
1985	Willie Roze, Wallingford, Connecticut	Outfielder
1985	E. Louise Albrecht, New Haven, Connecticut	Pitcher
1986	Chris Miner, Omaha, Nebraska	Infielder
1986	Peggy Kellers, Harrisonburg, Virginia	Catcher
1987	Lorene Ramsey, Pekin, Illinois	Pitcher
1987	Rose Marie Adams, Orange, California	Infielder
1991	Marilyn Rau, Phoenix, Arizona	Catcher
1991	Marlys Taber, Mundelein, Illinois	Shortstop
1992	Diane Schumacher, West Springfield, Massachusetts	First Base
1992	Carolyn Fitzwater, Portland, Oregon	Second Base

WOMEN'S SLOW PITCH

1976	Alberta Kohls Sims, Alexandria, Kentucky	Outfielder
1978	Norma Eschenbrenner Ante, Cincinnati, Ohio	Outfielder
1979	Donna Wolfe, Covington, Ohio	Outfielder
1982	Judy Hedgecock, Satellite Beach, Florida	Pitcher
1983	Ida Jean (Hoppy) Hopkins, Cleveland, Ohio	Shortstop

COMING TO TERMS WITH THE GAMES OF SOFTBALL

⁹ **Glossary**

It has long been assumed that the vocabulary of softball and that of baseball are identical or almost so. This wrong assumption is commonly made by those who think of softball as a pale reflection of baseball. Folks who play the game and spend odd hours with their heads poked in rule books or the latest issue of *Balls and Strikes* know better.

Though many of the terms are the same, they commonly have a different meaning in the context of softball. Some of these differences are slight, others substantial, and still others will have separate meanings within the context of softball depending on whether or not they apply to the slow pitch, fast pitch, modified pitch or 16 inch game. In other cases a term may have a separate meaning, depending on whether it is applied within the context of the Amateur Softball Association (ASA) or the United States Slo-Pitch Softball Association (U.S.S.S.A.). For instance, a base on balls is awarded in the ASA for four balls, while it only takes three in the U.S.S.S.A.

Over time, the rules of softball have become truly complex and about as easy to read as a computer manual. The 1993 Amateur Softball Association *Guide and Playing Rules Book* contains 296 pages, of which 216 are densely-packed pages of rules covering every conceivable contingency. The rules, however, are the rules and nothing can substitute for diligent study. However, some of the rules amount to definitions and some of those key definitions are repeated here. In other words, this glossary is not a substitute for the rules, but rather, is meant to give a good idea of what those rules are and what the terms that define them mean. The rule book definitions will be carefully noted as such, as they carry with them the responsibility of rules interpretation. In cases of particularly complicated definitions, the "play" interpretations are included and carefully marked as such.

There is also softball slang and more. Just keeping track of the variations on the basic game and various names given to it over the years is a task in itself. Among others, these include: Army ball, big ball, church ball, diamond ball, fast ball, indoor baseball, indoor-outdoor, kitten ball, lightning ball, mush ball, night ball, Over the Line, playground ball, playground baseball, recreation ball, serve us ball (also, service ball), 16 inch and twilight ball.

It is also true that much of organized softball is based on tournament play, so terms such as double elimination, loser's bracket and round-robin come into play.

What follows is a glossary incorporating far-flung slang, historic terms and terms right out of the rule book.

It is worth keeping in mind that with the exception of Over the Line softball the numerous modern variations in the game—slow pitch, modified fast pitch, co-ed and 16 inch—are based on rules and definitions created for fast pitch prior to the Second World War, so special attention will be paid to pointing out those terms that apply *only* to one form or other of the game.

aboard   A player on base is said to be "aboard."

airway   A term used to describe the path that a ball goes through in underhand pitching.

alley softball   An urban form of softball played in alleys and described in the chapter on Alley Games in *The Great American Book . . .Games* by Fred Ferretti:

Softball, alley style, carries rigid rules. A softball hit off the wires and caught is an out. A ball that hits or even grazes a house wall and is caught before hitting the ground is an out. A ball that lands atop any shed, house, or garage roof is an out. So is a ball landing in any yard.

And what was safe, you ask? Any line drive to dead center (straight down the alley), so long as it isn't caught. Pull hitters shun alley Softball.

---

altered bat   Defined in the ASA *Guide and Playing Rules Book*: "A bat is considered altered when the physical structure of a legal softball bat has been changed. Replacing the handle of a metal bat with a wooden or other type handle, inserting material inside the bat, applying excessive tape (more than two layers) to the bat grip, or painting a bat at the top or bottom for other than identification purposes are examples of altering a bat. Replacing the grip with another legal grip is not considered altering the bat. A 'flare' or 'cone' grip attached to the bat is considered an altered bat." ASA Rule 7, Sec. 1d specifies the following penalty for entering the batter's box with an altered bat: "The ball is dead; the batter is out; and, without warning, he is ejected from the game. Baserunners may not advance."

appeal play   The ASA *Guide and Playing Rules Book* states: "An appeal play is a play on which an umpire may not make a decision until requested by a manager, coach, or player. The appeal must be made before the next legal or illegal pitch, or before the defensive team has left the field. At the conclusion of the game, an appeal can be made up until the umpires leave the field of play."

The ASA definition also includes this amplification: The defensive team has left the field when the pitcher and all infielders have clearly vacated their normal fielding positions and have left fair territory on their way to the bench or dugout area."

An example: With a runner on first, the second batter hits a double. The first runner goes to third but fails to touch second. The umpire observes this, but no appeal is made. The second batter goes to second. Since no appeal was made, it is as if the first batter actually touched second.

arbiter An umpire.

arc A key measurement that essentially *defines* slow pitch softball. It is the point at which the ball reaches its highest point in its trajectory from the pitcher's hand to the plate. It is measured in feet from the ground to that high point and there is a maximum and minimum arc in organized slow pitch. Some unofficial leagues allow an unlimited arc, which gives some pitchers a tremendous advantage over the batter, especially when it can peak at 20 to 25 feet and still cross the plate. In the official game, anything above the maximum arc or below the minimum arc will be declared an illegal pitch and a ball will be awarded by the umpire to the batter as long as he doesn't swing at the pitch. The prescribed ASA arc is between 6 feet and 12 feet from the ground. The U.S.S.S.A. arc, on the other hand, is between 3 feet from the release point and 10 feet from the ground.

Army ball One of a number of names for softball and its many early variations; it probably stems from the fact that an early form of the game of softball was played on Army bases before, during and after World War I. The other names include: baseball (q.v.), big ball, church ball, diamond ball, indoor baseball, indoor-outdoor, kitten ball, kitty-ball, lightning ball, mush ball, night ball, panty waist, playground ball, playground baseball, recreation ball, serve us ball and twilight ball.

assist A fielding credit earned by a player who helps a teammate make a putout. Should the teammate fail to make the putout because of a misplay, the first player is still given credit for an assist.

away (1) The number of outs, such as "one away" instead of "one out." (2) A game played at a field other than one's home field.

backstop While a catcher is often called "the backstop," the term is more often applied to the fencing behind the plate.

back up To take a position to the rear of a teammate to retrieve any balls that the teammate might fail to catch.

bag A base. Also called "sack," "hassock," "pillow," "canvas," etc.

balance point The point in the pitching delivery in which the right hand is at its highest point above the head and the left foot is at its highest point above the ground.

balk Making a motion to pitch without immediately delivering the ball to the batter. This is really more of a baseball than a softball term, but it is useful in describing an illegal pitch in fast or slow pitch softball.

ball (1) A pitched ball that does not enter the pitcher's strike zone and that the batter does not attempt to hit. (2) The game ball. Softballs for the dominant forms of the game must weigh between six and a quarter and seven ounces and be between 11⅞ and 12 inches in circumference.

base The four "stations" on a ball field which runners on the offensive team must touch in succession before scoring—first base, second base, third base and home base, known as home plate. The three bases are each 15 inches square. Home plate is 17 inches wide.

baseball (1) The game that sired softball in the form of indoor baseball. (2) A term that has been used to describe women's fast pitch softball, more specifically, "baseball modified." It is of some significance that despite the title of Viola Mitchell's 1942 *Softball for Girls*, the terms softball and baseball were used interchangably.

base on balls (1) The penalty imposed on a pitcher who delivers four balls to a batter. The batter is allowed to go to first base. Officially defined in the ASA rules: "A base on balls permits a batter to gain first base without liability to be put out and is awarded to a batter by the umpire when four pitches are judged to be balls." For slow pitch *only* the ASA adds this to the definition: "If the pitcher desires to walk a batter intentionally, he may do so by notifying the plate umpire who shall award the batter first base." (2) The U.S.S.S.A. definition of a base on balls in slow pitch softball is that it occurs when "three pitches are adjudged to be balls."

base path A base path is an imaginary line three feet (0.91 meter) on either side of a direct line between the runner and the base he is advancing to. A runner who steps outside the base path to avoid a tag is out. The runner can move outside if he or she is trying to avoid a fielder who is attempting to catch a batted ball.

baserunner A baserunner is a player of the team at bat who has finished his turn at bat, reached first, second or third base, and has not yet been put out. In fast pitch, the base runner is allowed to lead off the base before the pitch or to steal during the pitch. In slow pitch, the runner must keep contact with the base until the pitched ball reaches home or is hit. If the runner runs early, the runner is out and "no pitch" is declared.

bat A regulation softball bat must be made of one piece of hard wood or of another approved material, no more than 2⅛ inches in diameter at its thickest part, no more than 34 inches long and not exceeding 38 ounces in weight.

bat ring A metal or plastic ring for measuring the diameter or circumference of a legal bat.

batted ball "A batted ball is any ball that hits the bat, or is hit by the bat, and lands either in fair or foul territory," is how it is defined in the ASA rules, which continue, "No intention to hit the ball is necessary."

batter The player who puts the ball in play. He or she must take position within the lines of the batter's box and must avoid interfering with the catcher.

batter-runner A batter-runner is a player who has finished his turn at bat but has not yet been put out or touched first base.

batter's box An area to either side of home plate (three feet wide and seven feet long under ASA rules) in which the batter must stand when it is his or her turn at bat. It is defined in the ASA rules this way: "The batter's box is the area to which the batter is restricted while in position with the intention of helping his team to obtain runs. The lines are considered as being within the batter's box. Prior to the pitch, he may touch the lines, but no part of his foot may be outside the lines." The U.S.S.S.A. batter's box is smaller (5½ feet long and 2½ feet wide), which gives the pitcher a slight advantage by limiting the batter's mobility.

battery The combination of the pitcher and the catcher.

batting average The number of hits divided by the number of times at bat. The result is usually expressed in three decimals.

batting order According to ASA Rule 1, Sec. 2: "The batting order is the official listing of offensive players in the order in which members of that team must come to bat. When the lineup card is submitted, it shall also include each player's position." If a player is caught batting out of order he or she will be called out if brought to the attention of the umpire prior to the first pitch to the next batter.

beat out To hit a ball to an infielder and reach first base ahead of that fielder's throw, for a hit.

beep ball Sound-emitting ball used in a form of softball played by the blind. ·

behind in the count Expression said of a pitcher when he or she has thrown more balls than strikes. It is also said of a batter when he or she is at bat and has more strikes than balls.

behind the back pitch One of the spectacular pitching variations permitted in U.S.S.S.A. slow pitch softball along with pitching between the legs and other variations. This ability stems from the U.S.S.S.A. rule that states that the pitcher must have one foot on the rubber at the time of the pitch, but that the other foot can be anywhere. The pitcher can do almost anything that he or she wants to do—including moving one's arm back and forth repeatedly before releasing the ball—as long as that one foot is in place. ASA rules permit none of this.

bench (1) Seating for players in uniform when not in the field. (2) To take a player out of the game; to be benched.

berndes An Over the Line term for an attempted home run that lands in the pull corner. (See also MISS.)

big ball One of a number of names for softball. See also ARMY BALL for a full listing of synonyms for softball.

bite Word yelled by players in Over the Line beach softball when trying to coax a ball to stay in on the court.

bleeder A batted ball that just trickles past the defensive players for a "weak" base hit.

blem Ball with a minor cosmetic defect; cannot be used in official game play. Blems are often sold as practice balls.

blocked ball As defined in the ASA *Guide and Playing Rules Book*: "A blocked ball is a batted or thrown ball that is touched, stopped, or handled by a person not engaged in the game, or which touches any object that is not part of the official equipment or official playing area."

The rules also contain this amplification: "If any illegal offensive equipment prevented the defense from making an out, the ball is dead, inter-ference will be ruled, the player being played on shall be declared out, and each other runner must return to the last base touched at the time of the dead ball declaration. If no apparent play is obvious, a blocked ball is ruled, no one is called out, and each runner must return to the last base touched at the time of the dead ball declaration."

A blocked ball is called when it strikes a spectator, but not when it hits a coach.

blooper A batted ball that arches over the heads of the infielders and drops in front of the outfielders for a base hit.

blue Any umpire from the color of his or her uniform. It is used in lines like "Oh, come on, blue" after a dubious call. It is not seen as derogatory; Dan McLaughlin, an umpire, wrote a column for *Sierra Softball* entitled "A Blue Point of View."

blue stitch Describing a ball with a COEFFICIENT OF RESTITUTION (or COR) of 50.

bobble Juggling the ball while attempting a catch, or dropping the ball for an error.

bong ball A very simple game for six or seven year olds, which, like TEE BALL, creates an awareness of the softball's fundamentals. The ball is hit off a tee with a fat plastic bat.

bottom The second part of an inning. For instance, the second half of the fourth inning (when the home team is at bat) is known as the "bottom" of the fourth. The first part of an inning (when the visiting team is at bat) is known as the "top."

box score The number of runs, hits and errors at the end of the game for each team.

bunt A bunt is a legally tapped ball in fast pitch *only*. It is not swung at, but intentionally met with the bat and tapped within the infield. It is, however, illegal in slow pitch; if it occurs the batter is called out and all runners have to return to their original bases.

burned A batted ball that is hit over the head of an outfielder. One of a series of contemporary slang softball terms collected by Umpire Bob

Pense, Jr., of Tidewater, Virginia, and published in *Balls and Strikes*. He adds: "In a fenced park, look out for that close call at third or home. If no outfield fences, Blue hollers for outfielders chasing the ball to bring back one coffee with cream and three sugars."

cabbageball   Another name for Chicago 16 inch softball.

called game   A game ended by the chief umpire because of the weather or some other such reason.

can   The literal name (not slang) for home plate in Over the line softball play.

catch   The ASA *Guide and Playing Rules Book* defines catch officially:

A catch is a legally caught ball which occurs when the fielder catches a batted, pitched, or thrown ball with his hand(s) or glove. If the ball is merely held in the fielder's arm(s) or prevented from dropping to the ground by some part of the fielder's body, equipment, or clothing, the catch is not completed until the ball is in the grasp of the fielder's hand(s) or glove. It is not a catch if a fielder, immediately after he contacts the ball, collides with another player, umpire, or a fence, or falls to the ground and drops the ball as a result of the collision or falling to the ground. In establishing a valid catch, the fielder shall hold the ball long enough to prove he has complete control of it or that his release of the ball is voluntary and intentional. If a player drops the ball after reaching into his glove to remove it, or while in the act of throwing it, it is a valid catch.

NOTE: A ball which strikes anything other than a defensive player while it is in flight is ruled the same as if it struck the ground.

The definitions section of the ASA rules also contains this series of amplifying examples in which B stands for batter and F for fielder:

PLAY (1)—A legal catch occurs when a fielder holds the ball (a) in his hands(s), (b) under his arms(s), (c) in his cap, (d) in his glove. RULING—(a) Yes, (b) No, (c) No, (d) Yes.

PLAY (2) The batter hits a line drive which, after passing the first baseman, strikes the umpire while the ball is over fair ground. The ball ricochets and is fielded by the third baseman while still in flight. RULING—This is not a catch. The batter would have to be thrown out or tagged out.

PLAY (3)—The first baseman and the second baseman both attempt to field a fly ball. Without touching the ground, the ball strikes the second baseman on the head and, while still in the air (hasn't touched the ground), is caught by the first baseman. RULING—This is a legally caught fly ball.

PLAY (4)—The batter hits a fly to the center fielder. The center fielder gets the ball in his hand(s) but drops it (a) when he falls to the ground and rolls over, or (b) when he collides with a fielder or a wall, or (c) when he starts to throw to the infield. RULING—In (a) and (b) it is not a catch. In (c) it is a legal catch if the ball was held long enough for the centerfielder to regain his balance but is then dropped in a motion associated with an intended throw.

---

catcher's box   The catcher's box is that area within which the catcher must remain until, according to ASA rules:

---

a. (fast pitch only) The pitch is released. The lines are to be considered within the catcher's box.

b. (slow pitch only) The pitched ball is batted, touches the ground or plate, or reaches the catcher's box. The lines are to be considered within the catcher's box, and all parts of the catcher's body and/or equipment must be within the catcher's box until the pitched ball is batted or reaches the catcher's box. The catcher is considered within the box unless he touches the ground outside the catcher's box.

Should the catcher step out of the catcher's box an illegal pitch shall be called immediately, and the batter will be awarded a ball, provided he does not swing at the illegal pitch.

Co-ed Softball   *A group of batters in a New Bedford, Massachusetts, co-ed softball tournament. They are all from the Donut and Deli Barn in Taunton, Massachusetts. They are Audrey Collins, Guy Butler, Howie Chaves and Cathy Fearing.* (Russell Mott)

change of pace/changeup   An intentionally slower pitch used to disrupt a batter's timing. A fast ball pitcher's ability to vary the speed of his delivery of pitches can be especially potent. The reality of this pitch can be quite stunning. Debbie Doom, the dominant female pitcher of the 1980s and the star of the 1991 Pan Am Games, is able to cut 15 m.p.h. off of her 65-m.p.h. fastball.

charged conference   A meeting of a team representative and player during a game for a reason other than an injury. There can only be one charged conference per inning with a batter or baserunner.

Here are the two forms of charged conference which appear in the ASA rules:

(a). *Defensive Conference.* The defensive team requests a suspension of play for any reason, and a representative (not in the field) of the defensive team enters the playing field and gives the umpire cause to believe that he has delivered a message (by any means) to the pitcher. When the manager crosses the foul line on the return to the dugout, the conference is over.

(b). *Offensive Conference.* The offensive team requests a suspension of play to allow the manager or other team representatives to confer with the batter and/or baserunners.

chatter   In softball, the continual encouragement (to your team) and the discouragement to the other team that goes on during a game. For instance, some of the chatter that you offer your

pitcher might be ritual lines like, "No batter here" and "They're scared of you out there."

choke (1) To grip a softball bat more closely to the "trademark" than is usual. "Choking the Bat" is often done to gain accuracy in hitting the ball or in cases when a bat is too heavy for the batter. (2) To misplay, usually in a crucial moment in the game, because of anxiety, apprehension or tension.

chopped ball A swing of the bat in which the batter strikes downward with a chopping motion so that the ball bounces high into the air. The purpose of a chopped ball is to allow the runner to reach first base by beating the throw. In slow pitch softball only the batter of a chopped ball is declared out and runners must return to their original bases.

claw A one-handed catch, Over the Line style.

clean-up batter Number four in the batting order, usually a power hitter.

Clincher A trademarked name for a line of softballs produced by the deBeer Company of Albany, New York. Introduced in 1931, the ball was created for longevity on urban pavement.

coach A coach is a member of the team at bat who takes his place within one of the coach's boxes on the field to direct the players of his team in running the bases. Two coaches are allowed. One coach can have in his possession in the coach's box a scorebook, pen or pencil and an indicator, all of which shall be used for scorekeeping or recordkeeping purposes only. No communication equipment is allowed.

coach's box An area where the coach stands and must remain during the game.

cock The action in which a pitcher holds the throwing hand at a right angle to the forearm in preparation for the wrist snap. (It is illegal in fast pitch.)

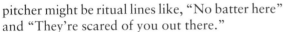

co-ed softball An official form of softball played by two teams, each composed of five men and five women who are positioned so that two men and two women are in the outfield, two men and two women are in the infield and one man and one woman pitch and catch.

coefficient of restitution The hardness of the softball or COR determined by throwing the ball against a rigid wall and measuring its rebound speed. The higher the COR the farther the ball will travel. The ASA requires a COR of 47 and the U.S.S.S.A. a COR of 50.

All manufacturers subscribe to a color code that enables anyone to determine the COR percentage of a ball. A ball with a red stitch has a COR of 47, a blue or white stitch a COR of 50 and a gold stitch a COR of 44.

complimentary runner A substitute baserunner who, by the mutual consent of the opposing managers, does not prevent the original runner from staying the game. (Not legal in ASA softball.)

COR (1) Short for coefficient of restitution, the hardness of the ball. (2) By extension, COR is used to refer to the center of the ball.

core The official name for the center of a softball. Traditionally made of long fibre kapok or compressed cork, most modern balls have cores made of cork and rubber or "polycore" cores made of polyurethane. The core is the largest part of the ball, having a diameter of approximately 3½ inches. Surrounding the core is a relatively thin layer of thread called the WINDING.

corner Portions of home plate; the part of the plate closest to a batter is known as "the inside corner." The part farthest from the batter is known as "the outside corner." The other bases are known as "the initial corner" (first base), the "keystone corner" (second base) and the "hot corner" (third base).

count The number of balls and strikes on the batter. A count of "one and two" means that the batter has one ball and two strikes on her.

counter A scored run; one that counts on the scoreboard.

cover One of the three components of a legal softball. It covers the other two components, the CORE and WINDING. Covers are generally made of first-grade leather, although some balls are wrapped with a synthetic leather cover. The cover is then cemented to the winding and hand stitched with a nylon thread; it is approximately ¹⁄₁₆ inch thick.

cripple-A league An early facetious name for slow pitch when it was still seen, as one writer put it, as "a game reserved for those who don't happen to care for violent exercise and big time competition."

crow hop "Fast pitch only" is the notation given along with this definition in the ASA *Guide and Playing Rules Book*: "A crow hop is defined as the act of a pitcher who steps or hops off the front of the pitcher's plate, replants the pivot foot, establishing a second impetus (or starting point), pushes off from the newly established starting point, and completes the delivery."

crowding the plate A batter moving close to the plate and refusing to back away with the pitch.

cut To swing at a pitched ball.

cut off To intercept a ball thrown to another teammate. A fielder will often cut off a throw aimed at home plate to trap a player running to another base.

cut-off player An infielder who gets into position to intercept a throw from the outfield.

cut the corner To throw a ball over the corner of home plate.

•D•

dead ball The ball is not in play and is not considered in play again until the pitcher has it in his possession, it is within eight feet (2.44 meters)

of the pitcher's plate, and "play ball" has been declared by the umpire.

deep (1) Term for pitched balls that fall behind the batter in slow pitch softball—analogous to "high" in baseball or fast pitch softball. A pitch that drops in front of a batter in slow pitch is called SHORT. (2) Describing a defensive player standing some distance beyond his or her usual playing position. It is the opposite of SHALLOW.

deep shot A homerun attempt in all forms of softball, but very common in Over the Line.

defensive conference See CHARGED CONFERENCE.

defensive interference See INTERFERENCE.

defensive team The team in the field.

defo A player who can take the 10th place in batting order in fast pitch *only* but plays only defense. See also DESIGNATED PLAYER.

delay steal An attempt to steal a base whereby the runner does not leave until the catcher releases the ball.

delayed steal An attempt to steal a base whereby the runner does not start her dash until the usual moment for attempting the steal has passed. (See also STEAL.)

deliver To pitch the ball.

designated player In current fast pitch only, a designated player may be used for any player, provided it is made known prior to the start of the game, and his name is indicated on the lineup sheet or score sheet as one of the nine hitters in the batting order. The starting DP may re-enter one time, as long as he or she goes back into the position in the batting order that he occupied when he or she left the game. The designated player or DP and the DEFO may never be on offense at the same time.

diamond The area formed by the four bases.

diamond ball One of a number of names for softball in its early days. (See also ARMY BALL for a full listing of synonyms for softball.)

die To be stranded on a base as the third out is made.

die-hards Term created to describe softball players who play in six or more competitive tournaments a year. There are approximately four million die-hards in the United States.

dink A short placement hit, Over the Line style.

dislodged base A base that is displaced from its proper position. A baserunner is not penalized for a dislodged base, nor is the runner expected to tag a base that is far out of its proper position.

do-or-die An outfield technique used to field a ground ball on the run, enabling the outfielder to release the ball quicker and produce more force behind it.

dome An Over the Line term that is usually preceded by the words "I'm in your," meaning the defense is getting a good read on the hitter.

double A hit that permits the batter-runner to safely reach second base without the aid of an error.

double-elimination Tournament format by which a team must be defeated twice before it is eliminated from play. It is the dominant format in the higher levels of the game, as it insures that a top team will not be eliminated too early in the tournament and that the weaker teams have two chances. In the second round of double-elimination play, winners meet winners and losers meet losers in a separate bracket of games known as the "losers bracket." A defeat in the loser's bracket eliminates the losing team from play. A first defeat for one of the original winners puts it into the loser's bracket where it can play as long as it wins.

To determine the number of games needed in double-elimination, multiply the number of teams by two and subtract by one. In some tournaments the two finalists play a best two out of three; in this case add two or three additional games.

Double-elimination differs from the other two tournament formats, which are "round robin" and "straight" or "single-elimination."

double play   A double play is a play by the defense resulting in two offensive players being legally put out.

double steal   A double steal occurs when two runners steal bases on the same play.

down   The number of outs; two down or two away means two outs.

DP   See DESIGNATED PLAYER.

drag bunt   Occurs when a batter executes a bunt at the last possible second in an attempt to catch the infielders by surprise, resulting in a base hit.

drifting   Timing the flight of a fly ball with movement of the body so that both will arrive at the same point simultaneously.

drilled, blitzed, schooled   Over the Line jargon for being on the bad end of a big inning.

drive   A hard-hit ball that travels in a fairly straight line.

drop, drop ball, drop pitch   In fast pitch *only*, it is a softball thrown with a straight downward spin with the ball dropping as it comes to the plate, forcing the batter to take a golf-like swing. Pitchers use it when they want the batter to hit a ground ball and top pitchers use it to get a strike. It has been likened to the "sinker" in baseball but drops more abruptly and graphically.

drop step   A defensive technique that allows the fielder to approach a grounder or fly in the most efficient manner and gain depth on those balls hit away from the fielder.

earned run   A run scored through offensive play rather than through a defensive error, charged against the pitcher.

earned run average   The average number of earned runs that a pitcher allows during a full game. To find the earned run average, divide the number of earned runs allowed by the number of innings pitched and multiply by seven.

easy out!   See NO BATTER, NO BATTER.

ejection   An infraction that requires removal from the game by the umpire, whereby the ejected player or coach can no longer participate. A flagrant act will require the player or coach to leave the grounds for the remainder of the game.

EP   See EXTRA PLAYER.

e.r.a.   Short for EARNED RUN AVERAGE.

error   (1) Any defensive misplay that allows a batter to remain at bat longer than she should, or a baserunner to remain on base longer than she should or a runner to reach base or take an extra base. However, a base on balls is not an error, nor is a wild pitch or a passed ball. (2) A misplayed ball charged against a fielder in the scoring of a game.

extension.   Extension happens when one stretches out into a full swing to hit the ball with the bat. When one takes a full cut at the ball one is said to have "good extension."

extra-base hit   A hit that allows the batter-runner to reach second or third base safely without the aid of an error.

extra player (EP) Commonly used in slow pitch, but only an option for slow pitch. ASA rules stipulate: "If a team uses the EP, it must be on the lineup card at the start of the game, and the team must end the game with 11 players or forfeit. All 11 players bat, but only 10 play defense. Changes with the defensive players may be made each inning; however, the batting order may not change. (i.e., the EP may sit on the bench one inning, play 3B one inning, play outfield one inning, sit on the bench again, and then play 1B. All would be legal as long as the EP remained in his same position in the batting order. This would be the same for any of the 11 starting players).

"Any of the starting 11 may leave the game once and reenter. A starting player and his substitute may not be in the game at the same time. If this occurs, the manager and the player listed in the wrong spot in the batting order are ejected by the umpire."

•F•

fair ball A batted ball that, according to the possibilities spelled out in the ASA rule book:

---

a. Settles or is touched on or over fair territory between home and first base or between home and third base.

b. Bounds over any part of the first or third base bag, regardless of where the ball hits after going over the bag.

c. While on or over fair territory, touches the person, attached equipment, or clothing of a player of an umpire.

d. Touches first, second, or third base.

e. First falls or is first touched on or over fair territory beyond first, second, or third base.

f. While over fair territory, passes out of the playing field beyond the outfield fence.

g. Hits the foul pole above the fence level.

NOTE: A fair fly shall be judged according to the relative position of the ball and the foul line, including the foul pole, and not as to whether the fielder is on fair or foul territory at the time he touches the ball. It does not matter whether the ball first touches fair or foul territory and complies with all other aspects of fair ball.

---

fair territory That part of the playing field between first and third base foul lines, including home plate.

fake bunt Assuming the bunting stance without attempting to bunt the ball. It is used to draw the infield in close and away from their bases. This term applies only in the fast pitch game where bunting is legal.

fake tag Term defined in the U.S.S.S.A. rule book as ". . . making the motions of a tag without the ball. This may be considered obstruction, and the offender may be ejected." ASA rules point out that a fake tag "occurs when a fielder without the ball deceives the runner by impeding his progress . . . causing him to slide, slow down, or stop running."

fastball An alternative name for fast pitch softball.

fast ball (1) In fast pitch softball, a ball that comes off the fingers with a straight but slightly downward spin. It drops slightly as it comes into the plate and is most effective when thrown to the corners of the strike zone. (2) In slow pitch softball, a fast pitch is illegal.

fast pitch softball, fast pitch An official and once dominant form of the game played by teams of nine players, in which the underhand pitch is delivered to the batter with great speed and, depending on the skill of the pitcher, a varying element of deception.

Fast Pitch   *Lisa Fernandez displaying the power that is behind the speed of fast pitch softball.* (Russell Mott)

---

fielder   Any player of the defensive team out on the field.

fielder's choice   A play in which a fielder, after taking a batted ball, elects to make a play on a baserunner rather than on the batter.

fielding average   To find a fielder's defensive average, add his/her total fielding chances (putouts, assists and errors) and divide this number into the total number of putouts and assists.

fielding chance   Term used to describe the opportunity to get one's hands on the ball during a softball game. Slow pitch offers many more fielding chances than fast pitch.

fifty-fifty   A lottery drawing held at a softball game or tournament where the winner gets half the money collected and the other half goes to the sponsor or a charity.

fifty-five five   In Over the Line softball, a line drive that clears the front line by five inches.

figure eight   A fast pitch delivery in which the arm is swung in a figure eight combining some of each of the SLINGSHOT and WINDMILL deliveries. The ball is moved back quickly, but not shot forward as in the slingshot; rather, it describes a figure eight pattern as it heads towards the batter. It is harder to master than the other two deliveries.

In *What Little I Know About Pitching and Hitting*, Eddie Feigner, the great barnstorming pitcher, described the figure eight along with other bygone deliveries.

There was once a time that any wind-up you could imagine was legal. Each pitcher had his own style. In addition to windmill and slingshot, there were other wind-ups that we used:

the **figure eight** (looked just like a figure-8 arm swing)

the **jerk pitch**

the **twist** (used when we were not allowed to wear gloves)

the **whip** (was a lot like the slingshot)

the **whirl-i-gig**

And some pitchers, back in the days when the game was played without a glove, would wind up with both arms and then would throw right- or left-handed. That was really a talent that very few had.

---

first base   The base to which the batter runs after hitting the ball. It is 60 feet from home plate for fast pitch, and 65 feet for slow pitch along the right field foul line.

floater   A ball that stays in the air for a long time, appearing to float.

fly, fly ball   A ball that is hit into the air, usually to the outfield.

force-out   An out occurring when a defensive player in possession of the ball touches any base before the runner. Thus, the ordinary out at first base is a force-out. Force-outs can occur at any of the four bases.

forfeit   An umpire may forfeit any game and award it to one team for a variety of reasons, such as delay of game, refusal to continue play, rule violation, etc. The score of a forfeited game is 7–0 in favor of the team not at fault.

In reality, few forfeits are actually called and most of these are for arguing or fighting.

foul ball   A foul ball is a batted ball that, according to the ASA *Guide and Playing Rules Book*:

---

a. Settles or is touched on or over foul territory between home and first base or between home and third base.

b. Bounds or rolls past first or third base on or over foul territory.

c. While on or over foul territory, touches the person, attached equipment, or clothing of a player or an umpire, or any object foreign to the natural ground and provided a fair ball declaration has not been made prior to the ball entering foul territory.

d. First falls or is first touched on or over foul territory beyond first or third base.

e. Touches the batter or the bat a second time while the ball is within the batter's box.

NOTE: A foul fly shall be judged according to the relative position of the ball and the foul line, including the foul pole, and not as to whether the fielder is on foul or fair territory at the time he touches the ball.

PLAY—Bat of batter breaks into pieces as a

result of hitting a pitch. The batted ball, bounding on foul territory in direction of third base, then hits the barrel of the bat, causing the ball to roll into fair territory in front of third base. One player fields the ball and throws it to the first baseman who tags first base before batter reaches it. RULING—Foul ball, but batter is not out for hitting ball a second time.

---

foul line   A three-inch white line extending from home plate out to the boundaries of the playing field. The two foul lines form right angles at home plate. The foul line itself is considered fair territory.

foul tip   A batted ball which goes directly from the bat, not higher than the batter's head, to the catcher's hand(s) and is legally caught by the catcher. It is not a foul tip unless caught, and any foul tip that is caught is a strike. In fast pitch and 16 inch slow pitch, the ball is in play. In slow pitch the ball is dead. It is not a catch if it is a rebound, unless the ball touched the catcher's hand(s) or glove first. The ASA rules give these examples:
    PLAY (1)—Ball goes directly from bat and rebounds from protector (a) of a fielder after having touched his glove, (b) of that fielder without first having touched his glove, (c) of umpire after having first touched glove of fielder, (d) of umpire without first having touched glove of fielder. In each case the ball rebounds into glove of fielder and is held. RULING—In (a) it is a foul tip and a strike. In (b), (c), and (d) it is a foul, with ball becoming dead when it touched the catcher in (b) or umpire in (c) and (d).
    PLAY (2)—(Fast Pitch *only*) With runner on second, batter hits foul tip. May the runner on second advance without retouching second? Also, does it make any difference if the catcher drops the batted ball? RULING—A foul tip is the same as any strike; hence, the runner may advance without retouching. If batted ball is not caught, it is not a foul tip and is ruled a foul ball, in which case no runner may advance.

frostie   A slow pitch pitch that arcs higher than 12 feet. It alludes facetiously to the frost that appears at higher altitudes.

full count   A count of three balls and two strikes on a batter.

fungo   A ball tossed in the air and batted on the fly to the field during fielding practice.

• **G** •

game   A softball game consists of seven innings. The team that has scored the most runs at the end of the time wins, unless there is a tie, in which case the game goes into extra innings. If the team batting in the bottom half of each inning scores more runs in six innings than the team batting in the top half of the inning scores in seven turns at bat, the game ends without having to play the last half of the seventh inning.

"giving" action   Pulling in or collapsing of the glove toward the body as the ball is caught in order to absorb the impact.

gold stitch   Describing a ball with a COEFFICIENT OF RESTITUTION (or COR) of 44.

good look   Expression in Over the Line for when a hitter gets a good read on the defense.

good ribby   What one says to a teammate who has just brought home a runner and is credited with a run batted in (RBI or ribby).

good wood   What one says when one makes solid contact with the ball, despite the fact that hardly anyone bats with wooden bats any more.

grand slam   A home run with the bases loaded.

grass cutter   A sharply hit ball which skims across the top of the grass.

grip The means by which one holds the bat; especially important in the slow pitch game, in which one's grip may have much to do with one's ability to drive the ball for distance.

groove To pitch the ball right in the middle of the strike zone.

Grip Carl Rose displays his characteristic grip, which is very much part of his ability to hit the ball phenomenal distances. Rose described his grip in this way to Balls and Strikes in 1992: "My grip is hard to describe. I put my left hand ring finger on the bat's knob. My left hand index finger is interlocked between my right index finger and middle finger."

(Russell Mott)

grounder A "grounder" or "ground ball" is a batted ball that hits the ground as soon as it leaves the player's bat and bounces in the infield as it moves toward the outfield.

ground rule A rule established locally to set the boundaries of a field, especially out of play areas.

ground rule double A hit that is automatically ruled a double because the ball first hit fair and then landed in an area which is out of play.

•H•

hardball A term for baseball, in contrast with softball, despite the fact that both balls are equally hard.

heat A hard-hit ball in the jargon of Over the Line.

helmet A protective hat worn by the batter, on-deck batter or runner. It should be of similar color to the uniform hat, have double ear flaps and have standard safety features. Helmets should not be altered from the original safety specifications.

hesitation A legal move allowed in 16 inch slow pitch. In 16 inch each pitch of the ball can be prefaced by one or two deceptive bluffs set to deceive and throw off the timing of the batter. Despite this, strikeouts are still rare.

high A pitched ball that passes the plate above the strike zone.

hit (1) To take one's turn at bat. (2) To reach a base through a single, double, triple or homerun.

hit-and-run An offensive play in which a baserunner begins running as soon as the pitcher starts her delivery. The batter then attempts to hit the ball, often through a spot vacated by the shortstop or second baseman. Often used as a device for avoiding double plays.

hit batsman A batter who is hit by a pitched ball in fast pitch. The batter is entitled to move to first base. However, she or he must make an attempt to get out of the path of the ball.

hit the dirt To slide.

hitting a ball a second time The ASA rules are clear on this:

When an umpire considers the act of a batter "hitting a ball a second time," he should place the act into one of three categories. These are:

A. If the bat is in the hand(s) of the batter when the ball comes into contact with it, and if the bat is over fair territory, **including over home plate**, and the batter is in the batter's box, it is a foul ball. If an entire foot of the batter is completely outside the lines of the batter's box, he is out. If the ball is over foul territory or in the batter's box when the second contact is made, it is a foul ball. When in doubt, don't guess the batter out. Call it a foul ball.

B. If the bat is out of the batter's hand(s) (dropped or thrown) and it hits the ball in fair territory, the ball is dead, and the batter-runner is out. If the ball hits the bat on the ground, the batter is not out. The umpire should then determine whether the ball is fair or foul based on the fair/foul rule. If the ball rolls against the bat in fair territory, it remains alive. If it rolls against the bat in foul territory, then rolls fair and it stops or is touched in fair territory, it is a foul ball regardless.

C. If a batter swings and misses the ball but accidentally hits it on the backswing, or intentionally hits it on the second swing, the ball is dead whether hit fair or foul, and is called a foul ball. If on the third strike in slow pitch, the batter is out.

The third contingency was created from an actual game situation in the 1930s. It was described in 1939 by the ASA's Leo Fischer in an article in the *Reader's Digest*: "A pitcher's speed sometimes gets the umpires into queer situations. In an Iowa game, a batter had two strikes on him, and the pitcher suddenly tossed one of those tantalizing slow balls. The hitter, taken by surprise, took a fast swing and then continued to clear around, hitting the ball on the second circuit for a home run. One side argued that the batter had struck out on his first swing. The opposition claimed that the run counted. The umpire wrote us for a decision."

hitting behind the runner When a batter intentionally hits the ball to an area behind the path of a runner.

hole The space between two fielders that is not covered by either of the two defensive players.

homerun limits See OVER THE FENCE HOMERUN RULE.

homerun rule Slow pitch softball restrictions on the number of home runs allowed in a game. Both the ASA and U.S.S.S.A. have different limits for different levels of the game; for instance in ASA "B" division play each team is allowed three homeruns per game, with excess homeruns being an out, while in U.S.S.S.A. play each "B" division team is allowed two homerun hitters who can hit as many homeruns as they like. Excess homeruns are counted as fouls.

home team The home team is the team on whose grounds the game is played and the one that bats in the second half or bottom of each inning. If the game is played on neutral ground, the home team shall be designated by mutual agreement or by the flip of a coin.

homer (1) An umpire who the visitors claim is making all the calls for the home team, not withstanding the evidence that these same visitors are 25 runs down, have committed nine errors and left bases full two out of four innings. (2) A homerun.

hook slide A baserunning maneuver in which the runner, trying to reach a base on a close play, slides feet first into the base and twists her body away from the defensive player to touch the base with her rear foot.

hot corner As in baseball, the preferred nickname for third base because of the number of balls batted to the third baseman.

illegal bat An illegal bat is one that does not meet the requirements stated in the rules of the ASA or other body and is not marked by the words "OFFICIAL SOFTBALL" by the manufacturer. Here is an example of the rule in action from the ASA rule book:

PLAY—Batter hits a double to centerfield. Umpire notices bat has been tampered with, i.e., baseball bat honed down to softball size. RULING—Dead ball, and Batter is called out. Remove illegal piece of equipment from the game. This is an illegal bat.

---

illegal pitcher A player legally in the game, but one who may not pitch as a result of: (a) being removed from the pitching position by the umpire as a result of two charged conferences in one inning, or (b) (slow pitch *only*) a pitcher who has been removed from the pitching position by the umpire as a result of pitching with excessive speed after a warning. Penalty: If an illegal pitcher returns to the pitching position and has thrown one pitch, he is ejected from the game.

illegal player A player who has entered the game without reporting. The player is ejected from the game when the violation is brought to the plate umpire's attention by the offended team after the first legal or illegal pitch.

illegally batted ball An illegally batted ball occurs when, according to ASA rules:

---

a. A batter's entire foot is completely outside the lines of the batter's box and on the ground when he hits a ball fair or foul.

b. Any part of the batter's foot is touching home plate when he hits the ball fair or foul.

c. The batter hits the ball with an illegal bat.

PLAY (1)—Batter hits a pitched ball while his entire foot is completely out of batter's box, in contact with the ground, and the ball goes directly into the stands behind home plate. RUL-

---

ING—Ball is dead. Batter is declared out.

PLAY (2)—Pitcher delivers ball to batter who has one foot touching home plate as he swings and completely misses pitch. RULING—A strike is called. This is not an illegally batted ball. The ball must be hit (fair or foul) to enforce the illegally batted ball rule.

---

illegally caught ball An illegally caught ball occurs when a fielder catches a batted or thrown ball with his cap, helmet, mask, protector, pocket, detached glove or any part of his uniform that is detached from its proper place.

industrial softball A generic name given to the many teams sponsored by companies for their employees. For many years softball has been a popular sport for both sexes in the recreation programs sponsored by industrial and commercial firms. One company spoke for many when it stated its reason for an active softball program ("Avco Lycoming Sports Excellent Softball Program," *Balls and Strikes*, April 1967) was that interdepartmental softball competition:

---

1. Promotes job efficiency, morale, and a strong sense of company loyalty. 2. Functions as a social "leveler," by affording friendly contact between employees at all personnel levels. 3. Promotes the physical and mental well-being of employees. 4. Promotes an excellent medium for observing the potential leadership abilities of employees.

---

infield The portion of the field included within the lines of the diamond and covered by infielders in position. Softball infields should be SKINNED—this is, they should be devoid of grass.

in flight Term used for any batted, thrown or pitched ball that has not yet touched the ground or some object or person on the field other than a fielder.

in jeopardy A term indicating that the ball is in play and an offensive player may be put out.

---

indoor baseball Softball in its first incarnation, which was baseball played inside a gymnasium.

indoor-outdoor One of a number of names for softball. (See also ARMY BALL for a full listing of synonyms for softball.)

ineligible player A player who does not meet the requirements of the ASA rules for amateur play. The determination of eligibility is not the responsibility of the umpire. The use of an ineligible player will constitute a forfeit.

infield The infield is that portion of the field in fair territory that includes areas normally covered by infielders.

infield fly An infield fly is a fair fly ball (not including a line drive or an attempted bunt) that can be caught by an infielder with ordinary effort when first and second bases or first, second and third bases are occupied before two are out. The pitcher, catcher and any outfielder who positions himself in the infield at the start of the pitch shall be considered infielders for the purpose of this rule. The infield fly is ruled when the ball reaches the highest point based on the position of the closest infielder, regardless of who makes the play. NOTE: When it seems apparent that a batted ball will be an infield fly, the umpire shall immediately declare, "INFIELD FLY: THE BATTER IS OUT" for the benefit of the runners. If the ball is near a foul line, the umpire shall declare, "INFIELD FLY: THE BATTER IS OUT IF FAIR."

The ball is alive, and runners may advance at the risk of the ball being caught or retouch and advance after the ball is touched, the same as on any fly ball. If the hit becomes a foul ball, it is treated the same as any foul.

If a declared infield fly is allowed to fall untouched to the ground and bounces foul before passing first or third base, it is a foul ball. If a

declared infield fly falls untouched to the ground outside the foul lines and bounces fair before passing first or third base, it is an infield fly.

Here is how the concept is played out in the ASA *Guide and Playing Rules Book*:

PLAY (1)—Runners (R1 and R2) are at second and first bases respectively with none out. Batter hits a high pop foul between home and first base which the first baseman loses sight of it in the sun. The infield fly is declared by the umpire(s). Ball lands on foul ground without being touched and rolls into fair territory halfway between home and first base. The pitcher picks up ball and throws to the second baseman covering first, who touches R2 with ball while runner R2 is off base. RULING—Infield fly. Batter and R2 are both out.

PLAY (2)—Runners (R1 and R2) are on second and first bases respectively with one out. Batter hits a high fly ball which, in the judgment of the umpire, may be handled by the second baseman with reasonable effort. The infield fly rule is declared by the umpire. The second baseman intentionally drops the fly ball. Seeing the ball dropped, R1 runs to third base but is thrown out. RULING—Batter is out on the infield fly. The ball remains alive. R1 is also out on the tag since the infield fly takes precedence over the intentionally dropped fly ball.

infield hit A base hit that does not go past the infielders to the outfield.

inning An inning is that portion of a game within which the teams alternate on offense and defense, and in which there are three outs for each team. A new inning begins immediately after the final out of the previous inning. Regulation softball games are seven innings in length, as contrasted with baseball games, which last nine innings.

in-shoot A fast pitch ball that curves towards the batter.

inside A pitch that misses the plate on the side closest to the batter.

interference (1) The act of an offensive player or team member that impedes or confuses a defensive player attempting to execute a play. Interference is deemed to have taken place by the umpire who declares the person guilty of interfering as out. (2) Interference also occurs if the catcher attempts to prevent the batter from hitting the ball.

The United States Slo-Pitch Softball Association *Official Rules Book* specifies four types of interference:

A. Defensive Interference—A defensive team interferes when a batter is hindered or prevented in striking at or hitting a pitched ball; interference may also be vocal.

B. Offensive Interference—When a player interferes with or impedes or confuses a defensive player, while he is attempting to make a play, by either physical or vocal actions.

C. Spectator Interference—Occurs when a person not engaged in the game touches a live batted or thrown ball which could prevent a blocked ball to occur.

D. Umpire Interference—Occurs when a fair batted ball strikes the umpire on fair ground before passing a fielder other than the pitcher.

"It only takes one" Softball "talk" or chatter used to encourage a hit that will lead to a rally.

"I've got it!" Name for one of the deceptive tricks of softball. Described by Judy A. Bluckner and Joanne Graf in their book *Championship Slow Pitch Softball*:

This technique can be used by a defensive outfield when there are runners on base and a fly ball or line drive is hit. If two outfielders are running toward a fly ball/line drive which neither of them will catch, the fielder closest to the ball should yell, "I've got it" in a loud confident voice. The purpose of this play is to freeze the runners momentarily. This will often prevent them from getting an extra base, because they have stayed to tag up in case of a catch. Perhaps, a specific remark would be used by the outfielders in this situation, instead of "I've got it," a common call when the fielder wants to ward off an adjacent fielder. Again, this play requires prior communication between members of the defensive team to prevent a mix-up.

Junior Olympic player Any player 18 years and under who has not reached the 19th birthday prior to September 1. Under ASA rules J.O. players must obey special rules and regulations. For instance, beginning in 1993 a J.O. fast pitch catcher was required to wear shin guards, which offer protection to the knee caps. Note: If one or more J.O. player(s) play on an adult team, adult rules will be in effect.

keystone sack Second base.

kitten ball (1) One of a number of historic names for softball. (2) The term still has application as 16 inch players talk disparagingly about folks who play with a 12-inch ball. A line from a 1976 issue of the periodical *Windy City Softball* tells of a "kittenball team from Indiana" being introduced to Chicago-style ball (and being whomped).

knuckle ball As used in fast pitch softball, a ball that breaks suddenly with little rotation. The ball is pushed out of the hand rather than rolled off the fingers.

Knuckle Ball Dave Owle, a Native American who pitches for the Birdtown team from North Carolina, men's fast pitch. Here he is demonstrating his grip for a knuckle ball in the summer of 1992, in Salem, Virginia. (Russell Mott)

• L •

last bullet Slang softball term for the upcoming third out in the last inning for the losing team.

lay one down To bunt the ball in fast pitch softball.

lead Term used in fast pitch only. A baserunner "takes a lead" when she moves off a base after a pitcher releases the ball in an effort to put herself closer to the next base. Her "lead" cannot be too great, or she may be tagged out. Taking a lead is illegal in slow pitch.

leadoff (1) The first batter for a team either at the start of a game or an inning. (2) A quick move off the base taken by a baserunner as soon as the ball leaves the pitcher's hand in slow pitch *only*. (3) Moving off the base before a ball is thrown in fast pitch *only*.

lead-off batter The first batter to bat in the inning.

leaping Term used in men's fast pitch only. An act by the pitcher that causes him to be airborne on his initial move and push from the plate. The momentum built by the forward movement of the pitcher causes the entire body, including both the pivot foot and the non-pivot foot, to be in the air and move toward home plate as the delivery is completed. With this style of pitching, the pitcher will release the ball simultaneously with his return to the ground. The pivot foot will then slide to the side and drag as the pitcher follows through or completes the delivery. This follow through should not be confused with replanting and gaining a second starting point (defined as the "crow hop"), but simply a finish or follow through of the leap style of pitching. At the completion of the leap, the non-pivot foot is planted but will not allow the pitcher to gain further distance towards the plate, therefore the slide and drag of the pivot foot is a legal act.

left the field See APPEAL PLAY.

legal touch A legal touch occurs when a baserunner or batter-runner who is not touching a base is touched by the ball while it is securely held in a fielder's hand(s). The ball is not considered as having been securely held if it is juggled or dropped by the fielder after having touched the runner, unless the runner deliberately knocks the ball from the hand(s) of the fielder. It is sufficient for the runner to be touched with the glove or hand(s) holding the ball.

The ASA rules contain three plays to illustrate this term:

PLAY (1)—Batter hits ground ball to first baseman who gathers in the ball, runs over to the first base line, tags the runner, then juggles, bobbles, and drops the ball. RULING—Illegal touch. Runner is safe.

PLAY (2)—The catcher has the ball in his glove when he tags runner with the glove. Ball does not come into contact with the runner. RULING—Touching with the glove or hand(s) holding the ball is the same as touching with the ball. The runner is out.

PLAY (3)—While lying on the ground with ball in right hand, the first baseman tags first base with left hand prior to batter-runner reaching first base. RULING—Batter-runner is out. Legal touch.

---

legally caught ball A legally caught ball is when a fielder catches a batted, pitched or thrown ball, provided it is not caught in the fielder's cap, helmet, mask, protector, pocket, detached glove or any part of his uniform that is detached from its proper place on his person. It must be caught and firmly held with a hand or hands. A player may not be contacting anything in a dead ball area at the time of the catch.

line drive A line drive is a fly ball that is batted sharply and directly into the playing field. In softball, a line drive is a ball with little arc that seems to travel parallel to the ground.

lightning ball One of a number of names for softball. (See also ARMY BALL for a full listing of synonyms for softball.)

live ball The *U.S.S.S.A. Official Rule Book* says it "... occurs when the umpire signals play ball. The ball remains alive until ball becomes dead for any reason. . . ."

• M •

maximum arc In slow pitch softball *only* this is the point at which the ball reaches its highest point in its trajectory from the release of the ball from the pitcher's hand to the plate. It is measured in feet from the ground to that high point, and there is a prescribed maximum arc in organized slow pitch that varies depending on which rules are being observed. The maximum arc in U.S.S.S.A. rules is 10 feet and 12 feet in ASA (See also MINIMUM ARC; UNLIMITED ARC.)

middle line of knuckles Softball batting grip alignment in which the second knuckle of each finger of each hand is in a straight line.

minimum arc In the slow pitch game this is the lowest apogee that the ball can reach in order to be considered a legal pitch. If it falls beneath the minimum arc the pitch will be declared an illegal pitch and a ball will be awarded by the umpire to the batter. The minimum distance varies between three feet from the release point in U.S.S.S.A.

Mush Ball *Batter Andre Peoples takes a swing at a 16-inch ball in the 1992 U.S.S.S.A. Wisconsin tournament. This photograph shows the 16-inch ball for what it is: a monstrous target. (Russell Mott)*

---

softball and six feet from the ground in ASA slow pitch softball. The U.S.S.S.A. rules allow the pitcher to release the ball from as low as he or she wants meaning that a ball released at ground level need only be three feet from the ground. (See also MINIMUM ARC; UNLIMITED ARC.)

miss An Over the Line term *only* for a mis-hit ball that spins off in the opposite direction intended.

mix up To vary the type and speed of pitches.

modified pitch, modified A form of softball that puts the batter back in the game by prohibiting the fastest and most difficult to hit deliveries in fast pitch softball: the SLINGSHOT and the WINDMILL.

move the ball Slang expression for hitting the ball. It is used in the fast pitch game. As Joan Joyce and John Anquillare explain in their book *Winning Softball*: "Hitting the ball places the pressure of performance on the fielder, while striking out does nothing to jeopardize the defense."

move up To advance to the next base.

mush ball (1) Name for the 16-inch softball to distinguish it from the smaller 12-inch version. (2) The 16 inch game. (See also PILLOW BALL and PUMPKIN BALL.) (3) One of a number of names for softball. (See also ARMY BALL for a full listing of synonyms for the game softball.) (4) The softball.

The most extended use of this metaphor for the ball itself comes from period before World War II when the softball itself came to be known as the "mush ball pill" in some circles.

• N •

night ball One of a number of names for softball. (See also ARMY BALL for a full listing of synonyms for softball.)

"no batter, no batter" The game's most popular—and, perhaps, as many claim most effective—taunt used by fielders to rattle opponent batters. As Stephanie Salter pointed out in "Softball Chatter Made Simple" in *Women's Sports and Fitness*, "Sarcasm must be dripping from the voice. An informal survey conducted by Beatrice Gallup of East Overshoe, Idaho, revealed that 36 percent of hitters challenged in this way promptly doubled to left on the next pitch." The second most popular taunt is EASY OUT! of which Salter says, "Same survey indicated that 42 percent of hitters challenged in this way promptly doubled to left on the next pitch."

no-hitter A game in which the pitcher does not give up a single hit, and usually no runs. A PERFECT GAME is one in which no opponent reaches first base on a hit, error, walk, etc.

• O •

obstruction Getting in the way of a batter or baserunner. Officially defined in the Amateur Softball Association *Guide and Playing Rules Book*: Obstruction is the act of:

———

a. A defensive player or team member which hinders or prevents a batter from striking or hitting a pitched ball.

b. A fielder, (1) not in possession of the ball,

(2) not in the act of fielding a batted ball, or (3) not about to receive a thrown ball which impedes the progress of a baserunner or batter-runner who is legally running bases.

———

offensive conference See CHARGED CONFERENCE.

offensive interference See INTERFERENCE.

offensive team The offensive team is the team at bat.

"Official Softball" Words used to designate approved softball equipment by manufacturers of bats and other equipment.

older game Baseball, as contrasted with softball, which is the YOUNGER GAME.

on-deck batter The offensive player whose name follows the name of the batter in the batting order. He shall take a position within the lines of the on-deck circle nearest his bench.

one pitch The name for the form of the game of slow pitch softball in which the batter begins his or her at bat with a count of three balls, two strikes and one foul. It is a fast game to play. The U.S.S.S.A. *Official Rule Book* carries a set of rules for this game.

one-two-three The side is retired without a batter reaching first base; or, three up–three down.

original softball Term used especially by fast pitch softball advocates and players to describe their form of the game.

O.T.L./OTL Short for Over the Line softball.

———

One Pitch *(Opposite) Rounding third in a one pitch tournament in Maine is David Pratt of South Paris, Maine, outfielder for Popeye's Variety. (Russell Mott)*

———

228

The Worth Book of Softball

out An "out" is the retirement of a batter or runner during play. The ways in which a batter or baserunner may be put out are numerous. Each team is allowed three outs during its time at bat in any one inning.

outfield The outfield is the portion of the field that extends from the bases that are stationed in the infield area to the distance marker that indicates inbounds and out-of-bounds; or, the area not normally covered by an infielder, and within the foul lines beyond first and third bases and boundaries of the grounds.

outside A pitched softball that misses the strike zone on the side of the plate farthest from the batter.

Over the Line (1) Three-player game that, depending on who you talk to, is either a form of softball or a cousin to it. Over the Line was created on the beaches of San Diego in 1954 by a group killing time waiting for a volleyball court. It is a beach game rather than one intended for traditional softball fields. Each team is composed of three players and each team pitches to its own batters. Kneeling next to the plate, the pitcher gently tosses the ball into the air for the batter to swing at and drive "Over the Line" which is, usually, 55 feet away. Hence the name of the game. The line is 60 feet wide. Any ball hit short of the line is considered a foul ball. (2) A ball hit over the front line in Over the Line softball.

overrun To run past a base or to slide past (overslide) a base placing the runner in danger of being tagged out. However, the batter is permitted to overrun first base while attempting to reach there after hitting the ball.

overslide An overslide is the act of an offensive player when, as a runner, he overslides a base he is attempting to reach. It is usually caused when

his momentum forces him to lose contact with the base, which then causes him to be in jeopardy of being tagged out. The batter-runner may overslide first base without being in jeopardy. In play a runner overslides first base (a) during advance from home plate or (b) on return to first base after an attempt to advance to second base. In either case he is tagged with the ball while off base. The proper ruling would be: (a) Safe (b) Out.

over-the-fence homerun rule Actually a series of rules created to limit the number of dingers at various levels of slow pitch *only* play. Here is the ASA slow pitch homerun rules:

A limit of over-the-fence home runs will be used in all men's and co-ed slow pitch divisions. There is no limit to men's Super Division or women and youth play.

a. All balls hit over the fence in a game BY A TEAM in excess of the following limits will be ruled an out. Major (12); Class A and Major Industrial (6); Major church, Class A industrial, Major co-ed, all Masters and Senior, and Class B have a limit of three (3) home runs. Class C, "A" Church and "A" co-ed have a limit of one (1). For each in excess of one the batter is ruled out, and all other players hitting a home run are ruled out and ejected from the game. For the first Class D classification home run, the batter is called out, and each subsequent player hitting a home run is declared out and ejected.

b. Any ball touched by a defensive player which then goes over the fence in fair territory should be considered a four base award and is not included in the total of over-the-fence home runs.

c. A home run will be charged for any ball hit over the fence whether runs score or not.

d. Anytime the batter is ruled out because of the excessive home run rule, the ball is dead and no runners can score.

Serve 'em Up (Opposite) Over the Line pitcher and batter show how one puts the ball over the line.
(Russell Mott)

overthrow An overthrow occurs when a thrown ball from a fielder goes beyond its intended receiver and lands outside the boundary lines of the playing field (DEAD BALL territory).

•P•

paint the corners A pitch that crosses the inside or outside part of home plate for a strike is said to "paint the corners."

parachute Over the Line slang for a missed WOOD CHOP.

passed ball A term used in fast pitch *only* referring to when a legally delivered ball that should have been held or controlled by the catcher with ordinary effort is missed. Baserunners can steal on a passed ball.

penalty Application of the rules, following an illegal act or violation.

pepper A game played with one batter and one or more fielders. The batter either bunts, or takes a half swing at the ball tossed by the fielder immediately after she fields the ball. The ball is continually thrown, batted and fielded in rapid succession.

perfect game A game in which the pitcher allows no hits, no runs and no players on base.

person U.S.S.S.A. *Official Rule Book*: "The Person of an Umpire or player includes all of its body, his clothing or his equipment."

pick off To trap or attempt to trap a runner off base with a sudden throw and tag.

pickup game Game created because someone has rounded up enough people to create two teams. Of all softball games played last year 42.654% were pickup games.

pillow ball (1) The 16-inch softball to distinguish it from the smaller 12-inch version. (2) The 16 inch game. (See also MUSH BALL.)

pinch hitter A player who is sent into the game to bat in place of another player.

pitcher's box The place from which the pitcher delivers the ball. In the pitcher's box it is the "rubber" or pitcher's plate, a rubber or wood block set flush with the ground, 24 inches long and six inches wide. This "rubber" is 40 feet from the outside corner of home plate in girls' and women's play.

pitchers' game Sobriquet for the fast pitch game since the 1930s. The argument has always been stated that this form of the game was not a TEAM GAME.

pitching The work of the pitcher. In fast pitch it is a matter of speed, control and deception, while the slow pitch game is based on location (i.e. getting the batter to put the ball in play in a way convenient to the defense) and timing (trying to get the batter off stride).

pitch-out A pitch purposely thrown wide of the plate to allow the catcher easier access to the ball. Used to stop a possible steal or hit and run.

pivot foot (1) Defined in ASA fast pitch rules: "The pivot foot is that foot which must remain in contact with the pitcher's plate. Pushing off with the pivot foot from a place other than the pitcher's plate is illegal." (2) Officially defined in ASA slow pitch rules: "The pivot foot is that foot which the pitcher must keep in constant contact with the pitcher's plate until the ball is released." NOTE: (16 inch slow pitch) After a hesitation, the pivot foot may be removed during a pick-off situation but must be replaced in contact with the pitcher's plate before the pitch is released.

play ball The term used by the plate umpire to indicate that play shall begin or be resumed when the pitcher has the ball in his possession and is within eight feet (2.44 meters) of the pitcher's plate. All defensive players except the catcher, who must be in his box, must be anywhere on fair ground to put the ball into play.

playground baseball Name given to an early version of softball in 1908 by the National Amateur Playground Ball Association. It was the linear descendent of INDOOR BASEBALL.

pop-up A short fly ball hit within the infield or in the related foul ground.

presenting the ball Action by the pitcher just prior to beginning the pitching motion. The pitcher stands with both feet on the pitcher's plate and ground with the ball in both hands.

protest An assertion by either team that either a playing rule has been misinterpreted, that the correct rule has not been applied by the umpire or that the correct penalty has not been given by the umpire for a violation. In *The Complete Book of Softball*, Robert G. Meyer asserts, "It usually costs money to make a protest to a league to reverse the decision of the umpire, and protests seldom work. If one is upheld, the game may be replayed from that point on or the league may change the decision as to who is the winner."

pull hitter The batter who gets maximum power by making contact with the ball after the wrists have snapped, driving the ball to the near field (left field for a right-handed batter; right field for a left-handed batter).

puppy, purse An Over the Line slang term for a soft hitting stroke.

put out The retiring of a batter or baserunner.

quick pitch, quick return pitch A pitch made by the pitcher with the obvious attempt to catch the batter off balance. This would be before the batter takes his desired position in the batter's box or while he is still off balance as a result of the previous pitch. When this is attempted the umpire is expected to declare that "no pitch" has been made. However, in many cases it is *not* called and some pitchers have learned to use it effectively.

•R•

radio pitch A super fast pitch. As described in *Softball Player's Magazine*, "Batters can hear it, but can't see it." It has been used to describe the fastball of Debbie Doom of El Monte, California. She dominated play at the August, 1991, Pan American games in Cuba where she hurled two *perfect games* in two outings. The Cuban fans called her "La Supersonica" (the Supersonic).

RBI Short for RUNS BATTED IN.

read Slang in Over the Line for watching the defense.

recreation ball One of a number of names for softball. (See also ARMY BALL for a full listing of synonyms for softball.)

red stitch Describing a ball with a COEFFICIENT OF RESTITUTION (or COE) of 47.

re-entry rule An Amateur Softball Association ruling that encouraged coaches to replace first string players with second stringers during a game since the rule permits a player to re-enter the game if his or her skill is later needed. Under U.S.S.S.A. rules the re-entry rule is only applicable in women's softball. In U.S.S.S.A. men's softball, once a player has been substituted, he's out of the game (as in baseball).

regulation game See GAME.

relay To return the ball from the outfield to the infield by using several short, fast throws rather than one long (and necessarily slower) throw. For most relays, an infielder moves out into the outfield, takes the throw from the outfielder and in turn throws it to another infielder.

rise, riser, rise ball, rise pitch A fast-pitched ball that suddenly goes up as it passes over the plate. The index finger is used to put a counterclockwise spin on the ball. A first rate fast pitch pitcher can throw one of these, have it approach the batter at waist height and suddenly cross the plate at the shoulder or chin.

This pitch is sometimes referred to as an "upshoot." It is the opposite of the DROP, DROP BALL, DROP PITCH.

rise-curve, rise-curve pitch　A pitch that combines the RISE, RISER, RISE BALL, RISE PITCH with a curve ball. It is very hard to hit; one such expert pitcher was Joan Joyce.

roster　The list of players carried by a softball team. There are various roster rules, including one that insists that co-ed teams carry an equal number of men and women.

roster size　The number of players on a softball team. Roster size is often determined by rules set by a league, tournament or governing body. The U.S.S.S.A. *Official Rule Book*, for instance, says, "In all Divisional, National and World Tournament play a team shall not exceed 20 players."

round-robin　A common type of softball tournament in which each team plays every other team at least once. The winner of such a tournament is the team that has won the highest percentage of its games.

This format has been combined with other tournament formats—for example, in the late 1930s and early 1940s when as many as 1,000 teams showed up for a tournament, round-robin was combined with STRAIGHT or SINGLE ELIMINATION. Groups of eight teams would play in a round-robin format and the winners of each of these rounds met in a single elimination series until a championship was determined. Round-robin is also known as LEAGUE PLAY.

rover　Extra player or shortfielder. The outfield area has three players (in fast pitch only) and four players (in slow pitch only) stationed in the outfield: (1) left field, (2) center field, (3) right field and (4) rover (slow pitch only). The rover, usually positioned in the shallow outfield, is also known as a ROVING FIELDER or SHORT FIELDER.

roving fielder　Proper name for the ROVER.

rubber　The 24-inch-wide plate from which the pitcher pitches. Its importance in the slow pitch game is significant in determining the difference between the ASA and U.S.S.S.A. legal pitch. ASA fast pitch rules state that the pitcher must stand with both feet on the rubber to begin the pitch, must move forward from the rubber and must keep one foot on the rubber at the time the pitch is released. In ASA slow pitch and U.S.S.S.A. play, the only rule that applies states that one foot must remain on the rubber but the other can be anywhere, which allows for all sorts of variant pitches.

rules　The complex sets of rules that define softball in its various incarnations. Most players lack the time or dedication to learn them all, but rather boil it down to those that are most essential. In the publication *Softball: A Game for Everyone*, the ASA listed certain key rules and ideas that might spell out the difference between winning and losing. That list:

The appeal play: In this instance an umpire will not render an adverse decision on the baserunner for missing a base or leaving a base too soon unless it is appealed.

Infield Fly Rule: With less than two outs a batter hits a fly ball other than a line drive or bunt that can be easily handled by an infielder. The baserunner advances at his own risk. The Infield Fly Rule can only be called when runners are on first and second or first, second and third with less than 2 outs.

Proper order of running bases: If a runner has advanced beyond a base on a legal catch of a fly ball, he must reverse properly by touching all bases in order.

Two runners occupying same base: The fielder touches the second occupant. The rightful occupant is the first runner, and the second runner is out.

Know when a run shall or shall not score on the third out: This is quite important. When a runner crosses home plate prior to the third out, other than a force out or when the batter-baserunner is retired at first base by virtue of failing to reach the base safely, a run shall score.

Know the legal position of the pitcher and catcher: The rules clearly state the position of the pitcher and the requirements prior to and during the delivery of the ball as well as the position of the catcher. You should acquaint yourselves with this information. Failure to do so could result in an illegal pitch.

Know the proper order of batting and what is the penalty for batting out of turn: If a player batted out of turn and it was detected by the opponent prior to a pitch to the next batter, the batter would be out. For this reason it is necessary to exercise good judgment to bat in the proper turn.

---

run The unit of scoring. The object of the game is to score runs. This is done when the batsman attempts to hit the ball into the fair field of play, and in doing so circles the three bases to return to the home base; a run is thus scored, provided the batter-runner is not tagged with the ball while circling the bases. A runner cannot move off the base until the ball is pitched (FP) or until 2 batted (SP).

run and hit A play in which the baserunner leaves with the pitch in anticipation of the batter hitting a base hit.

runner The term "runner" means BASERUNNER.

runs batted in (RBI) A batter is credited with batting in a run when a baserunner scores when she makes a base hit or a sacrifice, forces in a run by walking or hits into a putout.

• S •

sacrifice fly The ASA rule book defines the term: A sacrifice fly is scored when, with fewer than two outs, (a) the batter scores a runner with a fly ball or line drive that is caught; or (b) the batter scores a runner with a fly ball or line drive that is dropped by an outfielder (or an infielder running into the outfield), and, in the scorer's judgment, the runner could have scored after the catch had the fly ball or line drive being caught.

scoring position Description of when a runner(s) is at second or third base and can score on another hit. Because the distances are shorter this term has a more emphatic meaning in softball than in baseball.

scratch hit A ball, usually weakly hit, which none of the fielders can reach in time to retire the batter.

shag Chasing down and catching batted fly balls during batting or fielding practice.

shagger Name for a youngster hired to retrieve over the fence homeruns in slow pitch softball tournaments and bring them back for re-use. A major tournament like the Smoky Mountain Classic or the Twitty City will witness as many as 1,000 balls going over the wall.

shake off A term describing a pitcher's refusal to throw the type of pitch the catcher signals for.

short A pitch that drops in front of a batter in slow pitch softball—analogous to "low" in baseball or fast pitch softball. DEEP is the term for balls that fall behind the batter.

short center The 10th player in Chicago-style 16 inch softball; the extra player, so called because he or she plays in what can be best described as short center field just outside the infield.

short fielder ROVER by another name.

short-handed rule A slow pitch provision that allows a player to leave the game and the team to end the game with one less player than it started with.

shutout To prevent the opposing team from scoring a run. Shutouts are extremely rare in slow pitch softball, but extremely common in fast pitch; this is one major difference between the two games.

single A hit that permits the batter to reach first base without the aid of a defensive error.

single-elimination Tournament format in which one defeat eliminates a team from further play. It is the speediest way of reaching a champion, but is unpopular at the higher levels of the game (where the top team can be eliminated after a round or two).

sit Term used in Over the Line to order the ball to stay in play, much as a golfer will order a ball to sit on the green. (See also BITE.)

16 inch A common name given to Chicago-style softball, which is played with a large ball 16 inches in diameter.

skinned The proper condition and description of a softball infield that is devoid—or skinned—of grass.

skunk rule Proviso in many Over the Line encounters in which a game is ended if a team is ahead by a certain number of runs at the end of an inning. The number of runs is usually eleven, but is sometimes changed.

slants Pitched balls, especially in the fast ball parlance of the 1930s and 1940s.

slap hit Unique to fast pitch softball, this term describes a maneuver in which a left-handed batter will take a step towards first base as the ball leaves the pitcher's hand. While this step is being taken the batter hits the ball to the left side of the infield with a slapping motion. With the shorter basepath and what is essentially a legal lead off the plate and good timing, the batter has a fairly good chance of making it safely to first base.

slingshot A fast pitch delivery in which the arm, gripping the ball, leaves its position at the waist, is whipped backwards to the stretching point and is then moved forward with as much speed and force as possible. The ball is released at its farthest point forward, with as much drive as possible. It is a single powerful stroke rather than a circular delivery producing more control but less speed than the WINDMILL delivery. (See also FIGURE EIGHT.)

slow pitch softball One of the two major disciplines of the game. It describes a team game in which the softball must be thrown in an arc rather than directly over the plate. ASA rules specify that the arc be between six and 12 feet above the ground while U.S.S.S.A. rules call for a pitching arc of between three and 10 feet.

slow pitching What slow pitch softball was called in its early years. Quoting from Leo H. Fischer's 1940 classic *Winning Softball*: "A type of softball which has attained popularity in many sections of the country and which is gaining in others is the variety known as 'slow-pitching.'" At this time, according to ASA founder Fischer, it was played with a 16-inch ball.

smothering the ball To hold or control the ball by covering it with the glove and body rather than making a clean catch.

snag In Over the Line this is a tough catch.

softball (1) The game itself. A spinoff of baseball featuring underhand pitching, which originated in the United States and is largely participated in by the United States, Canada, Japan, Philippines,

---

Piece Work Stella McEwin, working at her table at Worth, Inc. in 1992. She is able to complete six or seven very taut softballs in an hour. (Russell Mott)

New Zealand, Australia and most of Latin America. There have been a number of attempts to define it in a few words. For instance, *The Oxford Companion to World Sports and Games* terms it, ". . . a nine-a-side bat-and-ball game originated in the U.S.A."

The history of the term as a name for the game begins long after the game itself had been created. The term softball was first used to describe the game in 1926 when a meeting was held in Colorado to standardize that state's rules under a common name. The term softball was suggested by Walter C. Hakanson, the Y.M.C.A. director for Denver and subsequent ASA Commissioner and president.

It took a while for the term to spread even in Colorado and it may have found its first popular application outside of that state in Canada. The earliest *printed* reference in the collection of the many citations in the extensive file on the term "softball" at Merriam-Webster, the dictionary company in Springfield, Massachusetts, is not in fact from Colorado but from the *Guelph Evening Mercury* of Guelph, Ontario, of August 26, 1927. A headline reads, "Guelph Softball Champions Eliminate Supremes of Galt" and there are articles on both men's and women's softball. These were high-spirited, high-scoring games. One of the women's games was described as "a heavy hitting affair with lots of good baseball injected into the fray." A team known as the Woolworths defeated St. James 16 to 11 with the aid of four homeruns.

The Merriam-Webster dictionaries use this 1927 Canadian citation as the moment of origin while the *Oxford English Dictionary* carries a 1926 Canadian citation for its point of origin. This one was from the *Victoria B.C. Daily Colonist* of July 2nd, in which the term appears but as two words: "The remainder of the morning was occupied by the younger members of the party in playing soft ball and other less strenuous games."

(2) The game ball of softball and a misnomer in the sense that the ball is not soft, but rather heavier and larger than a baseball and just about as hard. Traditionally, the softball was made of a core of tightly packed and molded kapoc, wound tightly with cotton winding, dipped in rubber cement, covered with horsehide and then hand-stitched. Rule 3, Sec. 2 of the ASA *Guide and Playing Rules Book* defines the required charac-

teristics of a legal softball as having three distinct parts: the CORE, WINDING and the COVER.

It is also worth noting that softball has a few meanings outside the game. In tennis a softball is a ball lobbed at low velocity for tactical reasons; for example a player may softball a shot to slow the pace of a volley or throw the other player off balance. The term has seen limited use for a changeup pitch in baseball. An article in the November, 1947, *Negro Digest* provides one such example:

Harry (The Cat) Brecheen, winner of three World Series games in 1946, was having a wonderful time on the mound for the Cardinals. Inning after inning he screwballed and softballed the Dodgers into submission.

According to the second edition of the *Oxford English Dictionary*, the oldest meaning of softball in English (usually written as "soft ball" or "soft-ball") refers to the process of making candy in which a soft globule of sugar is formed by dropping hot sugar into cold water. The soft ball is created to test the degree to which the sugar has been cooked. The term is very much still in use, and it is the soft ball that shows up in James Beard's *American Cookery* (1972). It is also defined in various cooking dictionaries as the stage that syrup reaches at 234 to 240 degrees F.

The most recent and currently popular use of the term is as an adjective or noun meaning easy and not at all provocative, such as a question that is easy to field and handle. It is a clear play on the "soft" of softball. The antonym of playing political softball is playing hardball. The earliest example of this term so used in print appears in the December, 1979, *Saturday Review* in which Tim O'Brien alleges that Justice Warren Burger will only grant in-depth interviews to those "who clear the subject matter with him in advance, promise to throw softballs, and then let the chief justice edit the finished product himself."

There are many examples of the term applied to many situations. For instance, asking a movie star "What makes a sex symbol?" is a "softball query" (*People*, March 1, 1982), while allowing a company to "persistently misrepresent itself" is "softball media coverage" (*Fortune*, August 9, 1982), and an easily discharged issue is a "political softball" (*U.S. News and World Report*, April 18, 1988.) On the other hand, a "softball interview" is a television phenomenon in which the camera is turned on, "letting the stars talk" (*People* August 20, 1984). In some cases, the softball question or query becomes simply "softball." Here is a writer for *U.S. News and World Report* (January 25, 1988) on the performance of Senator Robert Dole as he began his drive for the Republican nomination.

"I'm worried that I won't have enough money to go to college. How will a Dole administration help me?"

This in the currently fashionable vernacular, was a *softball*—which Dole swung on and missed, never looking the student in the eye and rambling on in unfathomable generalities.

---

softball loop A league of teams that played the game in an earlier time. It appears as early as 1934 in Maurice H. Weseen's *Dictionary of American Slang*. It was favored by headline writers, as in this 1940 banner: "NEW PITCHER DISCOVERED IN SOFTBALL LOOP."

softball pitcher (1) Man, woman or child who pitches the ball in a softball game. (2) In boxing, this refers to a light puncher; and the opposite of the "long ball hitter" who is a heavy puncher.

softball throw Athletic field event during which a ball is thrown for distance.

softballer One who has played softball since the 1930s. A September 26, 1939, *Time* magazine feature on the game is simply titled "Softballers."

spectator interference See INTERFERENCE.

split Defensive Over the Line softball formation in which two defenders play on the front line.

squeeze, squeeze play Fast pitch only: Advancing a runner from third to home plate by bunting the ball. The baserunner starts running as soon as the ball is pitched. If the batter hits the ball properly, the defensive team has very little time to retire the runner.

squib hit A fair ball hit off the end of the bat. A squib hit is often difficult for the defense to handle because it has spin and wobble.

starting pitcher The player listed as pitcher on the lineup card or official scorebook.

statue defense Over the Line softball slang describing a situation when the defense doesn't move—and, more to the point, doesn't have to move.

stealing Fast pitch and modified only: Stealing is the act of a baserunner attempting to advance during a pitch to the batter.

straight away (1) The term used to describe the normal defensive position of a team, wherein each player remains in her usual fielding area rather than shifting to the right or to the left. (2) Offensively, it refers to hitting out towards the center field.

straight elimination Another name for SINGLE ELIMINATION.

strike zone ASA fast pitch only: "The strike zone is the space over any part of home plate between the batter's arm pits and the top of his knees when he assumes a natural batting stance."

ASA slow pitch only: "The strike zone is that space over any part of home plate between the batter's back shoulder and his front knee when he assumes a natural batting stance."

The definitions in the United States Slo-Pitch Softball Association *Official Rule Book* defines the strike zone as ". . . that space directly above Home Plate which is not higher than the Batsman's highest shoulder, nor lower than the bottom of Batsman's front knee, when the batsman assumes his natural batting stance. Any part of the pitched ball is a strike."

Another element to the slow pitch strike zone is that it has a third dimension making it a cube or box, rather than the two-dimensional strike zone in baseball or fast pitch softball. In his book *The Strategy of Pitching Slow Pitch Softball*, Michael Ivankovich makes the point: "In order to be a strike the pitch must cross home plate, dropping behind the batter's front knee, but in front of the back shoulder. If the pitch drops on home plate, it is a ball. . . . Any pitch that misses that invisible box, falling either too short, too deep, or too wide on either side of the plate, is a ball."

strikeout Three strikes resulting in an out. Fast pitch softball produces many; but they are a rarity in the slow pitch game.

strikeout rule An ASA slow pitch rule that says the batter must hit the ball fair if he or she has two strikes. Should the batter hit the ball foul after two strikes, it's an out. In U.S.S.S.A. play, a batter can hit one foul after the second strike; but the second foul is ruled an out. The U.S.S.S.A. rule gives the batter a decided advantage.

sucker pitch A short pitch that a player throws with exaggerated motion hoping that the batter will mis-time his or her swing.

suspended game A game called before being completed which will be completed, at a later time or date. The terms of a suspended game are determined by the umpires.

• T •

tag According to U.S.S.S.A., a tag is the "action of a fielder in touching a base with any part of his body, while holding the ball firmly and securely in his hand or glove. Also touching the runner with the ball, or with the glove holding the ball, while continuously holding the ball firmly and securely during and immediately following the tag."

tag up The action of a baserunner in touching a base while a fielder is catching a fly ball. The runner must do so if she desires to advance to the next base without danger of being put out at the base from which she leaves. If she leaves this base

before a fielder catches the ball, she can be put out, providing a defensive player touches this base with the ball in her possession before the runner returns to tag the base.

taking the pitch If a batter does not swing at a pitch, the action is called "taking the pitch."

tally A run.

team game The term used during the long quest to take fast pitch softball out of the realm of being a PITCHER'S GAME. Typical sports section headlines from the 1950s promised that extending the distance from the mound to home plate would create such a game. A *San Francisco News* headline of April 25, 1925 proclaimed: "THREE FEET CHANGES SOFTBALL FROM PITCHERS' TO TEAM GAME."

tee ball A form of softball for youngsters in which there is no pitching and the ball is placed on a tee to be hit.

three-foot line A line half the distance between home and first base, or 32½ feet long for slow pitch, three feet from the first base foul line, extending from first base toward home plate. It designates the area where the batter-runner should run as she approaches first base.

tiltmeter In Over the Line, when a fan on the sideline nods off while watching a game.

time (1) The term used by the umpire to order the suspension of play. Players can request time, but it can only be granted by an umpire. (2) The ability to coordinate one's bat swing to the pitched softball.

timing The ability to coordinate one's bat swing to the pitched softball. An essential skill in softball batting, especially in slow pitch where the ability to throw off a batter's timing is one of the few things that the pitcher can do to get the batter to lack solid contact with the ball.

Title IX An educational amendment that became law in 1979; it was designed to outlaw sex discrimination in athletics. The initial act ordered schools to provide reasonable competitive athletic outlets for female students. It was a once and future boost for women's softball. It has become a term of reference for women who play softball. Stephanie Salter wrote about the game in the July, 1987, *Women's Sports and Fitness*: "My problem, you see, is that I adore the game of softball but play it so badly I could die of shame. When people insist I play, I tell them I am 37 years old, that I grew up before Title IX, and it is simply too late for me to emulate Joan Joyce."

tooled An Over the Line slang description for what happens when a team gets an excessive number of cheap hits.

top To hit the top portion of the ball so that it bounces downward sharply, resulting in a weak ground ball.

trampoline effect The action that takes place when a softball is hit from bats made of thin-walled aircraft aluminum and is literally launched off the surface of the bat—much like a person bouncing off a trampoline.

trap To catch a ball immediately after it has taken its first bounce.

triple A hit that permits the batter to safely reach third without the aid of an error.

triple play A triple play is a continuous action play by the defense on which three offensive players are put out between the time a ball leaves the pitcher's hand and is returned to him in the pitcher's box. It can only occur with at least two runners on base and no one out; hence it is rare.

turn at bat A turn at bat begins when a player first enters the batter's box and continues until he is put out or becomes a batter-runner.

twilight ball One of a number of names for softball. (See ARMY BALL for a full listing of synonyms for softball.)

two bagger A double.

umpire interference See U.S.S.S.A. definition under INTERFERENCE.

under the leg pitch One of the pitches allowed in U.S.S.S.A. slow pitch softball along with the BEHIND THE BACK PITCH.

undertaker's rule Name for an ASA rule adopted in 1941 that required all pitchers in both day and night games to wear all black or all dark blue uniforms with no letters or trimming on the front of the uniform. It was so called because it made the players look like undertakers. It was repealed in 1947.

unlimited arc A term in slow pitch referring to a form of pitching by which a pitcher is able to throw the ball as high as 25 feet or more on its way to the plate. The unlimited arc is not allowed by either the ASA or U.S.S.S.A. under current rules; but is permitted in some unofficial leagues. In his book *The Strategy of Pitching Slow Pitch Softball*, Michael Ivankovich points out that the unlimited arc that had been allowed at various points in the evolution of the slow pitch game gave the pitcher *too much* of an advantage, which was akin to the advantage that pitchers claim in the fast pitch game. According to Ivankovich, "Some pitchers were able to drop strikes from 20'-25' and more making it extremely difficult on the batter." (See also ARC.)

unwritten rules A term referring to the standards of different leagues and tournaments as to what is allowed and not allowed by the umpires and officials. For instance, the extent and passion with which a call by an umpire can be disputed varies considerably.

upshoot A pitch more commonly known as the RISE, RISER, RISE BALL, RISE PITCH.

• V •

visiting team The team playing on the opponent's home field that bats in the top half of an inning. See also HOME TEAM.

Voice of Softball Honorable title given to Ray Molphy who has been the announcer at almost every major slow pitch event since the late 1970s.

• W •

wait out An offensive strategy by a batter who refuses to swing at the pitcher's throws until she either gets a base on balls or makes the pitcher throw a good ball to hit.

waste pitch A slang expression referring to a pitch intentionally thrown outside the strike zone, in an attempt to trick the batter into swinging at a ball that he or she will have great difficulty hitting.

wheels Legs—a player with exceptional running speed is said to have them.

who's buying? Traditional question asked by the winning team of the losing team, alluding to any of a number of beer measures (round, rounds, pitcher, keg, etc.).

white stitch Describing a ball with a COEFFICIENT OF RESTITUTION (or COR) of 50.

wild pitch Fast pitch only: a legally delivered ball so high, so low or so wide off the plate that the catcher cannot catch or stop and control it with ordinary effort. When a wild pitch or passed ball lodges in or goes under, over or through the backstop the ball is dead and all baserunners are awarded a base. The batter is awarded first base only on the fourth ball.

windage In his book *What Little I Know About Pitching and Hitting*, Eddie Feigner describes the importance of windage in the fast pitch game:

In pitching, technically, you lead the target. Often, you'll be working against a wind that will move the ball. You'll also be throwing a ball straight in the strike zone that, with the spin, will move up or out or down or away from the strike zone. This is windage and ahead-of-target practice that you must work at. From the 46-foot mound, softball pitchers really have to learn windage. They will not be able to throw the ball by the batter unless they are very strong and very tall. When I pitch from second base, there are times in a wind that I throw a ball just out of dead reckoning, as far as fifteen feet to the right or left of home plate, and the ball comes down in the strike zone from the spin on the wind.

---

winding One of the three components of a legal softball (along with the CORE and the COVER). This cotton/polyester thread is tightly wrapped around the core and measures about $\frac{1}{16}$ inch. The ball is then dipped into a special chemical solution to solidify and strengthen the winding.

windmill The name for a fast pitch that begins with a full circle WINDMILL WINDUP and delivery. It results in fast balls of the highest momentum and speed and is used by pitchers with a high level of skill. According to Edward Claflin in his *Irresistible American Softball Book*: The first windmill pitch ever seen in softball was at a picnic game in Detroit in 1922. It was thrown by Mike Lutomski, a school principal, and was declared illegal by Hubert Johnson, the unofficial rules boss in Detroit. So many playground kids adopted the windmill style that Johnson had to reverse his decision and declare it legal in 1926. See also SLINGSHOT and FIGURE EIGHT.

windmill windup The force behind the windmill pitch. To paraphrase Harry D. Wilson's 1942 instructional manual *Play Softball*: The left foot swings back; this throws the weight on the right leg as the arm goes up overhead. The left foot starts forward on the second twirl and the weight goes forward on the left leg as the ball is released. Balance is maintained by the left arm. A slight hesitation as the ball is released may deceive the batter and cause him to swing too soon.

working on a cripple   A phrase collected by umpire Bob Pense, Jr., of Tidewater, Virginia, and published in *Balls and Strikes*: "Batter has 2–2 count, of which the second strike was a foul ball. The next pitch, the 'cripple,' if hit, must be fair. If foul, batter is out."

wormburner   A low hard shot, especially in Over the Line and fastpitch softball. It was defined by Stephanie Salter in the July, 1987, issue of *Women's Sports and Fitness* this way: "Pitch thrown extremely fast and so low that it scrapes over the plate. Appears at crucial moments in game, usually when pitcher has lost her 'stuff.' Hazardous to animals, plant life, catcher's shins and umpire's feet."

wood chop   A type of soft short pull which has been refined to a higher art in Over the Line beach softball. (See also PARACHUTE.)

younger game, the   What softball partisans often called the game during its pre–World War II period of expansion. Baseball was thought of as the OLDER GAME.

young pups, new breed   Up-and-coming players, in the slang of Over the Line softball.

• Z •

zone   (1) Over the Line slang for one's mindset when hitting well. (2) A pitcher's good area: the area or zone where his or her delivery is most effective.

10 Year by Year: A

The early history of the game is supplied in great detail in earlier sections of this book. Here is a thumbnail chronology beginning with the origins of the game:

1887 In the gymnasium of the high-Gothic Farragut Boat Club at the edge of Lake Michigan in Chicago in the 3000 block of Lake Park Avenue, a group of young men led by George Hancock created a new game they called indoor baseball. By mid-winter the game caught on all over Chicago and was being played in gymnasiums and lodge halls around the city. This has been softball's own account of its creation ever since.

1895 Eight years after Hancock first invented the game, the first women's team was organized

PELICANS

GULLS

CLYDE FAIRFIELD PHOTO

HALF CENTURY SOFTBALL CLUBS-ST. PETERSBURG FLORIDA ~

Softball Chronology

at Chicago's West Division High School, signifying the beginnings of the women's game.

- The game was re-invented for the outdoors by a fire department officer named Lewis Rober, Sr., who needed a game to keep his men in shape and involved in their idle time. This version was known as kitten ball.

1908 The National Amateur Playground Ball Association of the United States came into being in Chicago. It created a handbook for the game, which seemed to be run more on a set of options than a set of rules. The most bizarre option allowed the first baserunner in each inning to determine which direction his team would move during that inning. In other words, the first runner could start by running to first base or to third.

1931 *The fabled Kids and Kubs baseball club in an earlier time when they were called the Pelicans and Gulls. Here they pose in St. Petersburg, Florida, their home base. They were founded in 1931, making them an even older organization than the ASA.*

(Ron Menchine Collection)

1926 A meeting was held in Colorado to standardize that state's rules under a common name and the term softball was suggested for the first time by Walter C. Hakanson, the Y.M.C.A. director for Denver, Colorado.

1931 The Kids and Kubs, otherwise known as the Three Quarter Century Club, came into being

in Florida. All players had to be over 75 years of age.

1932   The first national tournament championships were held. The Wemcoes (Lake Hills, Wisconsin) and the Miller High Life team (Kenosha, Wisconsin) were the two top teams.

1933   Softball became softball with the tournament at the Century of Progress Exposition in Chicago. On the opening day of this tournament the *Chicago American* stated:

It is the largest and most comprehensive tournament ever held in the sport which has swept the country like wildfire. Champions will be decided in three classes—fast pitching, slow pitching, and girls.

• Backed by William Raldolph Hearst and his newspaper, the *Chicago American*, a national softball tournament, with separate divisions for fast pitch, slow pitch and a women's league, was held in conjunction with the World's Fair. Seventy thousand spectators attended these championship games. Entry fee for each team in these first nationals was $2.50.

• The Amateur Softball Association of America (ASA) was founded in Chicago. To this day the ASA, with its headquarters in Oklahoma City, is the national governing body of softball in the United States and remains the largest membership organization recognized by the U.S. Olympic Committee.

1945   *(Opposite) Clyde "Diz" Kirkendall of Findlay, Ohio, was the demon pitcher for the Fort Wayne Zollner Pistons. His Pistons' record from 1945 through 1948 was 108–16.*

(Amateur Softball Association)

1936   This is the first year in which it is claimed that more than one million Americans play softball.

1937   In the 1937 national tournament 88 teams from the United States and Canada participated. This was the first series to be broadcast over a national network, with both Columbia and the National Broadcasting Company doing play-by-play broadcasts of the important games.

1938   More than 10 million Americans played the game with many times that number listed as spectators. There were 8,000 softball diamonds in the nation and it was called a craze.

1939   The National Professional Indoor Baseball League came into being with baseball's Tris Speaker as Commissioner. It lasted a matter of days, resulting in many ASA suspensions and marking the first of a number of failed attempts to create a professional softball loop.

1940   The Amateur Softball Association claimed that more than five million active players were in the game. Sporting goods manufacturers credited expenditures of some 20 million dollars annually for the sport.

1943   The head of the Joint Rules Committee on Softball reported that the game had totally come into its own during wartime for both the military and civilian population. The differences concerning name and playing rules had disappeared, he said.

1946   The National Fastball League came into being uniting the nation's top male corporate teams. It was considered to be the top male fast pitch league ever put together.

• A man named Meryl King started a four-man softball team to take on all comers. He changed his name to Eddie Feigner and the King and His Court were off and running.

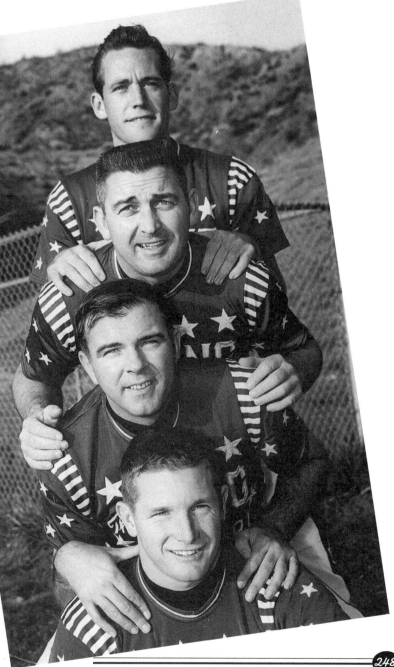

1947   The Zollner Piston team of Fort Wayne, Indiana, became the first team to win the national softball title three years in a row. After this, they elected not to enter the nationals again.

● The International Softball Congress, founded by Carrol Forbes, began holding its own tournaments in the West in direct competition with the ASA. The first I.S.C. World Champion, Farm Fresh Market, was crowned at Phoenix.

1948   The Jax Maids of New Orleans were made ineligible for amateur play because they played against professional teams. The Maids were the 1947 Women's World Champions. ASA teams were warned that if they play the Maids they will not be allowed to compete under the ASA banner in the future.

1949   For the first time the men and women had their tournaments in different cities. Previously they had appeared in the same venue.

● Herb Dudley, pitching for the Clearwater Bombers, from Clearwater, Florida, struck out 55 batters in a 21-inning national championship game.

1950   The Bombers of Clearwater, Florida, won the nationals at Austin, Texas.

● The National Fastball League disbanded temporarily because of the onset of the Korean War; but the game was eagerly proclaimed the favorite of the U.S. forces in that "police action."

● The Amateur Softball Association brought forth a remarkably detailed picture of the game: 2,952 lighted parks out of 15,212 playing areas.

● Bertha Ragan of the Orange Lionettes pitched 143 consecutive innings (the equivalent of 20 complete games plus three innings). This feat and others to follow helped focus attention on the remarkable abilities of women softball pitchers.

1951   The first National Softball Week was declared: July 22–28.

- Softball was deemed to be among the safest of sports. A study, published in the *Journal of the American Medical Association* of sport fatalities between 1918 and 1950 revealed that baseball (25 dead), boxing (21), basketball (7) and football (22) compared most poorly to polo, golf, cricket, relay racing and softball, which each had lost one participant. The lone softball tragedy had occurred when a player let a bat slip and hit another player in the head.

- Madeline Lorton, 25, of the Bronx, New York, became the first licensed woman umpire in organized softball. She umped at 35 games in her first season. There were approximately 5,000 male umpires at this point in softball history. It would take until 1967 before the game got its second female umpire.

1952 Softball invaded the Polo Grounds, home of the New York Giants, for a charity tilt in which the Zollner Pistons beat Grumman Aircraft 30–0.

- The International Softball Federation (I.S.F.) had its first meeting. Although the Amateur Softball Association was recognized as the governing body of amateur softball, the I.S.F. controlled international competition, including the Pan-American Games. One of its earliest goals was to see softball included in the list of Olympic sports.

1953 Slow pitch moved out of the shadows as a separate national championship and was added to the ASA finals. The tournament was held in Cincinnati and the winners were the Cincinnati Fire Department, who would win it again for the next three years. The program had started in the Fire Department a few years earlier when slow pitch had been introduced as part of a physical fitness plan for out-of-shape firefighters.

1954 Everybody seemed to be playing the game. Softball was declared to be the nation's leading industrial sport. On the East Coast, show business folks created their own league—the Broadway Show League—which would long outlast any play then being performed. On the West Coast Over the Line softball came into play. In Oklahoma

City, the first American Indian Tournament was held and the Fort Cobb Indians won.

1955 The Long Beach Nitehawks men's fast pitch team won their first of six consecutive Congress tournament championships.

1957 The ASA developed the Softball Hall of Fame in Oklahoma City, Oklahoma.

1958 The National Softball Congress ceased operation.

- Bertha Tickey and Joan Joyce teamed up to win the first of three consecutive national championships for the Raybestos Brakettes of Stratford, Connecticut. Tickey's many accomplishments during her career included 11 national championships, being an 18-time participant on the National All-Star Team and recipient of eight Most Valuable Player awards at the National Tournaments.

- A headline in *Sporting Goods Dealer* magazine noted that "SLOW PITCH SOFTBALL IS MOVING FAST IN SALES LEAGUE."

1959 In Cleveland, the ASA Cleveland Metro Chief announced a "mixed couples" league to encourage co-ed participation. Co-ed softball thus got an official start. The game is the same as regular softball except that spikes are not allowed, and half the players taking the field for any team must be male and the other half female.

- Softball made inroads overseas. A typical and, perhaps, overstated headline in *Balls and Strikes* proclaimed: "SOFTBALL FLOURISHES IN EAST PAKISTAN."

1960 Slow pitch eclipsed fast pitch softball for the first time in popularity.

1961 A big media year: CBS and ABC both televised softball events. *This Week* magazine proved that a fast-pitched softball travels faster than a baseball thrown by a big league pitcher.

1962 Joan Joyce, considered by many to be the greatest female softball pitcher of all-time, faced Ted Williams, who was considered by many to be the greatest hitter in baseball history, before 18,000 people in Waterbury, Connecticut. Forty pitches and 10 minutes later, Williams retired with one base hit and one foul ball. He did not touch another pitch. Joyce's fast ball was reportedly clocked at over 100 miles per hour.

1963 The Amateur Softball Association celebrated its 30th year.

1965 Softball was being played in more than 50 nations, up from a mere four in the early 1950s.

• Joan Joyce, while attending college in California and playing for the Orange Lionettes, led her team to the National Women's Fast Pitch Championship against her old teammates, the Raybestos Brakettes.

• The first I.S.F. World Championships were held in Melbourne, Australia. The Australians defeated the highly favored United States 1–0 in the final game. It was said that this event had great importance in making women's softball an international game and that this was the first step towards the Olympics and Pan American Games.

1966 The U.S., represented by the Aurora Sealmasters of Illinois, won the first Men's Fast Pitch World Championship Tournament in Mexico City. Twelve nations took part in play with the U.S. taking 10 straight victories.

1967 A long-awaited event: *Sports Illustrated* published its first softball article on September 11th. The Amateur Softball Association director Don Porter stated, "We trust it is not the last."

1968 In a Pittsburgh motel room a group of disenchanted slow pitch enthusiasts formed a new group, The United States Slo-Pitch Softball Association (U.S.S.S.A., or U-triple S.A.), beginning with a handful of teams. The upstart group argued that the Amateur Softball Association was in charge of both fast and slow pitch and that it was primarily interested in the faster game and was unwilling to consider improvements in slow pitch. Almost immediately the new group adopted 65-foot baselines and a smaller batter's box. As

U.S.S.S.A. literature of the time put it, "The Amateur Softball Association did not greet the newly formed slow-pitch organization with enthusiasm."

• The second men's world fast-pitch championship was held, with the U.S. again victorious, despite a 2–0 loss to Puerto Rico.

1969 The first softball clinic was held for U.S. troops in Vietnam.

1970 Over 15 million Americans were playing some form of softball regularly.

• A second world tournament was held for women. A crowd of 30,000 watched as the U.S. team was defeated by the Japanese 1–0. The host Japanese team had rattled off 12 straight victories.

1971 Softball was deemed to have become the leading team participation sport, eclipsing bowling for the first time.

1972 An educational amendment known as Title IX, designed to outlaw sex discrimination in athletics, was passed. The initial act ordered schools to provide reasonable competitive athletic outlets for females. With the offering of softball scholarships to educational institutions of higher learning, women's softball began to flourish at colleges and universities throughout the country. Title IX was implemented in 1979.

• The 1972 I.S.F. Men's World Championship at Manila was won by Canada.

1973 The Amateur Softball Association opened its Hall of Fame in Oklahoma City.

1973 (Opposite) Sculpture, entitled Play at Home, in front of the Amateur Softball Association headquarters in Oklahoma City. The building houses the sporty Hall of Fame, replete with an astroturf floor. This Hall of Fame celebrates all forms of the game.

(Russell Mott)

1974 The United States won the 1974 Women's World Championship in Stratford, Connecticut, emerging on top of a field of 15 national teams. The U.S. team had lost to Australia and Japan in the two earlier world championships. The 1974 tournament featured a round-robin plus a playoff series.

1975 The United States Slo-Pitch Softball Association (U.S.S.S.A.) sued the Amateur Softball Association (ASA) for violation of antitrust laws because the latter would not let the former play against the other's teams. It was later settled out of court with the decision that any U.S.S.S.A. team can play any ASA—and vice versa—without penalty. (Years later, in the early 1990s, the two organizations shared little more than disdain for one another. Many players and umpires, oblivious to the squabble, played and worked in both realms.)

• Joan Joyce of the Raybestos Brakettes retired from amateur softball. Joyce's career included 105 no-hitters and 33 perfect games, plus numerous national and world championships. She won 507 of 540 games in her career.

1976 The International Women's Professional Softball Association (WPSA) was founded and made its debut on May 28. Player contracts ranged from $1,000 to $3,000 per year. Joan Joyce led the Falcons from the Eastern Division and defeated the San Jose Sun Birds from the Western Division in the first World Series.

• The United States shared the I.S.F. Men's World Championship title with Canada and New Zealand.

1977 The American Professional Slo-Pitch League (A.P.S.P.L.) began with attendance averaging around two thousand in such cities as Baltimore, Cincinnati, Pittsburgh, Chicago, Columbus and Detroit. The Detroit Caesars won the first World Series in four straight games from the Baltimore Monuments.

• Jimmy Galloway, known as "Mr. Softball," joined the A.P.S.P.L. after being selected to the amateur All-American slow pitch team eight times.

1979 The Broadway Show League celebrated its 25th Anniversary. At this point in its history, it was totally restricted to "people who earn their living in show business." The league's top team was led by rock star Meat Loaf.

• The U.S.S.S.A. adopted the 11-inch softball for its Women's and Youth Programs.

• On October 22 the ASA registered its 100,000th adult softball team.

• For the first time in its history softball was played at the Pan American Games. The U.S. Women's National Team took the gold.

1980 Up from 15 million in 1970, the total number of Americans playing softball on a regular basis jumped to 25 million.

• The International Women's Professional Softball Association (I.W.P.S.A.) shut down in May after teetering along for four years on the brink of financial ruin.

1981 A co-ed slow pitch championship was added to the ASA's list of national championships, signaling the arrival of this version of the game.

1982 The University of California, Los Angeles (U.S.C.A.) won the first women's NCAA softball championship.

1983 The total number of women's teams registered with the ASA was 37,651, a stunning rise from the 5,361 teams ten years earlier (1973).

1987 Softball's 100th anniversary was celebrated with a game played on June 29th on the campus of the Michael Reese Hospital in Chicago where the Farragut Boat Club stood a century earlier. At the end of the game runners ran a torch relay from Chicago to the headquarters of the ASA in Oklahoma City.

• Softball also celebrated its 100th anniversary as Michele Granger, a junior from Valencia High School in southern California, pitched the United States to an undefeated Pan-American Games Championship in Indianapolis.

• A major effort to get softball's Centennial honored on a commemorative stamp failed, turning into what sports editor Buck Johnson of the *Chattanooga Times* called "an ugly political mess."

• Mike Macenko, with a national record of 844 homeruns, led Steele's Silver Bullets, of Grafton, Ohio, to its third consecutive ASA Supernational Slow-Pitch Title.

• Bruce Meade, the only player to ever hit a softball out of the Houston Astrodome (460 feet), led the Smythe Sox (Houston, Texas) to their second successive U.S.S.S.A. world slow pitch championship.

1988 Twenty years after its founding the United States Slo-Pitch Softball Association boasted a membership of 83,599 teams.

1990 At 40 million, softball stood as the nation's most popular team sport. A Gallup Poll revealed that 16 percent of all men, women and children played the game.

1991 On June 13, the International Olympic Committee added softball to its list of medal sports for the 1996 Olympic Games in Atlanta.

• Footville, Wisconsin (pop. 700) celebrated the 60th anniversary of the lighting of its softball park. It was the oldest and still existing park of its kind in the nation, having first turned on the lights for two kitten ball games on August 6, 1931.

• The Raybestos Brakettes, Women's Major Fast Pitch of Stratford, Connecticut, kept plugging along with a 64–2 record for the year.

• The NCAA Women's College World Series witnessed its first "threepeat" winner as Sharron Backus led UCLA to victory for the third time in a row over Fresno State.

• Banned from baseball, Pete Rose returned to the batter's box in a charity slow pitch softball game in West Hartford, Connecticut. In six at bats he managed a home run and a single playing for the Conn Kings in their 21–7 loss to the Peter Pan cafe.

• U.S. women, led by pitchers Lisa Fernandez (5–0), Debbie Doom (3–0) and Michele Granger (1–0) dominated play in the Pan American games in Cuba. They were undefeated in nine games during which they allowed 13 hits and three runs. The three pitchers achieved two perfect games, two no-hitters and 110 strikeouts in 60 innings.

1992 This was the 60th year in a row that membership in the Amateur Softball Association increased over the previous year. More than 250,000 teams were registered, up about 7,500 from 1991.

• Forty-eight of the world's top men's fast pitch softball teams converged at the Big Cottonwood Regional Softball Complex in Salt Lake, proving that the I.S.C., in its 45th season, is still a force to be reckoned with and so is fast pitch softball.

Finale Jennifer Brewster, number 13, has just hit a homerun for UCLA and the National Championship is theirs. And, as they say, the rest is indeed history. Left to right: Sue Enquist, co-head coach; Jennifer Brewster; Yvonne Gutierrez; Kirk Walker; Jo Alchin; Heather Compton; Kathi Evans; Kelly Inoue; Cindy Valero; and Lisa Fernandez, number 16. (Russell Mott)

Appendix of

Softball has many levels of local organization; but the most important are these five national and international groups.

The Amateur Softball Association Since 1933, the game's major force. It describes itself as the national "governing body for amateur softball in the U.S."

Its main periodical is *Balls and Strikes* and its publications include the annual *Official Guide and Rulebook*, which contains the latest rule changes and modifications, and *The ASA Umpire Manual*.

The ASA's Oklahoma complex features a Hall of Fame and Museum, gift shop, archives and the Hall of Fame Stadium, the site of a number of softball events including recent NCAA Women's College World Series and the Big Eight Conference tournaments.

This organization and its long-time Executive Director Don E. Porter are responsible for making women's fast pitch softball an Olympic medal sport.

The ASA has a number of allied members, including the NCAA, N.J.C.A.A., N.A.I.A. and Special Olympics, and is affiliated with the International Softball Federation (see below).

Executive Director: Don E. Porter
Telephone: (405) 424-5266
Address: The Amateur Softball
    Association
2801 N.E. 50th Street
Oklahoma City, OK 73111

Executive Director: Milt Stark
Telephone: (714) 998-5694
Address: International Softball Congress
6007 E. Hillcrest Circle
Anaheim Hills, CA 92807

International Softball Federation   Group directly linked to the ASA that unites softball associations in 80 nations from Anguilla to Zimbabwe. The I.S.F. promotes international development and competition. *World Softball* is the quarterly publication of the I.S.F. It is written in English and Spanish and is the best source for international softball news and rankings.

President: Don E. Porter
Telephone: (405) 424-6714
Address: International Softball Federation
2801 N.E. 50th Street
Oklahoma City, OK 73111

Softball Organizations

Cinderella Softball Leagues   An organization that seeks to promote and develop softball for females 18 and under. Conducts tournaments and stages its own World Series.

President: Tony Maio
Telephone: (607) 937-5469
Address: Cinderella Softball Leagues
P.O. Box 1411
Corning, NY 14830

The International Softball Congress   Since 1946, an "exclusive" association for men's amateur fast pitch softball, whose main activity is running tournaments that lead up to the I.S.C. World Tournament, which vies directly with the Men's ASA National Championship. The two national championships involve most of the same teams.

   The I.S.C. maintains its own Hall of Fame in Kimberly, Wisconsin.

The United States Slo-Pitch Softball Association
Founded in 1968, it is exclusively concerned with slow pitch—or as it insists on spelling it, "slo-pitch"—softball.

   Its major publication is *The Slo-Pitch Game* (a tabloid published eight times a year) and it produces an annual *Official Rule Book* incorporating the latest rule changes and modifications. The U.S.S.S.A. rules differ somewhat from the ASA's slow pitch rules.

Executive Director: Al Ramsey
Telephone: (804) 732-4099
Address: The United States
    Slo-Pitch Softball Association
3935 South Crater Road
Petersburg, VA 23805

Bibliography

As such things go, softball is short on its own literature. The Library of Congress computer spills out a mere 78 titles, including such curiosities as Mario Monetti's *Il Softball* and its Dutch counterpart *Honkbal* by G. Hogenbos. In addition there are many articles, a number of Ph.D. theses, instructional films and videotapes.

What follows first is a listing of the major works of nonfiction, the second is a listing of the very small number of fictional works, the third is a listing of periodicals and the last is a sampling of Ph.D. theses available.

1. Nonfiction

Amateur Softball Association of America. *Official Guide and Rule Book*. Oklahoma City, OK: ASA, 1988.

American Association for Health, Physical Education and Recreation. Division for Girls and Women's Sports. *DWGS Guidebooks*. Washington: DWGS, 1945 and forward.

Athletic Institute, *How to Improve Your Softball*. Chicago: Athletic Institute, 1953.

Backus, Sharron. *Inside Softball for Women*. Chicago, IL: Contemporary Books, 1979.

Bancroft, Jessie H., and William Dean Pulvermacher. *The Handbook of Athletic Games*. New York: Macmillan, 1916.

Bealle, Morris A. *The New 1962 Compact Edition of the Softball Story*. Washington, D.C.: Columbia Publishing Co., 1962.

———. *The Softball Story*. Washington, D.C.: Columbia Publishing Co., 1957.
(Both of these books by Bealle are invaluable references and very scarce as they were produced in limited quantity by Mr. Bealle's own small publishing house. The books are significantly different despite the impression given by the 1962 title. The latter book has much more information but is compact in that there is more type on each page.)

Blundell, William E. "Over-The-Line Is the Game; the Scene Is Beyond the Pale." *The Wall Street Journal*, August 2, 1983.

Bridges, Jennifer. *Unpublished Softball Beginnings*. Thesis submitted at Indiana University, 1983.

Brown, Bruce. *Dr. Whacko's Guide to Slow-Pitch Softball*. New York: Collier Books, 1991.

Claflin, Edward. *The Irresistible American Softball Book*. New York: Dolphin Books, 1978.
(The only book about the game as a social institution in the last 20 years.)

Clark, Tim. "The Greatest Dynasty in the History of Softball." *Yankee*, August, 1982.

Condor, Bob. "20 Things You Absolutely, Positively Must Know About Softball." *Sportswise*, March–April, 1984.

Cooney, Ellen. "Diamonds Are Forever: Why Softball's Magic Never Fades," *Women's Sports and Fitness*, August, 1985.

Crichton, Kyle. "Not So Soft." *Collier's*, August 10, 1935.

Crysdale, Sharon J., and Karen S. Harris. *Complete Handbook of Winning Softball*. Boston, MA: Allyn and Bacon, Inc., 1982.

Feigner, Eddie. *What Little I Know About Pitching and Hitting*. Walla Walla, WA: Saxum Publishing, 1980.

Feldman, Jay. "A Ball By Any Other Name." *Sports Heritage*, January, 1987.

Feretti, Fred. *The Great American Book . . . Games*. New York: Workman Publishing Co., 1975.

Fischer, Leo H. *How to Play Winning Softball*. New York: Prentice-Hall Inc., 1940.

———. "Softball Steps Up." *Reader's Digest*, June, 1939.

Fortune, Annette. *Complete Softball*. Windsor, CT: Jet Press, 1982.

Grossman, Edward. "From the Diary of a Softballer." *Commentary*, August, 1980.

Hamilton, Neil A. *Visions of Worth*. Melbourne, Florida: Preservation Publishing Co., 1988.

Hancock, George W. *Hancock's Indoor Base Ball Guide*. Chicago: George W. Hancock Publishers, 1889, 1890, 1891.
(These are extremely difficult to find. The Library of Congress has all three.)

Hannon, Kent. "It's Easy Come, Easy Go." *Sports Illustrated*, June 13, 1977.

Himli, Ibrahim. *Pioneers in Leisure and Recreation*. Reston, VA: American Alliance for Health, Physical Education, Recreation and Dance, 1989.

Hoehn, Robert G. *Playing Slow Pitch Softball*. New York: Sterling Publishing Co., 1979.

Houseworth, Steven D. and Francine V. Rivkin. *Coaching Softball Effectively*. Champaign, IL: Human Kinetics Publishers, Inc., 1985.

Ivankovich, Michael. *The Strategy of Pitching Slow Pitch Softball*. Maple Glen, PA: Diamond Publishing Co., 1986.

Jares, Joe. "She's Still Wonder Woman." *Sports Illustrated*, July 26, 1976.

Johnson, Connie P. and Margie Wright. *The Woman's Softball Book*. New York: Leisure Press, 1984.

Jones, Billie J., and Mary J. Murray. *Softball Concepts for Coaches and Teachers*. Dubuque, IA: Wm. C. Brown, 1978.

Joyce, Joan, and John Anquillare. *Winning Softball*. Chicago, IL: Henry Regnery Company, 1975.

Kawarsky, Irvin. *The Evolution and History of Softball in the United States*. A thesis submitted in partial fulfillment of the requirements for the degree of Master of Science in Education in Drake University, Des Moines, 1956.

Kneer, Marian E. and Charles L. McCord. *Softball: Slow and Fast Pitch*. Dubuque, IA: William C. Brown, 1991.

Lee, Mabel. *A History of Physical Education and Sports in the U.S.A.* New York: John Wylie and Sons, 1983.

Leviton, Daniel. *The Evolution of the Rules of Softball*. Thesis submitted in partial fulfillment of the requirement for the degree of Master of Science, Springfield College, June, 1956.

McCallum, Kent. "He can rise, drop and pop it at 104 mph." *Sports Illustrated*, May 28, 1979.

McCrory, G. Jacobs. *Softball Rules in Pictures*. New York: Perigee Books, 1987.

Manus, Willard. "Softball in the City." *Holiday*, June, 1967.

Meyer, Gladys C. *Softball for Girls and Women*. New York: Charles Scribners Sons, 1982.

Meyer, Robert G. *The Complete Book of Softball: The Loonies Guide to Playing and Enjoying the Game*. New York: Leisure Press, 1984.

Michener, James A. *Sports in America*. New York: Random House, 1976.

Mitchell, Viola. *Softball for Girls*. New York: A.S. Barnes, 1943.

National Association for Girls and Women in Sport. *Softball Guide*. Reston, VA: The American Alliance for Health, Physical Education, Recreation and Dance. (Published biannually).

Noren, Arthur T. *Softball*. New York: A.S. Barnes, 1940.

Oetgen, Albert. "Softball Ranks as American Religion for Some." Knight-Ridder Newspapers, June 1, 1986.

Perry, George R. *Slow Pitch Softball*. South Brunswick, NJ: A.S. Barnes, 1979.

Petroff, Tom. *Softball Hitting: Fast and Slow Pitch*. North Palm Beach: The Athletic Institute, 1990.

Reach, Jim and Bernard Schwartz. *Softball for Everyone*. Winston-Salem, NC: Hunter Books, 1989.

Salter, Stephanie. "Softball Dreamin': The Best, the Funniest, the Friendliest Game of Summer." *Women's Sports and Fitness*, July, 1987. (One of the best depictions of the modern women's game includes scouting reports on Dr. Ruth Westheimer and Cher.)

Sobel, Brian. *Fastpitch Softball*. Mountain View, CA: World Publications, 1980.

Spalding Athletic Library. *Official Rules of Playground Ball*. New York: American Sports Publishing Co., 1908–1930.

———. *Official Rules of Softball*. New York: American Sports Publishing Co., 1933–1940.

Sullivan, George. *The Complete Guide to Softball*. New York: Fleet Publishing Co., 1965.

Thomas, Lowell and Ted Shane. *Softball: So What?* New York: Frederick A. Stokes Co., 1940.

(Softball's mother lode of early lore and humor, it describes a game that moves eastward "like a prairie fire.")

"Indoor Baseball." *Time*, November 27, 1939.

"Softballers." *Time*, September 26, 1939.

Tunis, John R. *Sport for the Fun of It*. New York: A.S. Barnes and Co., 1940.

United States Slo-Pitch Softball Association. *Official Rule Book*. Petersburg, VA. (all editions through 1992).

———. *The U.S.S.S.A. 1991 World Series Almanac*. Petersburg, VA, 1991.

Walker, Dick. *Be the Best: Softball*. Mahwah, NJ: Troll Associates, 1990.

Walsh, Loren. *Coaching Winning Softball*. Chicago, IL: Contemporary Books, 1979.

———. *Contemporary Softball*. Chicago: Contemporary Books, 1978.

———. *Inside Softball*. Chicago: Regnery, 1977.

Walters, Jonathan. "Field of Dreamers." *USA Weekend*. May 4, 1990.

Webb, Jim. *Learning to Pitch Softball (Things Every Pitcher, Catcher, and Coach Should Know)*. Astoria, IL: Summertime Books Co., 1982.

Weinberg, David. "Executive Action." *Rolling Stone*, July 21–August 4, 1983.

Wilson, Harry D. *Play Softball*. Chicago: Little Technical Library (Ziff-Davis), 1942.

Yoder, Robert. "Miss Casey at the Bat." *Saturday Evening Post*, August 22, 1922.

Zipter, Yvonne. *Diamonds Are a Dyke's Best Friend*. Ithaca, NY: Firebrand Books, 1989. (The subtitle says it all: "Reflections, reminiscences, and reports from the field on the lesbian national pastime.")

Zolna, Ed, and Mike Conklin. *Mastering Softball*. Chicago: Contemporary Books, 1981.

Zoss, Joel, and John Bowman. *Diamonds in the Rough*. New York: MacMillan, 1989.

2. Fiction

Softball has generated about 100 books including eight works of juvenile fiction and several other novels. Here they are listed with plot summaries for some.

Bliss, Ronald G. *Indian Softball Summer; or, Kickapoos Never Say Goodbye*. New York: Dodd, Meade, 1974.
(Summary: The team's prospects seem bleak when they start the softball season with only eight players, one an Indian who has never played the game before. Then they discover the Indian is a girl.)

Christopher, Matt. *Supercharged Infield*. Boston: Little Brown, 1985.
(Summary: Penny Farrell, captain and third baseman of the Hawks softball team, tries to uncover the reason for the strange behavior of two teammates who have also suddenly turned into super athletes.)

Cooney, Ellen. *All the Way Home*. New York: G.P. Putnam and Sons, 1984.

Dessent, Michael H. *Baseball Becky*. San Diego: Oak Tree Publications, 1982.
(Summary: When uncoordinated Becky joins a softball team she learns a great deal about competition.)

Killien, Christi. *The Daffodils*. New York: Scholastic, 1992.
(Summary: When the Daffodils softball team elects a "sophisticated" new girl to lead them, former captain Nichole struggles with the growing pains of her team and her teammates to prove herself a winner on and off the field.)

Sayles, John. *Pride of the Bimbos*. New York: Harper Perennial, 1992.
(Summary: First published in 1975, this was John Sayles' first novel before he became a filmmaker. It is a raucous, adult book about a five-man softball team that barnstorms in drag under the name of the Brooklyn Bimbos.)

Schulman, Janet. *Camp KeeWee's Secret Weapon*. New York: Greenwillow Books, 1979.

(Summary: Jill's softball talent helps her find her niche at Camp KeeWee.)

Tester, Sylvia Root. *Carla-Too-Little*. Chicago: Child's World, 1976.
(Summary: Told by her family that she is too little for their various teams, Carla is offered a position as softball bat girl.)

Vail, Virginia. *Good Sports*. Mahwah, NJ: Troll Associates, 1990.
(Summary: The girls at Webster's Country Horse Camp despair of winning the upcoming sports and riding competition with a rival boy's camp, until Libby's unconventional grandmother shows up to coach them in softball.)

Walden, Amelia Elizabeth. *Play Ball, McGill*. Philadelphia: Westminster Press, 1972.
(Summary: When things begin to go wrong at home and in her social life, the star pitcher of a high school softball team feels her game is also being affected.)

Washington, Rosemary G. *Softball Is for Me*. Minneapolis: Lerner Publications Co., 1982.
(Summary: Explains how a girls' softball team learns to bat, catch and throw in order to get ready for their first game of slow pitch softball.)

3. Softball Periodicals

The main publications consulted in the preparation of this book were:

Balls and Strikes   Since the 1930s, the official publication of the ASA. In recent years it has undergone a major redesign and revitalizaiton. (c/o The Amateur Softball Association, 2801 N.E. 50th Street, Oklahoma City, OK 73111)

The Slo-Pitch World   Very detailed information on the slow pitch softball played under the U.S.S.S.A. banner. (c/o The United States Slo-

Pitch Softball Association, 3935 South Crater Road, Petersburg, VA 23805)

Softball Masters   For "all softball players," it is an independent review of all that is going on in the sport. (507 Columbus St., Montgomery, AL 36104)

World Softball   Quarterly publication of the International Softball Federation. Features are written in English and Spanish and it is the best place for international softball news and rankings. (c/o International Softball Federation, 2801 N.E. 50th Street, Oklahoma City, OK 73111)

Other periodicals that proved useful in showing the width and breadth of the game included: *The Sandbagger, Cincinnati Softball News, Softball West, Sierra Softball, Slo-Pitch News, The Softball News of the Diamond State* ("Delaware's award-winning softball newspaper,") *Chicago Metro Softball, Softball News, Southern California Softball Magazine, Southwest Softball, Let's Play Softball, Nebraska Softball News* and *Georgia Softball*.

4. Softball Theses

No softball bibliography would be complete without acknowledging the fact that scores of academic theses have been written on the subject. More than 100 of them are held by the ASA headquarters in Oklahoma City. To give the reader an idea of how diverse these academic studies are here is a sampling of the theses written by authors with last names beginning in the letters *A* and *B* taken from *Dissertation Abstracts International, Complete Research in Health, Physical Education and Recreation, Masters Abstracts Index* and *Research Quarterly*.

Adams, Madeline F. "The Relationship between Family Size, Ordinal Position in the Family, and Participation in Women's Amateur Softball in Texas." Masters thesis, Texas Woman's University, 1973.

Allen, William H. "Study of an Introductory Method of Rounding First Base." Masters thesis, Southeast Missouri State College, 1976.

Bearse, William F. "The Energy Cost of Playing Defensive Shortstop in Slow-pitch Softball." Ph.D. dissertation, Eastern Kentucky University, 1972.

Biersner, Robert J.; William G. McHugh; and Linda K. Bennett. "Cognitive and Emotional Factors Representative of Reinforcement Patterns Among an Amateur Softball Team." *Human Factors* 19:595–9.

Blackwood, Nancy S. "A Comparison of an Aluminum Softball Bat and a Wooden Softball Bat as Measured by Batting Power." Masters thesis, Central Missouri State University, 1972.

Boyce, Gary C. "Effect on the 'Flexibat' T.M. on Bat-head Velocity." Masters thesis, Michigan State University, 1979.

Brechtelsbauer, Kay M. "The Effects of Augmented Knowledge of Results of Increasing the Velocity of a Batted Softball." Ph.D. dissertation, Southern Illinois University at Carbondale, 1980.

Index

Softball team names appear in *italics*; illustrations are indicated by **boldface** page numbers; glossary terms are designated by a "*g*."

• G •

The Worth Book of Softball